Of One-Eyed and Toothless Miscreants

Of One-Eyed and Toothless Miscreants

Making the Punishment Fit the Crime?

Edited by
MICHAEL TONRY

OXFORD
UNIVERSITY PRESS

OXFORD
UNIVERSITY PRESS

Oxford University Press is a department of the University of Oxford. It furthers
the University's objective of excellence in research, scholarship, and education
by publishing worldwide. Oxford is a registered trade mark of Oxford University
Press in the UK and certain other countries.

Published in the United States of America by Oxford University Press
198 Madison Avenue, New York, NY 10016, United States of America.

CIP data is on file at the Library of Congress
ISBN 978-0-19-007059-5

1 3 5 7 9 8 6 4 2

Printed by Integrated Books International, United States of America

Contents

Preface

THIS VOLUME PRESENTS fruits of the labors of many people. It began in mid-2016, when Douglas Husak and I realized that neither of us had any clear understanding of what it means to say that a particular punishment is proportionate to a particular crime. We knew that a sizable multinational social science literature shows wide agreement among citizens about the relative seriousness of a small number of grave crimes. We knew that most people believe imprisonment is more punitive than a fine or a community punishment and that longer prison terms are more punitive than shorter ones. We also knew, contradictorily, that many offenders prefer to receive a prison sentence rather than a community punishment and that, for some in criminal milieus, a prison term is considered a rite of passage or a cost of doing business.

We realized that we could not persuasively explain why some crimes seem more serious than others. Is it, for example, because they more greatly interfere with their victims' ability to live satisfying lives, because they impose greater costs as economists measure them, because they involve greater pain or loss, or because of something else? Likewise with punishments. Are some more severe than others because they more greatly interfere with offenders' ability to live satisfying lives, because they impose greater pains (however measured), because they have greater economist costs, because they constitute greater intrusions on liberty, mobility, or autonomy, or because of something else? We could not answer the questions "Proportionate to what?" or "Proportionate in what sense?"

For nearly half a century, most theorists have described themselves as retributivists of one sort or another. All retributive theories call for proportionality between crimes and punishments. That so central a concept remains so poorly understood is a surprising lacuna.

There appear to be three main reasons proportionality is undertheorized. The first is historical. Interest in retributive theories revived in the 1960s and 1970s in reaction to fundamental injustices in the indeterminate sentencing systems then ubiquitous in the United States and common elsewhere. Reformers were much more interested in changing unjust policies and practices than in elaborating theories. Emphasis on proportionality, they hoped, would lead to greater consistency and reduce the unwarranted disparities, racial injustices, and procedural unfairness that characterized indeterminate sentencing.

The second reason is disciplinary. Most influential writers on retributive punishment theories in subsequent years were philosophers who were more interested in general principles than in practical applications. H. L. A. Hart long ago distinguished three fundamental questions: How can the existence of punishment systems be justified, who should be punished, and how much? Philosophers have attended mostly to the first question. A passage written by the late Dan Markel is illustrative:

> One question is: What might justify the state's creation of legal institutions of punishment? This is what we call the "justification" question. The second question is: Once the state has determined someone's liability for a crime, how much and what kind of punishment should the state mete out in response? This is the "sentencing" question. That a retributivist theorist gives a retributive . . . answer to the justification question does not require her to offer a precise answer for each sentencing question. . . . *A retributive conception of proportionality need not have much in the way of precision to say about the particular details of punishment's implementation* [emphasis added].

The third reason is that there are no easy answers. Human beings cannot convincingly say what specific punishment a particular offender deserves. This is the epistemological problem of cardinal or absolute desert; God may know what individuals deserve, but mortals can only expostulate. Nigel Walker observed that an ideal retributive approach to punishment would require the omniscience of the Recording Angel, a personage in Muslim theology, to calculate what any flawed human being deserves in light of every detail of his or her existence. Deserved punishments in this sense are unknowable, but human beings can do better than we now do.

We must become much clearer about what makes crimes more or less serious and punishments more or less severe if punishment systems are to be made more just. Husak and I decided to bring together groups of young and more senior theorists to see if, collectively, we could achieve greater clarity. Many of the essays in this volume were initially presented and discussed at a conference in Minneapolis in April 2017. Revised versions of some of those essays and others newly commissioned were discussed at length and in detail at Worcester College, Oxford, in April 2018. Participants besides the writers at one or both meetings included Andrew Ashworth and Lucia Zedner, both of All Souls College, Oxford; Jacco Bomhoff, London School of Economics; Vincent Chiao, University of Toronto; Alessandro Corda, Queen's University Belfast; Chad Flanders, St. Louis University; Richard Frase, University of Minnesota; Zachary Hoskins, University of Nottingham; and Andreas von Hirsch, University of Frankfurt. Husak and I provided additional suggestions to each writer.

The process played out over an extended period and involved substantial effort by many people. Thanks are due to the Robina Institute of the University of Minnesota Law School for providing funding to support the venture and to the law school and Worcester College for providing facilities and amenities that made the meetings possible. I am especially grateful to Doug Husak for being a partner in proportionality throughout, to Julian V. Roberts for arranging the Worcester College meeting, and to Su Smallen for providing her usual immaculate editorial work.

Husak and I believe this venture has moved the ball forward. Readers will decide for themselves.

Michael Tonry
Isola d'Elba, February 2019

Contributors

Göran Duus-Otterström is Associate Professor of Political Science at Aarhus University and the Institute for Futures Studies.

Douglas Husak is Professor of Philosophy at Rutgers, the State University of New Jersey, New Brunswick.

Adam J. Kolber is Professor of Law at Brooklyn Law School.

Tapio Lappi-Seppälä is Professor of Criminal Law and Criminology and Director of the Institute of Criminology and Legal Policy at the University of Helsinki.

Richard L. Lippke is Professor of Criminal Justice at Indiana University.

Matt Matravers is Professor of Law and Director of the Morrell Centre for Toleration at York Law School, University of York.

Julian V. Roberts is Professor of Criminology, Faculty of Law, at the University of Oxford.

Jesper Ryberg is Professor of Ethics and Philosophy of Law at Roskilde University.

Michael Tonry is McKnight Presidential Professor of Criminal Law and Policy at the University of Minnesota.

Is Proportionality in Punishment Possible, and Achievable?

Michael Tonry

PROPORTIONALITY THEORY'S INFLUENCE is waning. It is beset by challenges. Some, such as difficulties in scaling crime seriousness and punishment severity, and linking them, are primarily analytical and of interest mostly to theorists. Others, such as trade-offs between proportionality and crime prevention, relate to real-world applications. Both sets of challenges can be explored in their own terms, and solutions can be sought. The bigger question, though, is whether the challenges are epiphenomenal and portend displacement of retribution as the most intellectually influential normative frame of reference for thinking about punishment.

Interest in retributive theory in English-speaking countries revived in the 1970s. For at least a century before that, consequentialist ideas were overwhelmingly dominant. Retribution, Columbia law professors Jerome Michael and Herbert Wechsler (1940) wrote, expressing the long-standing conventional view, may represent "the unstudied belief of most men," but "no legal provision can be justified merely because it calls for the punishment of the morally guilty by penalties proportioned to their guilt, or criticized merely because it fails to do so" (pp. 7, 11).[1] The revival of retributivism in the 1970s

---

1. Wechsler was the reporter and primary draftsman of the Model Penal Code. His consequentialist beliefs and the Code's normative premises were made clear in an article on its sentencing provisions: "The rehabilitation of an individual who has incurred the moral condemnation of the law is in itself a social value of importance, a value, it is well to note, that is and ought to be the prime goal" (1961, p. 468).

appeared to be sudden. University of Chicago law professor Albert Alschuler (1978) bewilderedly observed of the eclipse of consequentialism: "That I and many other academics adhered in large part to this reformative viewpoint only a decade or so ago seems almost incredible to most of us today" (p. 552).

In retrospect, however, the roots of change were evident much earlier. C. S. Lewis in 1949 wrote a searing critique of what he called the humanitarian theory of punishment and urged its replacement by the "traditional or Retributive theory." Anthony Burgess's dystopian 1962 novel *A Clockwork Orange*, about the use of aversive conditioning to restrain violent impulses, offered, he later wrote, "a moral lesson, and it is the weary traditional one of the fundamental importance of moral choice" (1986, p. x). Legal scholars in the 1950s began to decry the dangers and abuses of the unregulated power that consequentialism gave practitioners over offenders' lives (e.g., Allen 1959). Philosophers chimed in. John Rawls (1955) and Edmund Pincoffs (1966) argued that consequentialism was fine for legislators, but judges should pay attention to blameworthiness. And, far from least, H. L. A. Hart's 1959 presidential address to the Aristotelian Society set out an analytical framework that could accommodate both consequentialist and retributivist ideas, and allowed that proportionality and equal treatment had roles to play even in utilitarian accounts of punishment.

Only time will tell whether retributivism is in terminal decline. My best guess is that the difficulties contemporary philosophers face are as much a reflection of a change in the zeitgeist, in prevailing sensibilities, in mentalités as of sudden realization that retributive ideas offer less guidance for thinking about punishment than was widely understood. In this essay, however, I mostly discuss fundamental challenges to proportionality theory. I begin in section I by discussing current disquiet. In section II, I step back to say a bit about the origins of what we now call proportionality theory. Section III discusses problems in scaling and linking offense seriousness and punishment severity. Section IV suggests ways to ameliorate current problems and anticipate future ones should a paradigm shift be under way.

There are two big questions. First, can proportionality theory provide satisfactory answers to core questions about crime seriousness, punishment severity, and links between them? Alas, it cannot. Second, should proportionality theory be consigned to the dustbin of history? The answer here is more positive. The post-Enlightenment values of fairness, equality, justice, and parsimony that underlie proportionality theory are widely accepted and influential (Tonry 2018). Their influence has shaped policy transitions that gave greater emphasis to proportionality than theretofore. One example was the shift in the 1970s and 1980s in the Netherlands and Scandinavia away from rehabilitationism and toward retributivism (Junger-Tas 2004; Lappi-Seppälä 2016). Another was the short-lived American sentencing reform movement from the mid-1970s to the mid-1980s (Tonry 2016, chap. 2).

Isaiah Berlin (1959) long ago showed that the implications of equally valid first principles often conflict. No one disapproves of the consequentialist goals of maintenance of public order and security, but their pursuit will always be in tension with other values. The theorist's job is to show how they can be reconciled. In this essay's conclusion, I suggest how that can be done.

I. Disquiet

Writers on punishment routinely describe proportionality as a fundamental requirement of justice. Douglas Husak (2019*a*), long one of America's leading criminal law theorists, observes that "sentencing according to the principle of proportionality is crucial if the state is to treat offenders as they deserve" (p. 97).The term has served for a half century as a metonym for retributive ways of thinking about punishment, as shorthand for the proposition that punishments should be based on, or limited by, offenders' blameworthiness, rather than on their rehabilitative prospects or reoffending probabilities, other putative effects of what is done to them, or consonance with public demands for vengeance.

Recent developments call the salience of proportionality theory into question. Policymakers in common-law countries seem unmoved by the proposition that justice forbids imposition of disproportionately severe punishments. To a lesser extent but perceptibly, something similar is happening in Scandinavia. The Criminal Justice Act 2003 in England and Wales created a presumption favoring imposition of indeterminate prison sentences on people convicted of any of 153 offenses, some (e.g., carnal knowledge of a sheep) not of self-evidently enormous gravity. Innumerable three-strikes, mandatory minimum sentence, and similar laws in the United States mandate longer prison terms for affected crimes than are routinely imposed for palpably more serious wrongdoing. Under California's 1994 three-strikes law, for example, some property misdemeanors and minor drug sales until recently triggered 25-year and life sentences. In Scandinavia, "Informed and principled argument about the penal value of different offense types has been replaced by references to the demands of the general sense of justice," as evidenced by media and public opinion, especially concerning violent and sexual crimes (Lappi-Seppälä 2019, p. 230).

No doubt influenced by these and similar developments and the belief that they respond to, or are reconcilable with, public preferences, scholars have begun to question the usefulness of the principle of proportionality. Nicola Lacey and Hanna Pickard (2015, p. 237), for example, referring to "powerful emotional dynamics" of populist crime politics, wonder whether "appeals to proportionality are little more than empty rhetoric." Husak (2019*b*), ceding ground to crime-control politics, is willing to privilege predictions of dangerousness over proportionality: "Retributivists should preserve the role of desert while weakening its strength. . . . If we have good reason to inflict different amounts of punishment on two offenders who have committed equally serious crimes, we should not be worried that our decision does not preserve proportionality" (pp. 44–45).

Setting real-world concerns aside, other philosophers doubt that proportionality theory can provide convincing answers to fundamental questions. Jesper Ryberg (2019) observes that proportionality theory's inability to deal satisfactorily with scaling of crime seriousness calls it into question "as the plausible principle of penal distribution" (p. 51). Göran Duus-Otterström (2019) describes insoluble problems in scaling punishment severities and cautions, "such are the difficulties . . . that it is understandable if critics of retributivism think that the problem is insuperable" (p. 48). Matt Matravers (2019) writes, "The problems of determining metrics for crime seriousness and sentence severity, and of fixing the scales of punishment . . . pose a serious challenge to the principle of proportionality" (p. 93).

Here is the bottom line. Neither retributive theories in general nor "the principle of proportionality" can satisfactorily explain how much punishment ("hard treatment" in the disciplinary argot) should be imposed for a particular crime or how much and what kinds of suffering any particular offender deserves to endure.

Proportionality theory does, however, support two injunctions with which, I believe, most people—citizens, scholars, and professionals alike— would say they agree. First, no one should be punished more severely than he or she deserves.[2] Second, all else being equal, people who commit more

---

2. Much apparent agreement is, however, likely to be unconsidered. Endorsing positive abstract principles—justice, equality, mercy, proportionality—is easy and comforting to the endorser's self-image. The proportionality principle is inherently comparative: whether a particular punishment can reasonably be said to be just requires comparisons with punishments of others for similar and different crimes. The slip is between comparative and casuistic reasoning. Probably few people urge especially severe punishments in individual cases, or judges justify them, on the basis that "X should be punished more than he deserves because . . ." Much more likely are

serious crimes should be punished more severely than people who commit less serious ones, and vice versa. Converting that principled agreement into real-world policies and practices, however, is not easy.

Prevailing ways of thinking do not take shape in vacuums. Even assuming, as public opinion research demonstrates (e.g., Roberts et al. 2003; Robinson and Darley 2007; Darley 2010; Robinson 2013), that most people believe offenders should be punished as much as, or no more than, they deserve, how crimes are ranked by seriousness and how severe people believe punishments should be depend on prevailing attitudes and beliefs. These vary substantially, as Lacey and Pickard illustrate by comparing punishment practices in Scandinavian and English-speaking countries. Comparison of contemporary practices in Maine and Vermont with those in Oklahoma and Louisiana provide an American demonstration. So over time would comparison of the lengths of American prison terms in the 1970s and the 2010s.[3]

The two injunctions provide contours for a just punishment system but provide no substantive guidance for specifying upper limits on deserved punishments or what crimes are more serious than others and by how much. Those specifications inevitably vary with prevailing beliefs, but once made, they provide bases for saying that particular punishments are too severe.

Achievement of general acceptance of the two injunctions is not an unworldly aspiration. Conventional beliefs change, even concerning contentious and emotional topics. Some American Southerners before the Civil War and during the Jim Crow period opposed racial inequality on moral grounds. Theirs eventually became the prevailing view. Early feminists and sympathizers, notably including Mary Wollstonecraft ([1792] 2009) and John Stuart Mill ([1869] 1997), argued, again against the odds, that subordination of women is wrong. That became the prevailing view. Consensual homosexual behavior remained a criminal offense in England until 1967 and in

---

noncomparative statements; "whatever X received was deserved because of his crime, antisocial personality, fecklessness, 'dangerousness,' or past criminality."

3. Mean times served at first release from state prisons in 1980 were 63 months for people convicted of murder, 33 months for people convicted of rape, and 25 months for people convicted of robbery (Cahalan 1986, table 3.25). By the 2000s, those numbers more than doubled: in 2009, murder, 158 months; rape, 92 months; robbery, 53 months (Bureau of Justice Statistics 2011). All of these numbers understate actual times served; the numbers for prisoners released in any year overrepresent people serving shorter sentences and underrepresent people serving long ones. Because many more people in recent years are serving sentences of life, life without parole, and mandatory minimum terms measured in decades, the underestimates were greater in 2009.

some American states until 2003. That is unimaginable now. Other countries' criminal law systems are committed to ideas of proportionality and equal treatment. Someday that may be true in the United States. Even if an as yet unrecognized paradigm shift in thinking about punishment is under way, the two injunctions will have roles to play.

II. Origins

Few people disagree with the Mikado's declaration that the punishment should fit the crime. It is not easy to explain what that means or to know when it happens. Punishments can meaningfully be said to be proportionate only if we can explain why some crimes are more serious than others, why some punishments are more severe than others, and how specific crimes should be linked to particular punishments. The contemporary literature has comparatively little to say about any of these matters. Immanuel Kant and Georg Wilhelm Friedrich Hegel briefly discussed them centuries ago.

For nearly a half century, most writers on punishment theory have described themselves as retributivists of one sort or another and have described the principle of proportionality as a requirement of justice. Details vary, but all retributivists agree that the seriousness of the crime should be the sole or a primary determinant of the punishment's severity. Herbert Morris (1981), for example, in a classic essay, referred almost in passing to "principles that are familiar dictates of retributivism—that only the guilty may be punished, that the guilty must be, and that the punishment inflicted reflect the degree of guilt" (p. 271).

Conceptualizations of "degrees of guilt" differ. Kant, the archetypal retributivist, referred to offenders' "inner wickedness" ([1797] 2017, p. 116). Andreas von Hirsch (1976) famously wrote of their "just deserts." Others refer to blameworthiness, wrongfulness, or moral culpability. All of these terms encompass the nature and gravity of the criminal behavior and the offender's mental state and awareness at the time.

In this essay, I usually refer to blameworthiness, by which I mean something akin to Morris's degree of guilt or Kant's inner wickedness. I assume that offenders should be punished only for harms they intended or foresaw. Foresight encompasses harms that the offender knew or expected would happen. Reasonable people might differ on whether Model Penal Code recklessness ("conscious disregard" of a "substantial and unjustifiable risk") counts as foresight (American Law Institute 1962). For sure, if the offender knew the risk was substantial and unjustifiable; otherwise, almost certainly not, I'd say.

This is not the mainstream view.[4] Matravers (2019) observes that crime seriousness "is usually taken to be a composite of harmfulness (or endangerment, as not all crimes lead to actual harm) and culpability" (p. 77). In the mainstream view, he writes, harm "is equated with the actual harm done or threatened, and 'culpability' is a matter of the blameworthiness of the agent (for example, whether he or she acted intentionally or only recklessly)" (p. 77).

The key phrase is "the actual harm done," which sometimes may not have been intended, foreseen, or foreseeable to the offender or to anyone else except possibly the victim. A trivial example is the pickpocket who intends to commit the minor misdemeanor of stealing pocket change from a person of seemingly modest means but whose hand emerges holding a $20,000 Rolex watch; in most legal systems, that is a serious felony. A decidedly nontrivial example is the mugger who steals a woman's purse and pushes her aside to get away. If she falls and is seriously hurt, the harm can be substantial. If she falls and has a miscarriage, the actual harm done in some American states is a homicide. The loss of the fetus is a calamity and a tragedy but not something the assailant sought, foresaw, or consciously risked. In neither hypothetical is there any question that the offender's behavior proximately caused the harms. Punishing the offender for them, however, makes him or her strictly liable and erases the distinction between crimes and torts.

Tort law is different. Negligent, reckless, and intending actors are liable for the harms they cause. They "take their victims as they find them," including, for example, when an assault victim has a "glass jaw" or for other reasons experiences greater than normal suffering or loss. There, however, the issue is only who should bear consequential and incidental costs. Likewise for victim compensation and social insurance schemes: Their aims are to provide assistance and support to victims to help them overcome the effects of miserable experiences and get on with their lives. The offender's mens rea and awareness or nonawareness of risk are irrelevant.

---

4. Many philosophers, particularly ones who do not particularly focus on punishment, accept the legitimacy of the emotional intuition that consequences matter. Thomas Nagel (1979) offers examples to show that we blame ourselves and others do also when harms occur that are causally related to our behavior (e.g., the minor auto repair not made that causes an accident). From this, he concludes that people may fairly be deemed more blameworthy when harm results than when it doesn't. Jeremy Waldron (2008) and David Enoch (2008) deconstruct legal treatments of moral luck in far more detail, distinguishing among moral, legal, and plain luck, but, like Nagel, they accept as morally germane the widely held intuition that resulting harms matter.

Kant, to my knowledge, did not discuss serendipitous harm.[5] However, he insisted that punishment be calibrated to the seriousness of the offense:

> But what kind and what amount of punishment is it that public justice makes its principle and measure? None other than the principle of equality (in the position of the needle on the scale of justice), to incline no more to one side than to the other. Accordingly, whatever undeserved evil you inflict on another among the people, that you [deserve]. . . . Only the law of retribution (*jus talionis*) . . . can specify definitely the quality and the quantity of punishment. ([1797] 2017, p. 115)

Analysts, however, have seldom delved into the questions of what makes one "undeserved evil" worse than another, how "the quality and the quantity" of punishment required by "the principle of equality" are to be determined, and how crime seriousness and punishment severity should relate to each other.

Kant recognized that the answers are not obvious. Much of his discussion concerns homicide and other grave crimes for which he believed death was axiomatic. For lesser crimes, he acknowledged that application of the principle of equality is more difficult. For these, what should be done to the offender "is what he has perpetrated on others, if not in terms of its letter at least in terms of its spirit" (p. 140). He observed that the nature and severity of deserved punishments should sometimes take account of offenders' personal circumstances, particularly class distinctions, which makes the link between crime and punishment even less certain.[6] This raises the question, which Kolber (2009*a*, 2009*b*) most exhaustively addresses, of whether severity of punishments should be understood objectively or in terms of their individualized effects on particular people.

Hegel ([1821] 1991) shared Kant's abstract conception of the measure of deserved punishment: "What the criminal has done should also happen to

---

5. Nagel (1979) uncontroversially observes that for Kant a good will, even if ineffectual in achieving good things, "would sparkle like a jewel in its own right" and from that posits, "He would presumably have said the same thing about a bad will: whether it accomplishes its evil purposes is morally irrelevant" (n. 22 [p. 60]).

6. Kant ([1797] 2017) expressed particular concern that "the existence of class distinctions would not allow for [application of] the retributive principle" and proposed harsher punishments for privileged offenders. Thus, "someone of high standing given to violence could be condemned not only to apologize for striking an innocent person socially inferior to himself, but also to undergo a solitary confinement involving hardship; in addition to the discomfort he undergoes, the offender's vanity would be painfully affected, so that through his shame like would be fittingly repaid with like" (p. 115).

him" (p. 127). However, he also acknowledged that, save for crimes deservedly punishable by death, relations between crimes and punishments cannot be mechanical:

> An insuperable difficulty arises. . . . It is very easy to portray the retributive aspect of punishment as an absurdity (theft as retribution for theft, robbery for robbery, an eye for an eye, and a tooth for a tooth, so that one can even imagine the miscreant as one-eyed or toothless); but the concept has nothing to do with this absurdity. (p. 128)

Instead, he wrote, "Thought cannot specify how each crime should be punished; positive determinations are necessary for this purpose." Cultural norms change: "With the progress of education, however, attitudes toward crime become more lenient, and punishments today are not nearly so harsh as they were a hundred years ago. It is not the crimes or punishments themselves which change, but the relation between the two" (p. 123).

Kant published only a few pages on punishment, Hegel several times more but still not many. They were writing in detail about a subject that, save for people such as Jeremy Bentham who rejected their retributive premises, had previously been discussed only in broad generalizations.

Kant and Hegel were positivist retributivists who believed that deserved punishments not only may but must be imposed and that anything greater, or less, is per se unjust. Hegel ([1821] 1991) was explicit: "An injustice is done if there is one lash too many, or one dollar or groschen, one week or one day in prison too many or too few" (p. 245). From this flows the horizontal proportionality requirement that equally blameworthy offenders be punished equally severely and, since criminal wrongs are more and less serious, the vertical requirement that offenders be punished more and less severely in proportion to their relative blameworthiness. Negative retributivists such as Norval Morris (1974) relax both the horizontal and the vertical proportionality requirements but insist that any punishment more severe than positive retributivism would allow is per se unjust.

III. Fundamental Proportionality Questions

In this section, I canvass efforts to answer the three questions raised by the passage from Kant. There are no satisfactory answers. Kant and Hegel were right: the best we can do is make "positive determinations" about punishment that take account of the "spirit" of proportionality.

A. Crime Seriousness

Efforts to specify the relative seriousness of crimes founder on three problems. There is no conventional or widely accepted metric of seriousness. The competing realities problem is that victims' and offenders' conceptions of a single crime may sometimes be very different. The moral luck problem—that crimes may cause an intended harm or a lesser or greater one—breaks the link between blameworthiness and harm.

1. *The Missing Metric.* We lack any widely agreed measure or metric of what makes one category of crime, or one particular crime, more or less serious than another. In other domains, metrics are common. The Richter scale measures the strength of earthquakes. The Saffir-Simpson scale measures hurricane force. Diamond prices, controlling for demand, vary in understood ways with carats, color, and imperfections. Acuteness of medical care need determines emergency ward priorities. Buyers' willingness to pay determines values in wholesale fish markets. All of these measures are imperfect, of course, and reflect consideration of complex interacting details, but all provide widely accepted indicators of importance or value. Nothing even vaguely comparable exists for crime.

No big deal, some might say. There is no need for a highfalutin metric. Everyone knows when one crime is more serious than another; intuitions are widely shared. Associate US Supreme Court Justice Potter Stewart, in *Jacobellis v. Ohio*, 378 U.S. 184, 197 (1964), analogously explained that it would be difficult to define hard-core pornography, but it isn't necessary: "I know it when I see it." He was mocked. A half century later, his observation is regularly trotted out, as here, to illustrate the limits and elusiveness of personal intuitions.

Widely shared intuitions about offense seriousness exist only at the extremes. Almost everyone agrees that robbery and rape are more serious than shoplifting, bicycle theft, or sale of marijuana. Agreement is harder to reach on whether rape is more serious than robbery or shoplifting is more serious than selling pot. When offense descriptions become finer-grained—intoxicated acquaintance rape compared with armed street robbery or shoplifting by professionals compared with bike thefts by addicts—the widely shared intuitions dissolve. Intuitions are idiosyncratic and vary widely, which is why book reviews often reveal more about reviewers than about books (and sentences often reveal more about judges than about offenders).

There are a number of possible metrics. One is objective burdensomeness, the amount of physical injury or property loss crimes cause in general or in specific cases. This, however, raises formidable problems of assessing, characterizing, scaling, and combining degrees of physical injury and property loss. A second possibility is to use the average or actual costs of victimizations of different crimes, as economists might measure them, but this raises, among many others, the formidable problem of estimating the monetary costs of physical and psychological injuries. A third, a bit nebulous, is crimes' effects on victims' capacities to live a satisfying life. A fourth, even more nebulous, is the extent to which crimes invade victims' core interests.

Little work has been done on any of them; on most, there has been none. Economists have carried out aggregate cost-of-crime and cost-benefit studies (e.g., Cohen 2005; Greenfield and Paoli 2013; Dominguez-Rivera and Raphael 2015). Almost all use data collected by economist Mark Cohen on damage awards for pain and suffering in private tort actions to estimate the intangible costs of crime. This is inherently arbitrary and unrepresentative; few crimes result in tort actions, and those usually involve notorious cases and deep-pocketed defendants (Tonry 2015). Table 1.1 shows the severity rankings that emerge from Cohen's analysis. Two patterns stand out. Intangible costs are the primary driver of offense seriousness. Many of the rankings are counterintuitive: robbery, a combination of assault and theft, is less serious than assault alone; drunk driving is more serious than robbery, assault, burglary, and auto theft; arson is more serious than anything except child abuse and rape. Offense scales based on economic analyses will vary with the variables included in the model and how they are estimated.

Von Hirsch and Jareborg (1991) proposed a "living standards" metric that takes account of crimes' effects on victims' "means and capabilities" for living a satisfying life. Crimes that significantly impede a victim's ability to support himself or herself or to maintain prior living standards, for example, are more serious than crimes that do not. Stealing an automobile from a wealthy person who owns several imposes lesser burdens than stealing the only car of a family of modest means. Burning down a vacation home usually causes less material dislocation than burning down a primary residence.[7] If offenders are aware of salient differences between victims, it is reasonable to say that greater harm was intended or foreseen in one case than in another. Sentencing policies often provide, for example, increased penalties for crimes against elderly, infirm, financially dependent, and otherwise vulnerable victims.

---

7. These examples are taken from a presentation by von Hirsch at the University of Minnesota Law School in 1992.

Table 1.1 Crime seriousness, by average economic cost
(1993 constant dollars)

Crime	Lost productivity	Medical, mental health costs	Social services	Property loss	Quality of life	Total*
Child sexual abuse	2,100	6,290	1,100	0	89,800	99,000
Adult rape, sexual assault	2,200	2,700	27	100	81,400	87,000
Child physical abuse	3,400	3,490	2,100	26	57,500	67,000
Arson	1,750	1,118	0	15,500	18,000	37,500
Assault, injury	3,100	1,567	46	39	19,300	24,000
Robbery, injury	1,500	1,565	44	1,400	13,800	19,000
Drunk driving	2,800	1,482	0	1,600	11,900	18,000
All assault	950	501	16	26	7,800	9,000
All robbery	950	436	25	750	2,300	8,000
Motor vehicle theft	45	5	0	3,300	300	3,700
Burglary	12	5	5	970	300	1,400

*Total includes an additional invariably small item, not shown: fire and police services.
Source: Cohen (2005, table 3.1).

That kind of case-level analysis is not, however, what von Hirsch and Jareborg have in mind. They propose that assessments of "standard harms" associated with different crimes be used to develop seriousness scales.[8] This may slightly sharpen intuitive analyses, but not by much except for a few types of crime such as sale of marijuana. Standard harms analysis provides a basis for

---

8. Husak (1994) and Ryberg (2004) explore implications and possible methods for incorporating the living-standards approach in characterizations of crime seriousness, as, in considerably greater detail, does Ryberg (2019).

saying that rape is more serious than auto theft, or burglary is more serious than shoplifting, but few people would disagree. It calls for punishing property crimes involving larger amounts more severely than property crimes involving significantly lesser amounts, but few people would disagree about that, either. It provides little basis for deciding whether intoxicated acquaintance rape is more serious than armed street robbery or burglary is more serious than auto theft. Individuals have idiosyncratic opinions about the harms typically associated with different crimes, but they must inevitably vary depending on the weights different individuals give to different kinds of harms.

All that is left are intuitive assessments of the sort that lead legislators to authorize higher penalties for some crimes than for others and sentencing commissions to rank offense seriousness. Public opinion surveys and laboratory experiments on people's views about the seriousness of crime provide little guidance for those decisions. They find broad agreement across time and space in assessments of the relative gravity of a small number of serious crimes (e.g., Sellin and Wolfgang 1964; Sebba 1978; Robinson and Darley 2007; Adriaenssen et al. 2018). However, findings do not remotely approach the level of detail needed to develop comprehensive scales of offense seriousness.

2. *Conflicting Realities.* Offense definitions are general, but victimization is specific. To a person with a glass jaw, a barroom assault may cause unbearable pain, life-threatening injury, and permanent disfigurement. The assailant may have intended only insult and minor fleeting pain or discomfort. To an offender, the measure of the seriousness of a crime is the wrongfulness of what he or she set out to do, foresaw, or consciously risked. The measure of the seriousness of a crime to a victim is what happened and with what consequences. A crime that results in great pain, hospitalization, extended recuperation, or ongoing mental-health problems is more serious to a victim than an identical crime without some or all of those consequences. Property crimes involving pocket change are less serious than property crimes involving Rolex watches. Closely comparable crimes may have starkly diverse effects: one victim may simply recall an unpleasant experience; one may suffer continuing anxiety, miss work, and incur sizable counseling bills; one may suffer post-traumatic stress disorder, never recover, and eventually commit suicide. Bystanders mostly see, and care about, the victim's reality. So, often, do prosecutors and judges.

3. *Moral Luck.* The moral luck problem is that although an offender may intend or foresee a specific harm, what happens is always to some degree serendipitous. A would-be assailant may produce no harm at all if an attempt fails and the intended victim was unaware of it; some harm if only lesser, incidental damage results; the intended harm; or a greater one. Criminal

law doctrines address some of this but not enough.[9] They embody diverse mixes of utilitarian and retributive considerations and provide standards for convictions, not punishments.

There is no consensus view about serendipitous harm among people who write about moral luck. Thomas Nagel (1979), with Bernard Williams (1981), an instigator of the modern literature, accepts the legitimacy of the emotional intuition that consequences matter. So do other influential philosophers (e.g., Wolf 2001; Waldron 2008). However, equally influential writers disagree (e.g., Kadish 1994; Feinberg 1995). Some paradigmatic hypotheticals appear to many retributivists to be easy. Few disagree with Andrew Ashworth (1988) that an intending murderer who fails only because a gun misfires or because the victim moves at the critical microsecond is as blameworthy as if he had succeeded. From Bentham onward, however, most common-law jurisdictions and most utilitarians, including the drafters of the Model Penal Code, have favored punishing attempts less severely than completed offenses.

Utilitarian views of moral luck are, however, beside the point for purposes of this essay. In principle, retributive views such as Ashworth's concerning unsuccessful completed attempts should be two-edged. If causing less harm than was intended or foreseen should not diminish imputation of blame, causing unintended, unforeseen greater harms should not increase it.

The mainstream "actual harm caused" view, that crime seriousness is a composite of harmfulness and culpability, offers an ironic "punishment of the innocent" parallel to a standard retributivist critique of utilitarianism. The critique is that utilitarians should approve of punishment of innocent people if that will produce a net decrease in human suffering. The classic hypothetical involves the rape of a white woman, apparently by a black man, in the American South during the Jim Crow period (McCloskey 1965). A sheriff believes he can prevent racial violence in which many people will be injured or killed if he frames an innocent black man seen near the scene of the crime. The question is whether he should do that. Most utilitarians say no, arguing either that only morally blameworthy offenders may be punished[10] or that

---

9. Examples: transferred-malice doctrine (the shot misses the intended victim but hits someone else); homicide doctrines such as felony murder and equation of intent to commit grievous bodily harm with intention to kill that make assailants criminally responsible for greater than intended harms.

10. Hart (1968) was perplexed that Bentham endorsed the insanity offense on the rationale that insane people cannot be deterred. Hart characterized this as a "non sequitur"; the audience for deterrent punishments is the general population, he wrote, not only mentally disturbed people such as the offender. Hart was a much keener analyst than I could ever be, but he

occasional punishments of the innocent would inevitably be discovered, nullifying any beneficial effects and undermining the criminal law's legitimacy and effectiveness.

Some utilitarians argue that knowingly punishing an innocent person when necessary to prevent greater aggregate suffering should not be considered "punishment" (Quinton 1969). Hart characterized this as an evasion, an impermissible "definitional stop" (1968, p. 5). To the person affected, punishment feels like punishment, whatever its rationale or name. If it looks like a duck, walks like a duck, and quacks like a duck, most likely it is a duck. Plutarch (1957) quotes Bion of Borysthenes (325–250 B.C.E.), who observed, of boys playing by a stream on a summer day, "Though boys throw stones at frogs in sport, yet the frogs do not die in sport but in earnest" (p. 355).

The parallel argument concerning serendipitous harm is that increments of punishment exceeding what offenders deserve are not really "punishment" but state impositions meant to acknowledge emotional reactions and protect the law's legitimacy. If Hart is right in ruling out the definitional stop to justify punishing innocent people, and I believe he is, neither retributivists nor anyone else should be able legitimately to offer a similar justification for punishing people for harms they neither intended nor foresaw.

Many people appear to believe, however, all else including the offender's blameworthiness being equal, that serendipitous harms make crimes more serious. The victim's bad luck is the offender's. Of a thousand equally blameworthy drunk drivers, 999 may arrive safely home without incident and one may be involved in an accident causing injury or death. The book is usually thrown at him or her, and demands for punishment are adamant. Cases involving no harm are a different matter. Public furors seldom occur when unsuccessful attempts are punished less severely than successful ones or when drunk drivers who arrive home safely are not charged with attempted vehicular homicide. All thousand are guilty of drunk driving and could appropriately be prosecuted and punished, but unless the one involved in the accident was otherwise more blameworthy than the 999, he or she should be dealt with in the same way. Doing otherwise is to punish by lottery.

---

seems to have overlooked that Bentham also endorsed ignorance-of-the-law and intoxication defenses on the rationale that affected offenders could not have known that what they did was a crime. Bentham anticipated Hart's distinction between the separate questions of who may be punished and how much. The non sequitur disappears if insane offenders are not liable to punishment because they are not blameworthy and can therefore not be convicted.

I HAVE BEEN unable to find any sustained analysis of other analytical models for characterizing crime seriousness. Other relevant literatures may exist, of course, but none of the few writings that attempt exhaustively to survey the subject mentions them (e.g., Greenfield and Paoli 2013; Ryberg 2019). We lack a metric and face the possibly overwhelming problems of different realities and moral luck.

B. Punishment Severity

How much hard treatment is due any particular offender? Efforts to develop scales of punishment severity founder on interpersonal comparisons of suffering. In physical sciences, objective scales are easy. Fahrenheit and Celsius scales of temperature give different values to a degree, but once it is specified, we know exactly what 17 degrees means. Likewise in many realms of day-to-day life. Once an hourly pay rate is set, we know exactly what is due to people who work 17 or 37 hours. Punishment is not like that. One axis of the American federal sentencing guidelines sets out 43 levels of offense seriousness and specifies for each a range of recommended punishments (mostly prison sentences). There is nothing remotely comparable to a Celsius degree or an hourly wage rate to indicate whether offenses are correctly classified or whether the designated punishments are the right ones. The US Sentencing Commission simply assumed that objective durations of confinement should be the coin of punishment. Any seemingly objective measure of severity, including years in prison or dollars, however, will have substantially different effects on different people. There is no widely agreed metric of punishment severity.

Financial penalties are illustrative. Fixed amounts burden the poor more than the rich, but so do fines scaled to income and wealth. Taking comparable shares of income, net worth, or both from the poor and the rich makes the poor poorer and leaves the rich richer and better able to replenish what is taken. Even if—and no existing system of fines, including day fines, does this—all of offenders' assets above what is required for a subsistence standard of living were taken, rich offenders' social capital makes financial recovery much easier and more likely.

Confinement presents comparable problems. A stay in the same prison for the same period imposes vastly different burdens on a middle-aged bread-winner, a claustrophobe, a seriously mental ill or terminally ill person, a young gang member for whom prison time is a rite of passage, and a career offender for whom it is a cost of doing business. The commonest solutions—to ignore the problem or base punishment severity on the suffering of an average person and accept unusual suffering as either a regrettable externality or something the offender, aware of his or her personal vulnerabilities, knowingly risked (Lippke 2019)—beg the question.

There is no literature, to my knowledge, on the metric of punishment or on how to measure or characterize the suffering of an average person or an individual while being punished. Most retributivists distinguish between authoritative state censure, condemnation, or blaming that occurs when an offender is found guilty and the "hard treatment" that punishment entails. The expression of censure can be standardized; hard treatment cannot. In the United States, imprisonment is the hard treatment invariably assumed for nontrivial crimes by individuals.[11] Whether that is because imprisonment restricts prisoners' mobility, autonomy, or liberty; diminishes their quality of life; reduces their life chances; humiliates them; stigmatizes them; degrades them; causes psychological suffering; or something else is seldom discussed or considered.

Imprisonment does some of those things to all inmates and all of them to some, but that does not make the metric question trivial. Nor does it make all those effects of imprisonment justifiable. If, for example, restriction of mobility were the gravamen of punishment, alternatives to imprisonment, such as home detention or confinement in comfortable but secure accommodation in conditions permitting exercise of all privileges of citizenship except mobility, would be available. All of the other effects would be unwanted externalities to be avoided or ameliorated. Prophylactic measures might include full-wage employment in confinement or by day release; extensive family visits, including conjugal visits; adequate medical and mental-health services; extensive educational, vocational training, and recreational opportunities; and nondisclosure of records of criminal convictions.

This is not as far-fetched as most Americans might imagine. It is at least the aspiration and to varying extents the reality in many Swiss, Dutch, German, and Scandinavian prisons. Federal District Court Judge James E. Doyle, in *Morales v. Schmidt*, 340 F. Supp. 544 (1972), reasoning that people are sent

---

11. The next few paragraphs pertain primarily to the United States and, to a lesser extent, other English-speaking countries in which imprisonment is extensively used and prison terms are often long. In much of Western Europe, most sentences to imprisonment are immediately suspended, only 4 to 20 percent of convicted offenders receive unsuspended prison sentences, the vast majority of prison sentences are for 2 years or less, and day fines, community service, and electronic monitoring are extensively used as prison alternatives (Aebi et al. 2014; Lappi-Seppälä 2016).

to prison as punishment, not for punishment, held that prisoners retain all rights of citizenship other than those entailed in restriction of mobility. The decision was overturned by a higher court.

Two scant punishment theory literatures nibble at the edges of a punishment metric. One explores ways to substitute other forms of punishment for imprisonment. The other considers whether decisions about punishment should take interpersonal differences in suffering into account.

1. *Interchangeability of Punishments.* Paul Robinson, Andreas von Hirsch and colleagues, and Norval Morris and I attempted in the 1980s to devise systems for equating periods or amounts of community punishment to periods of imprisonment. None of us succeeded. Von Hirsch, Wasik, and Greene (1989) proposed a limited system for substituting community punishments for imprisonment but only when the former were as burdensome as the putatively equivalent term of imprisonment would have been. That necessarily limited substitution to only the most minor crimes.

Morris and I (Morris and Tonry 1990) attempted to develop a "punishment units" scheme in which all punishment forms could be expressed. Our aim was to devise a system in which offenders would be sentenced to a specific number of units, say, 120. Each of 1 month's imprisonment, 2 month's probation, 2 weeks' home confinement, a fine of 5 days' after-tax income, and 20 hours of unpaid community service might be valued as 10 units. Any punishment or combination of punishments that totaled 120 units would do. Judges would specify the pertinent purposes "at" rather than "of" sentencing. By this, we intended that the judge would think about, and be required to explain, what he or she hoped to accomplish by imposing that specific sentence on that particular person.

We gave up. The insuperable problem was that in American political and legal culture, then and now, only imprisonment counts. Some state sentencing commissions experimented with punishment units and invariably considered or established equivalences that limited substitution to only the shortest prison sentences. Washington State, for example, made 24 hours' community service equivalent to 1 day of confinement; 240 hours could thus substitute for 10 days' confinement. By contrast, successful community service pilot projects in the United States and the United Kingdom substituted 240 hours' service for 6 months' imprisonment; the rationale was that anything more was administratively infeasible (McDonald 1986). In the end, a bit lamely, we urged increased use of community punishments that were "roughly equivalent" to imprisonment.

Robinson (1987, 2017) also developed a punishment-units scheme. Like von Hirsch, Wasik, and Greene (1989), he would permit use only of community punishments that were as burdensome as a prison sentence would have been. As a practical matter, this limited his scheme to choices among community punishments or between highly burdensome community punishments and very short prison sentences. Some notion of suffering ordinarily resulting from imprisonment as the generic metric of punishment severity is implicit in Robinson's and von Hirsch, Wasik, and Greene's proposals. Adam Kolber (2009*b*) appears to mean something similar when he uses the word "distress."

2. *Subjective Measures of Suffering.* Kolber (2009*a*, 2009*b*) provoked a furor among punishment theorists when, in an emperor's-new-clothes argument, he insisted that severity of punishment, on any coherent account, should be assessed in relation to the suffering or distress of individual offenders. He made two main claims: "First, a successful justification of punishment must take account of offenders' subjective experiences when assessing punishment severity. Second, we have certain obligations to consider actual or anticipated punishment experience at sentencing" (2009*b*, p. 132). A few people agree (Masur, Bronsteen, and Buccafusco 2009; Hayes 2016). It is fair to say, however, that his claims mostly provoked spirited objections (e.g., Markel and Flanders 2010; Lippke 2019).[12]

The objections are odd. Only modern retributivists assume that punishment decisions should take no account of individual differences. Kant assumed that punishments should be adjusted to take account of their differing effects on individuals and provided several examples ([1797] 2017, p. 115). Bentham insisted that the offender's "sensibilities" be considered ("sensitivities" in our time). That is, the punishment must take account of how it would affect that particular individual. People have different sensitivities and react in different ways to the same experience, including experiences of punishment. Accordingly, "That the quantity actually inflicted on an individual offender may correspond to the quantity intended for similar offenders in general, the several circumstances influencing sensibility ought always to be taken into account" ([1789] 1970, p. 169).[13] Nigel Walker (1991)

---

12. Matravers (2019, p. 91) suggests that the issue is a false one. He writes, citing Dworkin (1977, p. 227), "There is a difference between 'equal treatment' and 'treatment as an equal.'" Disregarding fundamental differences between individuals that materially affect their experience of a punishment "fails to notice this distinction, and in subjecting them [all] to identical (equal) treatment . . . fails to treat them as equals (that is, 'with the same respect and concern')."

13. Bentham ([1789] 1970) devoted three substantial chapters of *An Introduction to the Principles of Morals and Legislation* to the tailoring of punishments to individual characteristic: "Of Circumstances Influencing Sensibility," "Of the Proportion between Punishments and Offences," and "Of the Properties to be Given to a Lot of Punishment."

observed that retributive theories of punishment, taken seriously, would require the omniscience of Saint Peter or Islam's Recording Angel to calculate what any flawed human being deserves in light of every detail of his or her existence that relates to assessment of moral blameworthiness concerning the specific crime.

AS WITH SCALING of offense seriousness, so with punishment severity. We lack any commonly agreed metric. Human beings will muddle through. Crimes will be committed, and punishments will be imposed, but proportionality theory can provide only the most general guidance on what those punishments should be.

C. Linking Crimes and Punishments

Linking crimes and punishments, even assuming we could scale both in morally convincing ways, founders on cardinal, or absolute, desert (Duus-Otterström 2019). Saint Peter or the Recording Angel may know precisely what a wrongdoer deserves, but we mortals do not. Antony Duff (2001) observed of efforts to specify absolute desert: "There is no Archimedean point, independent of all existing penal practice, from which we could embark on such an enterprise" (p. 134). Hegel ([1821] 1991) declared that "it is impossible to determine by reason . . . [what] the just punishment for an offence is" (p. 245). Even if, as individuals, we believe we know, others believe differently. We could vote on a range of possibilities for a particular offense or average everyone's intuitions, but the result would be an arithmetic amalgam, little more morally compelling than drawing straws. The fallback is to switch to ordinal, or relative, desert, develop intuitive scales of offense seriousness and punishment severity, and draw lines between the two: specify the crime and follow the lines (von Hirsch 2017). This works mechanically but begs lots of questions, including how severely the most and least serious crimes deserve to be punished and how much more punishment one crime deserves relative to another. Here, too, Saint Peter and other angels presumably know the answers. We mortals have access only to our diverse intuitions.

IV. Conclusion

Proportionality is at the core of retributive theory but by itself cannot specify the contours of a just punishment system or a just punishment. Utilitarian proportionality in principle can do both. Bentham's rules for determining punishments of individuals for specific crimes are complex but, with perfect knowledge of the empirical world, could in principle indicate uniquely appropriate punishments. Retributive proportionality theory, by contrast, can provide no general or specific guidance until judgments are made about the most severe punishments that may be imposed in general and for specific kinds of crimes. Those judgments vary widely with time and place and reflect diverse historical, cultural, and political influences.

Punishments will not be proportionate in the retributive sense unless policymakers and practitioners want them to be. In recent decades in some countries, they have often not much cared. Many, maybe most, people in Western countries, however, would say they support the two retributive injunctions that no one be punished more severely than he or she deserves and, all else being equal, that more serious crimes be punished more severely than less serious ones. Assuming those avowals are substantive, and not merely rhetorical, proportionality theory has roles to play but subject to conditions.

A. The Top of the Punishment Scale

The first role concerns maximum punishments. Limits have to be set, negotiated; there is no place to look for an objective indicator. Andreas von Hirsch and Norval Morris argued about this for years. Morris (1974) believed that relatively broad agreement can be reached, in any place and time, about punishments that are too severe and, sometimes, too slight for particular crimes; those limits of "not undeserved punishment" set the boundaries within which a sentencing system must operate. Von Hirsch (1976) initially proposed 5 years' imprisonment as the maximum for all but exceptionally serious crimes, with proportionately lower caps for the less serious. He repeatedly expressed frustration about Morris's view and urged him to be more concrete. They never reached a meeting of the minds. That is not surprising. Von Hirsch is a positive retributivist, committed to ordinal proportionality. Morris was at heart a utilitarian who, like H. L. A. Hart, believed that the law must reflect widely shared public attitudes if it is to retain its legitimacy.

Lacey and Pickard (2015) are probably right; in times and places where broad agreement does not exist about punishment severity, commitment to proportionality may remain mostly rhetorical. That is not true everywhere. In many Western and Northern European countries, statutory maximum punishments for most crimes are in low single digits (in years) and for the most serious, except sometimes murder, are 10, 12, or 14 years (e.g., for

Scandinavia, Lappi-Seppälä 2016). Because maximums by definition apply to the most serious of a type of crime, and most crimes are not very serious, much lesser punishments are normally imposed. Low caps and modest proportionate punishments in such places are not likely to be controversial.

The psychological dynamic is different in the United States and England and Wales, where maximum statutory punishments for many crimes are expressed in decades or lifetimes and sentences of 10 or more years are common. American sentencing commissions ducked principled questions when setting sentence lengths. They undertook statistical analyses of sentencing patterns a year or two before they began work and largely based guidelines on what they learned (e.g., Parent 1988). They usually ignored statutory maximums and achieved crude proportionality; former sentencing patterns presumably roughly paralleled prevailing attitudes about crime seriousness, at least among prosecutors and judges. Even that approach, however, did not work for long in Minnesota. In the aftermath of several notorious murders in the early 1990s, the legislature in a stroke doubled the lengths of presumptive sentences for many crimes (Frase 2005).

The empirical approach rests uncomfortably within a proportionality frame. In principle, articulable normative rationales should underlie scaling of crime seriousness, establishment of maximum sentences, and punishment severity. American punishment practices, for victim-reality reasons, probably punish violent crimes more severely than systematic analyses starting from normative premises would justify. The empirical approach may nonetheless be the likeliest to succeed. In principle, were it politically possible, it would be better to negotiate an overall cap and seriousness rankings.

B. Rough Equivalence

Matravers (2019) observes, "As anyone who has graded papers in legal theory—and many other domains—knows, it is a rough and ready business in which one seeks for rough equivalence and not precise differences," and suggests that may be the best to be hoped for concerning punishment (p. __). Morris and I (1990), in our effort to facilitate substitution of community punishments for imprisonment, similarly concluded that rough equivalence is the only achievable goal.

That is a weak aspiration, but given that there are no widely agreed metrics to use in scaling offense seriousness or punishment severity, it may be the best we can do. And that is not so bad. Any classification of crimes is necessarily a classification of legal definitions that apply to wide ranges of behavior.

Robberies, for example, involve different kinds of offenders, victims, locations, threats, weapons (if any), injuries (if any), and property values (if any) and may be accomplished or unsuccessfully attempted. Each difference can vary in character and intensity. Some of those differences can be captured to some degree by creating subcategories of offenses, but major differences between events falling within the same category will remain. Particular punishments likewise vary objectively in nature, intensity, and detailed characteristics and subjectively in their effects on individuals. And every punishment decision must be made by an individual or group of individuals with distinct personalities, beliefs, and idiosyncrasies. No system of rules or punishment standards can encompass all the material differences. If an overall cap and a morally persuasive system of offense seriousness ranking has been set, rough equivalence in treatment of different cases is probably the best human beings can do.

C. Varieties of Retributivism

For the reasons set out in this essay and in essays by others that I have quoted, no punishment system based on positive retributivist premises is achievable without fundamental compromises. Reasonably principled systems based on negative retributivist principles may be. Norval Morris's "limiting retributivism" proposals are more timely now than when he made them. He called for setting maximum punishments for every type of crime and, sometimes for the most serious or emotionally galvanizing, minimums. Within those limits, the presumptively appropriate punishment, following Bentham's frugality principle (Morris's parsimony), would be the least severe allowable. That presumption could be overridden when there were valid, evidence-based reasons to believe a more severe punishment would be an effective crime preventive. In his time, Morris (1974) believed the state of the evidence did not justify increasing punishments for deterrent, incapacitative, or rehabilitative reasons. The National Academy of Sciences Committee on Causes and Consequences of High Rates of Incarceration concluded that the evidence concerning deterrence and incapacitation is little better in our time (Travis, Western, and Redburn 2014, chaps. 3, 5). The evidence concerning rehabilitation has improved (Petersilia and Rosenfeld 2007). Well-managed, targeted, and funded programs can reduce reoffending. This provides no justification, however, for imprisoning people or imprisoning them for longer than they otherwise would be: treatment programs are more effective in the community than in prison. It may often provide justification for diverting people from prison.

Proportionality theory by itself cannot provide adequate guidance for creating just systems of punishment. The theoretical implications are clear. Lots of careful work needs to be done to enrich understanding of what makes particular crimes more serious than others and particular punishments more severe than others. Little has been done so far, and it has not provided useful tools. Scaling decisions will continue largely to result from negotiations among people who have different intuitions, but those negotiations can be better informed and more sensitive to normative considerations than they are now. Theorists could help.

The policy implications are also clear: punishments should always be the least severe possible. Numerical sentencing guidelines did not exist in the United States when Morris wrote. They do now, in the federal system and 16 states (Frase 2019). They set ranges of ostensibly appropriate sentences for particular categories of crimes. Positive retributivism can provide little useful principled guidance on fixing punishments within those ranges. The necessary conceptual work has not been done. Morris's limiting retributivism can provide guidance: impose the least severe presumptively appropriate punishment unless there are good, evidence-based—not intuition-based—reasons to do something more. When there are mitigating circumstances relating to the offender or the offense, do less. Should paradigms shift, the proportionality implications are the same: do the least harm to wrongdoers and only for good evidence-based reasons.

References

Adriaenssen, An, Letizia Paoli, Susanne Karstedt, Jonas Visschers, Victoria A. Greenfield, and Stefaan Pleysier. 2018. "Public Perceptions of the Seriousness of Crime: Weighing the Harm and the Wrong." *European Journal of Criminology*. https://doi.org/10.1177/1477370818772768.

Aebi, Marcelo F., Galma Akdeniz, Gordon Barclay, Claudia Campistol, Stefano Caneppele, Beata Gruszczyńska, Stefan Harrendorf, Markku Heiskanen, Vasilika Hysi, Jorg-Martin Jehle, Anniina Jokinen, Annie Kensey, Martin Killias, Chris J. Lewis, Ernesto Savonna, Paul Smit, and Rannveig Bórisdóttir. 2014. *European Sourcebook of Crime and Criminal Justice Statistics: 2014*, 5th ed. Helsinki: Helsinki European United Nations Institute.

Allen, Francis A. 1959. "Legal Values and the Rehabilitative Ideal." *Journal of Criminal Law, Criminology, and Police Science* 50:226–32.

Alschuler, Albert. 1978. "Sentencing Reform and Prosecutorial Power." *University of Pennsylvania Law Review* 126:550–77.

American Law Institute. 1962. *Model Penal Code: Proposed Official Draft.* Philadelphia: American Law Institute.

Ashworth, Andrew. 1988. "Criminal Attempts and the Role of Resulting Harm under the Code, and in the Common Law." *Rutgers Law Review* 19:725–72.

Bentham, Jeremy. 1970. *An Introduction to the Principles of Morals and Legislation*, edited by J. H. Burns and H. L. A. Hart. Oxford: Clarendon. (Originally published 1789.)

Berlin, Isaiah. 1959. *Four Essays on Liberty.* Oxford: Oxford University Press.

Bureau of Justice Statistics. 2011. *BJS—2009—Time Served of Releasees*, file ncrp0909. csv. Washington, DC: US Department of Justice.

Burgess, Anthony. 1962. *A Clockwork Orange.* London: Heinemann.

Burgess, Anthony. 1986. "Introduction: A Clockwork Orange Resucked." *A Clockwork Orange.* New York: W. W. Norton.

Cahalan, Margaret. 1986. *Historical Corrections Statistics in the United States, 1850–1984.* Washington, DC: US Department of Justice, Bureau of Justice Statistics.

Cohen, Mark A. 2005. *The Costs of Crime and Justice.* London: Routledge.

Darley, John M. 2010. "Citizens' Assignments of Punishments for Moral Transgressions: A Case Study in the Psychology of Punishment." *Ohio State Journal of Criminal Law* 8:101–17.

Dominguez-Rivera, Patricio, and Steven Raphael. 2015. "The Role of the Costs-of-Crime Literature in Bridging the Gap between Social Science Research and Policy Making: Potentials and Limitations." *Criminology and Public Policy* 14(4):589–632.

Duff, R. Antony. 2001. *Punishment, Communication, and Community.* New York: Oxford University Press.

Duus-Otterström, Göran. 2019. "Weighing Relative and Absolute Proportionality in Punishment." In *Of One-Eyed and Toothless Miscreants: Making the Punishment Fit the Crime?* edited by Michael Tonry. New York: Oxford University Press.

Dworkin, Ronald. 1977. *Taking Rights Seriously.* Cambridge: Harvard University Press.

Enoch, David. 2008. "Luck between Morality, Law, and Justice." *Theoretical Inquiries in Law* 9:23–60.

Feinberg, Joel. 1995. "Equal Punishment for Failed Attempts." *Arizona Law Review* 37:117–32.

Frase, Richard S. 2005. "Sentencing Guidelines in Minnesota, 1978–2003." In *Crime and Justice: A Review of Research*, vol. 32, edited by Michael Tonry. Chicago: University of Chicago Press.

Frase, Richard S. 2019. "Forty Years of American Sentencing Guidelines: What Have We Learned?" In *American Sentencing*, edited by Michael Tonry. Vol. 48 of *Crime and Justice: A Review of Research*, edited by Michael Tonry. Chicago: University of Chicago Press.

Greenfield, Victoria A., and Letizia Paoli. 2013. "A Framework to Assess the Harms of Crimes." *British Journal of Criminology* 53:864–85.

Hart, H. L. A. 1959. "Prolegomenon to the Principles of Punishment." *Proceedings of the Aristotelian Society*, n.s., 60:1–26.

Hart, H. L. A. 1968. *Punishment and Responsibility: Essays in the Philosophy of Law.* Oxford: Clarendon.

Hayes, David J. 2016. "Penal Impact: Towards a More Intersubjective Measure of Penal Severity." *Oxford Journal of Legal Studies* 36:724–50.

Hegel, Georg Wilhelm Friedrich. 1991. *Elements of the Philosophy of Right*, edited by Allen W. Wood. Translation by H. B. Nisbet. Cambridge: Cambridge University Press. (Originally published 1821.)

Husak, Douglas. 1994. "Is Drunk Driving a Serious Offense?" *Philosophy and Public Affairs* 23:52–73.

Husak, Douglas. 2019a. "The Metric of Punishment Severity: A Puzzle about the Principle of Proportionality." In *Of One-Eyed and Toothless Miscreants: Making the Punishment Fit the Crime?* edited by Michael Tonry. New York: Oxford University Press.

Husak, Douglas. 2019b. "Why Legal Philosophers (Including Retributivists) Should Be Less Resistant to Risk-Based Sentencing." In *Predictive Sentencing: Normative and Empirical Perspectives*, edited by Jan W. de Keijser, Julian V. Roberts, and Jesper Ryberg. Oxford: Hart.

Junger-Tas, Josine. 2004. "Youth Justice in the Netherlands." In *Youth Crime and Youth Justice: Comparative and Cross-National Perspectives*, edited by Michael Tonry and Anthony N. Doob. Vol. 31 of *Crime and Justice: A Review of Research*, edited by Michael Tonry. Chicago: University of Chicago Press.

Kadish, Sanford H. 1994. "The Criminal Law and the Luck of the Draw." *Journal of Criminal Law and Criminology* 84:679–702.

Kant, Immanuel. 2017. *The Metaphysics of Morals*, edited by Lara Denis. Translation by Mary Gregor. Cambridge: Cambridge University Press. (Originally published 1797.)

Kolber, Adam. 2009a. "The Comparative Nature of Punishment." *Boston University Law Review* 89:1565–610.

Kolber, Adam. 2009b. "The Subjective Experience of Punishment." *Columbia Law Review* 109:182–236.

Lacey, Nicola, and Hanna Pickard. 2015. "The Chimera of Proportionality: Instituti onalising Limits on Punishment in Contemporary Social and Political Systems." *Modern Law Review* 78(2):216–40.

Lappi-Seppälä, Tapio. 2016. "Nordic Sentencing." In *Sentencing Policies and Practices in Western Countries: Comparative and Cross-National Perspectives*, edited by Michael Tonry. Vol. 45 of *Crime and Justice: A Review of Research*, edited by Michael Tonry. Chicago: University of Chicago Press.

Lappi-Seppälä, Tapio. 2019. "Humane Neoclassicism: Proportionality and Other Values in Nordic Sentencing." In *Of One-Eyed and Toothless Miscreants: Making the Punishment Fit the Crime?* edited by Michael Tonry. New York: Oxford University Press.

Lewis, C. S. 1949. "The Humanitarian Theory of Punishment." *20th Century: An Australian Quarterly Review* 3(3):5–12.

Lippke, Richard. 2019. "Penal Severity and the Modern State." In *Of One-Eyed and Toothless Miscreants: Making the Punishment Fit the Crime?* edited by Michael Tonry. New York: Oxford University Press.

Markel, Dan, and Chad Flanders. 2010. "Bentham on Stilts? The Bare Relevance of Subjectivity to Retributive Justice." *California Law Review* 98:907–88.

Masur, Jonathan, John Bronsteen, and Christopher Buccafusco. 2009. "Happiness and Punishment." *University of Chicago Law Review* 76:1037–81.

Matravers, Matt. 2019. "The Place of Proportionality in Penal Theory: Or Rethinking Thinking about Punishment." In *Of One-Eyed and Toothless Miscreants: Making the Punishment Fit the Crime?* edited by Michael Tonry. New York: Oxford University Press.

McCloskey, H. J. 1965. "A Non-Utilitarian Approach to Punishment." *Inquiry: An Interdisciplinary Journal of Philosophy* 8(1–4):249–63.

McDonald, Douglas. 1986. *Punishment without Walls.* New Brunswick, NJ: Rutgers University Press.

Michael, Jerome, and Herbert Wechsler. 1940. *Criminal Law and Its Administration.* Chicago: Foundation.

Mill, John Stuart. 1997. *The Subjection of Women.* New York: Dover. (Originally published 1869.)

Morris, Herbert. 1981. "A Paternalist Theory of Punishment." *American Philosophical Quarterly* 18:263–71.

Morris, Norval. 1974. *The Future of Imprisonment.* Chicago: University of Chicago Press.

Morris, Norval, and Michael Tonry. 1990. *Between Prison and Probation.* New York: Oxford University Press.

Nagel, Thomas. 1979. *Mortal Questions.* Cambridge: Cambridge University Press.

Parent, Dale G. 1988. *Structuring Criminal Sentences: The Evolution of Minnesota's Sentencing Guidelines.* New York: Lexis.

Petersilia, Joan, and Richard Rosenfeld, eds. 2007. *Parole, Desistance from Crime, and Community Integration.* Washington, DC: National Academy Press.

Pincoffs, Edmund. 1966. *The Rationale of Legal Punishment.* Atlantic Highlands, NJ: Humanities.

Plutarch. 1957. "Whether Land or Sea Animals Are Cleverer." In *Moralia,* vol. 12. Translation by Harold Cherniss. Cambridge: Harvard University Press.

Quinton, Anthony M. 1969. "On Punishment." In *The Philosophy of Punishment,* edited by H. B. Acton. London: St. Martin's.

Rawls, John. 1955. "Two Concepts of Rules." *Philosophical Review* 64(1):3–32.

Roberts, Julian V., Loretta J. Stalans, David Indermaur, and Mike Hough. 2003. *Penal Populism and Public Opinion: Lessons from Five Countries*. Oxford: Oxford University Press.

Robinson, Paul H. 1987 "Hybrid Principles for the Distribution of Criminal Sanctions." *Northwestern University Law Review* 82:19–42.

Robinson, Paul H. 2013. *Intuitions of Justice and the Utility of Desert*. New York: Oxford University Press.

Robinson, Paul H. 2017. "Democratizing Criminal Law: Feasibility, Utility, and the Challenge of Social Change." *Northwestern University Law Review* 111:1565–95.

Robinson, Paul H., and John E. Darley. 2007. "Intuitions of Justice: Implications for Criminal Law and Justice Policy." *Southern California Law Review* 81:1–67.

Ryberg, Jesper. 2004. *Proportionate Punishment: A Critical Investigation*. Dordrecht and New York: Kluwer Academic.

Ryberg, Jesper. 2019. "Proportionality and the Seriousness of Crimes." In *Of One-Eyed and Toothless Miscreants: Making the Punishment Fit the Crime?* edited by Michael Tonry. New York: Oxford University Press.

Sebba, Leslie. 1978. "Some Explorations in the Scaling of Penalties." *Journal of Research on Crime and Delinquency* 15:247–65.

Sellin, Thorsten, and Marvin E. Wolfgang. 1964. *The Measurement of Delinquency*. New York: Wiley.

Tonry, Michael. 2015. "The Fog around Cost-of-Crime Studies May Finally Be Clearing: Prisoners and Their Kids Suffer Too." *Criminology and Public Policy* 14(4):653–71.

Tonry, Michael. 2016. *Sentencing Fragments*. New York: Oxford University Press.

Tonry, Michael. 2018. "Punishment and Human Dignity: Sentencing Principles for Twenty-First-Century America." In *Crime and Justice: A Review of Research*, vol. 47, edited by Michael Tonry. Chicago: University of Chicago Press.

Travis, Jeremy, Bruce Western, and Steve Redburn, eds. 2014. *The Growth of Incarceration in the United States: Exploring Causes and Consequences*. Washington, DC: National Academies.

Von Hirsch, Andreas [Andrew]. 1976. *Doing Justice: The Choice of Punishments*. New York: Hill and Wang.

Von Hirsch, Andreas. 2017. *Deserved Criminal Sentences*. London: Hart.

Von Hirsch, Andreas [Andrew], and Nils Jareborg. 1991. "Gauging Criminal Harm: A Living-Standard Analysis." *Oxford Journal of Legal Studies* 11(1):1–38.

Von Hirsch, Andreas [Andrew], Martin Wasik, and Judith A. Greene. 1989. "Punishments in the Community and the Principles of Desert." *Rutgers Law Review* 20:595–618.

Waldron, Jeremy. 2008. "Lucky in Your Judge." *Theoretical Inquiries in Law* 9(1):185–216.

Walker, Nigel. 1991. *Why Punish?* Oxford: Oxford University Press.

Wechsler, Herbert. 1961. "Sentencing, Correction, and the Model Penal Code." *University of Pennsylvania Law Review* 109(4):465–93.

Williams, Bernard. 1981. *Moral Luck: Philosophical Papers 1973–1980*. Cambridge: Cambridge University Press.

Wolf, Susan. 2001. "The Moral of Moral Luck." *Philosophic Exchange* 31(1):4–19.

Wollstonecraft, Mary. 2009. *A Vindication of the Rights of Women*. Oxford: Oxford University Press. (Originally published 1792.)

2

Weighing Relative and Absolute Proportionality in Punishment

Göran Duus-Otterström

TALK OF RETRIBUTIVE justice in punishment draws on two quite different values: the idea that punishments should be arrayed so that offenders get the right relative amount of punishment and so that they get what they deserve in an absolute sense. These values reflect two different senses of proportionality, which I refer to as relative and absolute proportionality. While the distinction between them is pretty well understood, we know much less about how to handle conflicts between them. My ambition in this essay is to discuss this issue. More specifically, I consider situations in which we face a choice between greater absolute proportionality and greater relative proportionality. Such situations present a problem for retributivism, the difficulty of which is yet to be fully appreciated.

I defend three claims. First, absolute and relative proportionality contribute independently to the ideal of proportionality in punishment. Some retributivists might be tempted to deny the value of one of the two types of proportionality, but doing so is ultimately implausible. Second, this means

Göran Duus-Otterström is Associate Professor of Political Science at Aarhus University and a researcher in the Institute for Futures Studies. Previous versions of this essay were presented at the University of Minnesota in 2017 and at Worcester College, Oxford University, in 2018. The author is grateful to all who participated in these two workshops for helpful comments and stimulating discussion, especially Jesper Ryberg, who caught some mistakes in an earlier version. Special thanks go to Doug Husak, Julian Roberts, and Michael Tonry for organizing the workshops and to Su Smallen for administrative and editorial assistance. Tonry provided extensive written comments on the penultimate draft.

that to resolve situations in which the two types of proportionality come into conflict, retributivists must figure out how to weigh absolute and relative proportionality. Third, figuring this out, however, is very difficult.

Before I begin, I want to make a couple of preliminary points about the scope of the essay. First, I confine myself to a retributivist account of proportionality, that is, one that holds that proportionality is about making penal severity a function of criminal seriousness. I recognize that there might be other ways of thinking about proportionality, but I set them to one side here.[1] I explore retributivist proportionality "from within." Second, I simply assume that we have adequate accounts of what constitutes criminal seriousness (but see Ryberg 2019) and penal severity (Husak 2019). That is an optimistic assumption, but it allows me to proceed to the questions I am interested in here, and my arguments do not depend on a particular view of crime seriousness or penal severity anyway, except that we should measure penal severity on the receiver side of punishment (Husak 2010, p. 444).[2] This means that when I say of two offenders that they are punished equally or unequally, I refer to the extent to which their interests are set back.

I. Relative and Absolute Proportionality in Punishment

Proportionality in punishment is the idea that the severity of punishments should be a function of the seriousness of crimes. Every version of this idea will build on the following principles:

Parity: Equally serious crimes should get equally severe punishments.
Difference: Unequally serious crimes should get unequally severe punishments.
Positive slope: The more serious a crime, the more severe the punishment should be.

It may immediately be wondered whether proponents of proportionality must be so strict. For example, it could be argued that it is not worrying if

---

1. In general, these approaches either mean something other than the retributivists do by proportionality (Bentham 1988) or justify retributivist proportionality on nonretributivist grounds (Rachels 1997).

2. Receiver-side conceptions of penal severity raise difficult questions about how individuated the impact should be (Kolber 2009; Tonry 2011, pp. 19–21).

two equally serious crimes get slightly different punishments. Such reactions could track legitimate skepticism about whether there can be such a thing as a precise judgment of proportionality even in principle.[3] More often, however, I think they are simply concessions that judgments of proportionality are imprecise in practice. This is perfectly consistent with saying that *parity* and *difference* express what proportionality requires in principle, that is, describe an ideal that we can, better or worse, approximate in practice. I proceed on the plausible assumption that *parity* and *difference* lay out what proportionality requires as a matter of ideal theory.

Proportionality is typically also thought to include a spacing requirement. It is at odds with proportionality if a crime that is much more serious than another crime receives a punishment that is only marginally more severe. Proportionality thus not only requires that the severity of punishments be a positive function of the seriousness of crime; the relative severity of punishments must also reflect the relative seriousness of crimes. This is captured by the following principle:

Spacing: Unequally serious crimes should get unequally severe punishments, and the difference in severity between punishments should correspond to the difference in seriousness between crimes.

It is this principle that is involved when we say things such as "crime X is twice as serious as crime Y and should therefore receive a punishment twice as severe as Y." Note that if we accept *spacing*, *difference* becomes redundant, since the former principle contains the latter.

When we combine *parity, positive slope,* and *spacing,* we get the view I refer to as relative cardinal proportionality, or relative proportionality for short. This view operates with two cardinal scales: one mapping crimes in terms of seriousness, the other mapping punishments in terms of severity.[4] That they

---

3. Some argue that criminal seriousness only establishes a range, not a point, such that any punishment in the range would be equally proportionate (Hestevold 1983) or not disproportionate (Morris 1974). I prefer to think of such ranges as flowing from epistemic limitations on our ability to identify proportionate punishments, but I recognize that is controversial (Duus-Otterström 2013). Unless otherwise indicated, I set aside this complication, but it should be noted that adopting a range conception of proportionality only mitigates the problems discussed here and does not make them go away. This is because we may need to choose between at least some people getting punishments that fall within the proportionate ranges and ensuring that everyone's relative punishment is correct.

4. To be precise, the term *cardinal scale* covers two types: interval scales and ratio scales. Both allow us to express distance between items, but only ratio scales have a predefined zero point.

are cardinal scales is essential, because only then can punishment respect the relative distance of items on the two scales. Suppose, for the sake of argument, that we could assign "seriousness scores" to different crimes. Suppose further that one crime has a seriousness score of 20 units and is punished by 12 months in prison, and another crime has a seriousness score of 40 units and is punished by 24 months in prison. According to relative proportionality, we can now deduce that a crime with a seriousness score of 30 units should be punished by 18 months in prison. I suspect, but do not try to prove here, that this means that the proportionality function is linear, that is, that any increase of n units on the crime scale should result in an increase of m units on the punishment scale irrespective of at which point on the crime scale n occurs.[5] The key point is that relative proportionality obtains when the punishment of any crime is as severe as it should be given the way other crimes are punished.[6]

Relative proportionality can be satisfied by many different penal schemes, ranging from draconian to very mild (Duff 2001, p. 133). This implication clashes with another plausible meaning of proportionality according to which, to be proportionate, a punishment must also be fitting in an absolute sense. That is captured by the following principle:

Fit: The punishments should be fitting in an absolute sense.

When we add *fit*, we get the view I call absolute cardinal proportionality, or absolute proportionality for short. Absolute proportionality is simply the idea of taking relative proportionality and then adding that the entire penal scheme must be placed at the right absolute level of severity, that is, be neither too harsh nor too lenient. It is this sense of proportionality that we rely on

---

The difference is not important here, but it presumably means that penal severity maps onto a ratio scale (since it starts with no punishment at all).

5. There are, of course, many potential reasons not to obey this function. Perhaps very trivial crimes should not be punished at all, since punishment here would not be worth the administrative cost. More relevantly, the state should not punish extraordinarily serious crimes extraordinarily severely, because this would require barbaric punishment. But it is important that these examples are consistent with regarding proportionality as a linear function. They only show that the state would be justified in departing from proportionality. For discussion, see Reiman (1985) and Ryberg (2004, pp. 131–42). For "extra desert" reasons for and against punishment, see Husak (2010, pp. 405ff).

6. This way of putting it makes clear that relative proportionality needs one or several "anchors" (Ryberg 2004, p. 129; von Hirsch and Ashworth 2005). One cannot get relative proportionality going without having a point from which to derive the rest of the scheme.

when we reject ideas such as incarceration for minor traffic offenses or trifling punishments for seriously violent offenses as intrinsically disproportionate.

The distinction between relative and absolute proportionality draws on Andreas von Hirsch's important work on proportionate sentencing (see, e.g., von Hirsch 1993; von Hirsch and Ashworth 2005, pp. 137–41). It may therefore be wondered why I do not follow von Hirsch in speaking about "ordinal" and "cardinal" proportionality instead. The answer is twofold. First, while we are, of course, free to stipulate what we mean by the terms we use, in standard usage, ordinal scales cannot express the difference in degree of items. Ordinal scales only allow for establishing the rank order of items (e.g., "Clare is taller than Bob") and not their spacing (e.g., "Clare is 5 feet, 10 inches tall and Bob is 5 feet, 7 inches tall"). Von Hirsch's conception of ordinal proportionality, however, clearly relies on mapping crimes and punishments on what in standard usage would be called cardinal scales (von Hirsch and Ashworth 2005, p. 140). I think departing from standard usage in this way creates unnecessary confusion.

A second and related reason to be particular about the terminology here is that some philosophers defend an approach to proportionality that is ordinal in the standard sense of the word (Davis 1983). Now I think such an approach is implausible, as it will fail to space crimes and punishments correctly. But it is nevertheless an approach to proportionality, and we make it more difficult to see what is distinctive about it if we talk about ordinality when we should be talking about cardinality.

II. Conflicts between Absolute and Relative Proportionality

Absolute and relative (cardinal) proportionality capture different aspects of the ideal of proportionality. Suppose we are to punish an instance of armed robbery. From the perspective of relative proportionality, the important thing is that our punishment is at an appropriate level of severity given how other crimes are punished (both other armed robberies and other crimes). There is no intrinsically appropriate punishment for armed robbery according to this perspective. Indeed, any punishment could be proportionate provided that it stands in the right relationship to the way other crimes are punished. From the perspective of absolute proportionality, however, this is not the case. Here the assumption is that there is an intrinsically appropriate punishment. If we knew that 24 months' imprisonment would be the fitting punishment, then this punishment would be proportionate no matter how other crimes are punished.

For a retributivist, the distinction between absolute and relative proportionality tracks a more fundamental distinction between comparative and noncomparative desert (Miller 2003; Temkin 2011; Kagan 2012).[7] Noncomparative desert concerns how people should fare in an absolute sense, that is, what someone deserves when viewed in isolation. Comparative desert, by contrast, concerns how people should fare in light of how other people fare. It is preoccupied with whether there are undeserved differences or similarities in how people fare. Both types of desert help capture what we mean when we ask whether someone deserves something. For example, when we wonder whether a candidate deserves a job, we may mean to ask whether he or she has worked hard enough to merit the job (noncomparative desert) or whether he or she has worked harder than other candidates have (comparative desert).

It should be clear from this that absolute and relative proportionality are independent values. It should also be clear that the two types of proportionality, as with noncomparative and comparative desert more generally, can come into conflict. They are certainly not in necessary tension or conflict as, say, liberty and security are sometimes claimed to be. This is important because it means that our inquiry does not amount to a kind of zero-sum game where gains in one value invariably mean shortfalls in other values. Indeed, we can have a situation in which both absolute and relative proportionality are fully satisfied. This compatibility does not rule out, however, that the two types of proportionality can come into conflict. For example, it may occur that relative proportionality is fully satisfied but no one gets what he or she deserves in an absolute sense. This happens whenever the scheme of punishment as a whole is either too lenient or too severe.

Since absolute and relative proportionality can come into conflict, retributivists must think about how to handle such conflicts. Supposing there

---

7. Comparative and noncomparative desert, in turn, sort under the distinction between comparative and noncomparative justice (Feinberg 1974). It should be noted that some could defend relative proportionality without cashing this out in terms of desert. This is because they might believe that while punishments should be apportioned in proportion to criminal seriousness, criminal seriousness does not bear on a person's desert—desert, it may be thought, is about how well a person should fare overall, which is not something the criminal law does or should concern itself with. But an act-based retributivist could, of course, maintain that criminal seriousness only bears on what offenders deserve in a more restricted sense. For "whole life" objections to retributivism, see Tadros (2011, pp. 60–73).

is a choice between satisfying relative and absolute proportionality, what should a retributivist choose?

I approach this question by considering a somewhat contrived but, I hope, illuminating example. Suppose there is a state whose sentencing scheme is perfectly calibrated as far as proportionality is concerned. The scheme is set up in a way that when it is conscientiously applied, it gives each offender the absolutely proportionate punishment. But now suppose the state decides that the sentencing scheme should be changed. Perhaps it wants to make it milder in order to cut public expenses. Perhaps it wants to make it more severe in order to increase general deterrence. The direction of the move is not relevant here. The important point is that for reasons other than proportionality, the state knowingly decides to move away from its perfectly proportionate scheme of sentencing.

Now consider that the state could choose between two ways of moving the penal scheme. According to what we may call a "full" move, the state moves the whole scheme without upsetting the relative positions of crimes and punishments. That is, the state adjusts the scheme upward or downward but maintains the ranking and relative spacing of the elements of the scheme. It is important to note that although the whole scheme would then undergo a repositioning, it would be just as good from the perspective of relative proportionality. But it would be worse from the perspective of absolute proportionality. In fact, because the whole system would move, no offender would get the punishment he or she deserves in a noncomparative sense.

Recognizing this flaw, the state might also decide to undertake what we may call a "partial" move. According to this option, while the state moves some parts of the sentencing scheme, it leaves other parts of the scheme intact. This would be better from the perspective of absolute proportionality. In subjecting some offenders to the punishment of the prior and perfectly calibrated system, it would ensure that at least some get what they noncomparatively deserve. This could be motivated by a wish to strike a balance between absolute proportionality and other penal aims.

A more concrete example might help to illustrate the difference. Suppose that an instance of armed robbery is twice as serious as an instance of assault. Suppose further that in the prior and perfectly calibrated scheme, those who performed such robberies got 24 months' imprisonment whereas those who committed such assaults got 12 months' imprisonment. Suppose finally that because it wanted to cut down on public expenses, the state decided to reduce sentences. A full move is one in which punishments were reduced in a way that preserved relative proportionality. For example, the sentences for armed robberies and assaults might be 12 and 6 months, respectively. A partial move, by contrast, is one in which parts of the previous scheme were preserved. For example, if the state decided to still punish armed robbers with 24 months' imprisonment but reduced the punishment for assault to 6 months, it would have undertaken a partial move.

Reflecting on this example creates an interesting puzzle for retributivism. In what follows, I sketch the different responses available to retributivists. They could argue that:

1. Relative proportionality has no value.
2. Absolute proportionality has no value.
3. Absolute and relative proportionality both have value.

Option 1 means that a partial move would always be better than a full move. Option 2 means that a full move would always be better than a partial move. Option 3, finally, means that there is no general answer regarding which move would be better; absolute and relative proportionality both have independent value and must be weighed on a case-to-case basis.

I believe that option 3 is the most plausible response. But I also argue that it raises a set of very difficult questions for retributivists related to weighing the two types of proportionality.

My discussion of the three options begins in section IV. However, it is interesting first to consider whether we can get the relevant guidance from values or principles that do not draw on proportionality or desert. To that end, in the next section, I briefly consider some nonretributivist reasons to prefer a full move. Readers who want to focus on retributivist proportionality can jump directly to section IV.

Before evaluating the responses, however, we should dispel a natural objection to the relevance of our inquiry. Some may think that retributivists do not have to consider which move to prefer because both moves are worse than the status quo ante. That is, why could a retributivist not simply respond that the state is forbidden to make either move? Although this response seems convincing at first glance, it is ultimately unpersuasive. It is no doubt true that either move is worse than no move as far as proportionality is concerned. However, that does not mean that retributivists can disregard conflicts between absolute and relative proportionality. For one thing, some retributivists will hold a pluralist view according to which proportionality is but one important aim of a penal scheme. This guarantees that it is quite legitimate to consider departures from ideal proportionality in punishment. It could also be that it is infeasible for the state fully to satisfy both senses of proportionality simultaneously, for example, because there simply is not enough prison capacity. Indeed, the state may be wholly uninterested in proportionality but pursue penal policies that nevertheless can be evaluated through the lens of proportionality. For these reasons, retributivists cannot avoid facing the question of handling conflicts between absolute and relative proportionality.

III. Nonretributivist Principles

We might think that the important thing for the choice between the two moves is not proportionality as much as it is that a partial move would offend against some other important principle or value. Considering this possibility is illuminating, because there might be overriding reasons, unrelated to proportionality or desert, to avoid partial moves.

One idea might be that we should prefer a full move because this ensures that punishments are predictable to would-be offenders. Now, predictability is certainly an important concern. Enabling would-be offenders to figure out potential punishments ahead of time is essential for giving people control over the legal force to which they are liable (Hart 2008). However, the penal scheme that results from a partial move is not in any way less predictable than the penal scheme of a full move. Indeed, if it is transparent and faithfully applied, any penal scheme based on determinate sentencing will be predictable in the relevant sense regardless of its proportionality.[8] We can easily imagine a system of punishment that is predictable (because it announces determinate sentences ahead of time) without being proportionate (because the punishments are not a function of crime seriousness). Put differently, all proportionate systems will be predictable, but not all predictable systems will be proportionate. Thus, a concern for predictability cannot swing the choice either way.

A second idea is that we should prefer a full move because it respects formal justice. Formal justice is the important principle that similar cases

---

8. The desire to ensure determinate sentencing played a prominent role in the turn to proportionality ("just deserts") in Western academia and Western penal practice. Proportionality as a guiding ideal of sentencing was seen as desirable in part because it took away some discretionary power from judges and other state officials, especially by reducing their ability to inflict indeterminate sentencing (Tonry 2011, pp. 8–9; von Hirsch 2011, pp. 256–59). The fact that proportionality-based systems of punishment will be ones of determinate sentencing is indeed an attractive feature of such systems, but proportionality is not a necessary condition for determinate sentencing.

should be treated similarly. Thus, it is preoccupied with the "impartial and consistent administration of laws and institutions" (Rawls 1999, p. 51). A partial move, it may be thought, would necessarily violate this principle. It would ensure that some offenders—those who are punished in accordance with the old penal scheme—are treated unequally compared with the rest.

This principle, too, fails to show that there is something wrong about a partial move. Recall that in making the partial move, the state decides to punish a whole class of offenders according to the old scheme. It is then difficult to see why these offenders are unequally treated in some morally problematic sense. They are subjected, to borrow Rawls's phrase, to an "impartial and consistent administration of laws."[9]

This is not to deny that there is merit to the worry from formal justice. But the worry is directed against certain kinds of partial moves, and it is instructive to bring this out. To illustrate, suppose that instead of preserving the old punishments for entire classes of offenders, the state sometimes metes out the old punishments for a given class of offenders and sometimes does not. Perhaps the state institutes a system according to which offenders run a 1-in-10 chance of being punished according to the old scheme or chooses to implement the old scheme only on Mondays. Since the state would then occasionally apply the old scheme, we can call this a "spotty" move. A spotty move would clearly be a violation of formal justice, because some offenders would get different punishments even though they are convicted of the same crime. (To connect with the previous point about predictability, it would also undermine people's ability to foresee what punishments they might face.) When a partial move is not spotty, however, it is difficult to see why unequal treatment would be the case, since all offenders of a certain type would then be treated in the same way.

A third and related option is to argue that a full move is preferable because it respects something like interpersonal fairness or proportional equality.[10] The idea here is that in punishing offenders, the state intentionally sets back their interests, often to a very significant extent. It is therefore extraordinarily important that punishment live up to rigid standards of fairness. In particular,

---

9. This would admittedly not be true in all cases, because it might be that the state fails to show due impartiality in choosing the classes of offenses for which the old scheme applies. Suppose, for example, that an offense is predominantly committed by members of a particular minority. The state's choice to preserve harsher punishments for this offense may then be based on a discriminatory attitude, which is clearly an instance of morally problematic unequal treatment.

10. For the classical discussion of proportional equality, see Aristotle (1998, pp. 106–17). For a celebrated analysis of fairness, see Broome (1990).

the state must not punish some offenders more or less than would be appropriate given how it punishes other offenders. For example, if one offender commits a worse crime than another offender does, it would be unfair if the two ended up getting the same punishment. Yet that can happen under a partial move.

This response draws on an important concern, as fairness is, no doubt, a crucial value for legitimate state coercion. It also shows that even nonretributivists may have strong reason to value relative proportionality. To value relative proportionality, we need not subscribe to the retributivist notion that punishments should be a function of criminal seriousness. It is sufficient that (rightly or wrongly) the state's practice of punishment is based on this notion. As soon as this is the case, it is a simple matter of fairness that it would be problematic if the state were to treat people unfairly given its own penal aims, as this would mean singling out some offenders for harsher treatment than others.

A commitment to fairness thus gives us a robust reason to prefer full moves to partial moves regardless of what we think of proportionality. For retributivists, on the other hand, the response hardly adds anything new, because for them, a commitment to interpersonal fairness in punishment is the same thing as a commitment to comparative desert. Retributivists will agree that a partial move would introduce some unfairness into the penal scheme but will maintain that this is precisely because it violates the dictates of comparative desert. Thus, they will reject that accounting for the unfairness requires going beyond the confines of their own theory. This is significant because it shows that retributivists cannot hope to solve the conflict between relative and absolute proportionality by drawing on an external standard of fairness. Saying that a partial move is "unfair" merely restates the challenge they face in handling the tension between the two types of proportionality.[11]

IV. Denying the Value of Relative Proportionality

Let us now consider responses that are internal to retributivism. A first option is to resolve the tension by denying that relative proportionality has any independent value. This option exploits an interesting feature about the relationship between absolute and relative proportionality, namely, that if we satisfy absolute proportionality, we automatically satisfy relative

---

11. But see Gordon-Solmon (2017) for an interesting critique, focusing on Kagan's (2012) theory of comparative desert.

proportionality. To see this, note that if each offender receives a punishment that is fitting given the seriousness of his or her crime, then it must be true that the punishments also express the differences in criminal seriousness between their crimes.[12] Suppose, for example, that Adam deserves 24 months' imprisonment and Bob deserves 12 months' imprisonment. If Adam and Bob get these noncomparatively fitting punishments, then the difference between the two punishments (12 months) cannot but reflect the difference in seriousness between the two crimes. To put the same point in the terminology of the aforementioned principles: if we satisfy *fit*, we would automatically satisfy *parity*, *spacing*, and *positive slope*.

In light of this, a retributivist could argue that what really counts is absolute proportionality. Relative proportionality is not a genuine value but a mere artifact of satisfying absolute proportionality. Thus, we need not think about cases such as the partial move versus the full move as a problem of weighing different values. We should prefer a partial move because that would be better from the point of view of the genuine value, which is absolute proportionality. After all, some would get the punishments they deserve in that outcome.

The problem with this response is that it does not seem like a very faithful depiction of the ideal of proportionality. Suppose the state decides to reduce general penal levels drastically, but for some reason or another, decides to retain the old punishments for armed robbery. Armed robbers would then get what they deserve as a matter of absolute proportionality, but their punishments would be greatly disproportionate given how other crimes are punished. Indeed, the situation might be one in which armed robbers receive stiffer punishments than do offenders who are much more deserving of stiff punishment. Something has then surely gone awry as far as proportionality is concerned. But according to the response we are now considering, there is nothing to regret about punishing the armed robbers according to the old scheme. Since this punishment is what the robbers deserve in an absolute sense, it would strictly be a change for the worse if they, too, were to be punished more leniently along with the other offenders. This is far too drastic, suggesting that relative proportionality does contribute independently to the ideal of proportionality.

---

12. Kagan (2012) notes the same thing in the context of discussing the relationship between comparative and noncomparative desert. He conjectures that "when noncomparative desert is perfectly satisfied, comparative desert is perfectly satisfied as well," noting that the two types of desert would otherwise "float free from each other in an implausible and philosophically unsatisfying way" (p. 352).

V. Denying the Value of Absolute Proportionality

A second option is to argue that it is absolute proportionality that lacks value altogether.[13] This option mirrors the previous one in that it resolves the tension by denying one of the putative values, but it suggests that the full move is comprehensively better. There is nothing to regret about making the full move, irrespective of whether it consists in a harshening or softening of the penal scheme.

One reason to endorse this option is that we might be skeptics about noncomparative desert. That is, we might deny that it is ever true that anyone deserves any punishment in particular when regarded in isolation. Claims about absolute fittingness, so this argument goes, are just artifacts of particular sociocultural conventions of a political community. Whatever may be wrong about making a full move, it certainly is not that offenders do not get what they deserve. Thus, this option rejects the assumption that there could be a penal scheme that is "perfectly calibrated" in terms of absolute proportionality.

I have written about this kind of "popular" retributivism elsewhere, so I do not say much about it here (Duus-Otterström 2018). The important thing for our present purposes is to note that even if it is true that we can never say that anyone deserves anything in particular, we also need an argument for why relative proportionality has genuine value. Why should we think it matters that the penal scheme satisfies relative proportionality? The most promising answer draws on communicative versions of retributivism, which have become influential in recent decades (see, e.g., Duff 2001; von Hirsch and Ashworth 2005; Bennett 2008; Wringe 2016). The distinctive claim of communicative versions of retributivism is that punishment seeks to convey, and is justified by conveying, the appropriate amount of censure of the offender. If we accept that claim, it seems that relative proportionality is all that matters. Von Hirsch and Ashworth (2005) write:

> When persons are (and should be) dealt with in a manner that ascribes demerit, their treatment should reflect how unmeritorious their conduct should be judged to be. By punishing one kind of conduct more severely than another, the punisher implies that it is worse—which is appropriate only if the conduct is indeed worse (i.e., more serious). Were penalties ordered in severity inconsistently with the comparative

---

13. For a defense of this outside the realm of punishment, see McLeod (2003).

seriousness of crime, the less reprehensible conduct would, unfairly, receive the greater reprobation. (pp. 135–36)

If the aim of punishment is just to express the relative blameworthiness of offenders, we could argue that it is simply beside the point whether a penal scheme ensures absolute proportionality (if there even is such a thing). What is important is that the penal scheme is arranged so that it communicates the degrees of "demerit," ensuring that greater criminal wrongs receive comparatively greater punishments.[14] There is then nothing to regret about the full move, since it leaves relative proportionality untouched.[15] The partial move, by contrast, necessarily gets some declarations about degrees of demerit wrong.

There are two problems with this response, one internal and one external. The internal problem is that it is not clear that the censuring aspect of a punishment is freestanding from the amount of hard treatment in the way the response assumes. Suppose that the state were to reduce the severity of all punishments to a considerable extent yet would manage to preserve the relative proportionality of the entire penal scheme. Contrary to what this response assumes, it is far from obvious that the new penal scheme would be able to communicate censure just as well as the old one did. The alternative possibility is that the system would become worse at communicating censure simply because a punishment's degree of censure depends on its degree of absolute severity (Duus-Otterström 2018; see also von Hirsch and Ashworth 2005, chap. 2). Put differently, even though the new penal scheme would get the differences between offenders right, it might fail to express the right amount of censure for crime as such. And if that is true, then communicative retributivists, too, must worry about the absolute proportionality of the penal scheme, not because it is needed to express the relative blameworthiness of different crimes but because expressing relative blameworthiness is not all there is to communicating censure successfully.

Communicative retributivists might argue that the aim of communicating censure successfully does not require more than establishing relative

---

14. It should be noted that not all communicative theories of punishment are retributivist. Here, however, I focus on retributive versions according to which what the offender deserves is a response that expresses the right amount of censure.

15. Several theorists have defended the decremental strategy of gradually lowering the scheme of punishment precisely for the reason that this would enable punishment to do what it is supposed to do—censure criminal wrongdoing—without causing as much suffering (von Hirsch 1993, pp. 36–46; Duff 2001, p. 134; Matravers 2014). For discussion, see Duus-Otterström (2018).

proportionality and thus deny that the internal problem is a challenge to their view. Yet they must still reckon with the external problem, which is that it is simply not very plausible that absolute proportionality should play no role for sentencing even if we assume that relative proportionality is sufficient specifically for the communicative aim of punishment. After all, if we only stress that punishments should be arranged to convey their relative blameworthiness, we have no resources to exclude clearly absurd ideas such as prison sentences for jaywalking. The belief that punishments should be fitting—or at least not demonstrably unfitting—is, of course, why absolute proportionality is usually held up as an important consideration in the first place. Thus, rejecting the value of absolute proportionality is also too drastic. It is worth noting that even if we believe, with the skeptics, that standards of absolute proportionality are ultimately supplied by sociocultural conventions, this does not provide a reason to think that tracking these standards is unimportant.

VI. Weighing Relative and
Absolute Proportionality

The third response is to argue that absolute and relative proportionality contribute independently to the ideal of proportionality. Since the two senses of proportionality can come into conflict, this means that we must consider the age-old question of pluralism: supposing a retributivist must choose between satisfying relative and absolute proportionality, both of which have normative force, what should he or she choose?

There are two main approaches to handling pluralism: lexical ordering and weighing. Lexical ordering is the idea that we can place values in a strict hierarchy, such that great gains in one value cannot justify even small offenses against other values. A famous example of this is John Rawls's (1999) contention that we must never infringe on some basic liberties for the sake of socioeconomic justice. Applied to our topic, lexical ordering would mean that although both types of proportionality have normative force, one takes strict priority over the other. But that does not offer an accurate picture of the normative concerns we have in thinking about proportionality in punishment. We have already seen why it is problematic to drop one of the values, and the weaker idea of giving lexical priority to one of them is vulnerable to similar objections. For example, it could mean that any gain in absolute proportionality would justify any loss in the relative proportionality of the penal scheme, which is highly implausible.

The remaining option, then, is to approach the question as one of weighing. Weighing is appropriate when we have several values that cannot be lexically ordered. We can then only proceed by assessing the relative weight of the two values. This kind of inquiry should be familiar. A good example is debates about how far liberty may be sacrificed for the sake of security (Waldron 2003). Another example, perhaps more vivid to academics, concerns meeting deadlines. When a deadline is approaching, we often find ourselves torn between delivering on time and sending out something good. In those cases, we must strike a balance between the two aims, and this is a question of weighing.

Weighing is unfortunately often very imprecise, leading to no more than intuitionistic guidance about individual cases (Rawls 1999, pp. 30–36). I see no reason to suppose that retributivists could do much better in relation to our question. Normative analysis involving more than value often ends up being a weighing exercise, and weighing invariably tends to be imprecise. Still, it is instructive to lay out the dimensions that go into weighing the two types of proportionality.

A first consideration concerns the common metric by virtue of which absolute and relative proportionality are commensurable.[16] Unless there is commensurability between the two values, it is simply impossible to weigh their relative importance, because a gain in one value could not be compared to the loss in the other value. Commensurability, then, is necessary to the very idea of weighing, and if it does not obtain, we must resort to lexical ordering after all (Steiner 2003).

Much is at stake here for retributivism, because if there is no commensurability between absolute and relative proportionality, and lexical ordering is implausible for the reasons mentioned above, then the theory is doomed to be indeterminate in many cases. For example, in the choice between the partial move and the full move, all the theory would be able to say is that the full move would be better from the perspective of relative proportionality and the partial move would be better from the perspective of absolute proportionality. It could never say which move would be better overall.

Kagan (2012, pp. 591–619) has provided a blueprint for how retributivists could develop commensurability. Investigating the tension between

---

16. I am here relying on a conception of commensurability according to which A and B are commensurate values if and only if A and B can be reduced to a common measure such that losses in one value can be outweighed by gains in the other. This is closely related to the idea that A and B are comparable. The relationship between commensurability and comparability is subject to debate. See Raz (1986); Chang (2014); Hsieh (2016).

comparative and noncomparative desert, Kagan argues that both types of desert contribute to the same overall value, which he calls "goodness from the point of view of desert." Indeed, he contends that comparative and noncomparative desert can be broken down into units of intrinsic good, each of which contributes exactly the same to the goodness of the overall outcome. As he writes, "regardless of how it is produced, one unit of intrinsic good is worth exactly one unit of intrinsic good" (p. 595). Thus, Kagan rejects that there can be indeterminacy in how we rank outcomes from the point of view of desert. The best outcome is simply the one that contains the most units of goodness from the point of view of desert.

If retributivists were to adopt this framework, they would be able to say that there is in principle an answer regarding whether a partial move would be preferable to a full move. The answer is that it depends on which move would create the most goodness from the point of view of desert. But this itself does not get us very far, for, as Kagan notes, we also need to know whether one type of desert tends to produce more units of intrinsic good than the other, and this is unclear. Thus, the difficult questions remain. Even though we may accept that the best outcome is the one that contains the most units of intrinsic good, it is an open question whether comparative desert is more important for overall goodness than noncomparative desert or vice versa.

The openness of this question ensures that the question of weighing reappears. Whenever we face a choice between absolute and relative proportionality, we must decide what moral importance to vest in the two types of proportionality, where "moral importance" refers to the tendency to produce the relevant units of value. Should we assume, as Kagan does in his discussion of weighing comparative and noncomparative desert, that the two are "roughly comparable" in moral importance?[17] Or should we say something stronger than this, for example, that they are of equal importance or that the importance of one is some determinate fraction of the other? We must then also assess the size of the shortfall in value that the two moves represent. Only if we have some sense of the moral importance of absolute and relative proportionality and know how much we would offend against these values could we come to a reasoned conclusion regarding whether a full move should be preferred to a partial move.

---

17. Kagan (2012) has a weak condition in mind here. He holds that rough comparability requires that "the weightier value does not so thoroughly swamp the less weighty value as to render that less weighty value of no practical significance at all" (p. 602).

When we lay out what it takes to weigh relative and absolute proportionality in this way, it should be clear that it involves considerable difficulties. Let me end with the briefest of suggestions about what I take to be the most promising avenue forward.

It is a reasonable guess that we are better at knowing what relative proportionality requires than what absolute proportionality requires. Neither laypersons nor sentencing commissions tend to find it an impossibly vexing task to rank and space crimes in terms of seriousness, and it is conceivable that we could reach a similar level of agreement when it comes to ranking and spacing punishments in terms of their severity.[18] We might take this as some indication that, in general, we are not hopeless at tracking relative proportionality. In comparison, we are more in the dark about absolute proportionality. We know, of course, that absolute proportionality rules out ludicrously lenient or severe punishments. Indeed, that a day fine is too lenient for murder and life imprisonment is too harsh for shoplifting is as certain as anything in moral theory. But we are quite uncertain, I think, about which punishments would be proportionate within the broad range that remains once we remove the absurd punishments. This difference in epistemic access to the two types of proportionality in itself provides a reason to pay more attention to relative proportionality, because it means that we would probably be more successful in satisfying that value, were we to try. If we pair this general reason to focus on relative proportionality with the view that violations against absolute proportionality are more morally problematic when they come in the form of overpunishment than in the form of underpunishment, as I have argued at length elsewhere (Duus-Otterström 2013), then a rough rule of thumb appears. A retributivist penal scheme should concentrate on satisfying relative proportionality and, in order to err on the side of underpunishment, should be rather lenient.

While this rule of thumb gives some guidance, it certainly does not resolve all the difficulties. Indeed, relying on our better epistemic access to relative proportionality is in a sense already to presuppose an answer to our question, because even if we grant that we are better at tracking relative proportionality, this does not mean much unless we presuppose that it carries roughly comparable moral importance to absolute proportionality. After all, we

---

18. For the point that laypersons tend to agree on the relative blameworthiness of core crimes, see, e.g., Robinson (2013). For the experience from early US sentencing commissions, see von Hirsch, Knapp, and Tonry (1987). For the attempts to develop a scale of penal severity and the problems facing such attempts, see Husak (2019).

would not take our more reliable ability to satisfy value X over another value Y as a reason to prioritize X if it turns out that Y is greatly more important. Consider marking term papers: while a student's ability to cite references correctly contributes to the overall quality of the paper, the fact that we are good at assessing how well students cite references is not a reason to let this profoundly influence the grade if we believe there are other qualities, such as being smart, that are more important. Stressing epistemic access, then, merely restates the central difficulty, which is to decide the relative weight of relative and absolute proportionality.

VII. Conclusion

I have argued that relative and absolute proportionality contribute independently to the ideal of proportionality in punishment, meaning that retributivists must figure out how these two types of proportionality should be weighed. I have also argued that figuring out how to do this is very hard. Indeed, such are the difficulties in weighing the two types of proportionality that it is understandable if critics of retributivism think the problem is insuperable. While such skepticism may well be overstated, the least we can say is that weighing relative and absolute proportionality should be added to an already long list of fascinating and vexing problems facing retributivist thought.

References

Aristotle. 1998. *The Nichomachean Ethics*. Translated by David Ross. Oxford: Oxford University Press.

Bennett, Christopher. 2008. *The Apology Ritual.* Cambridge: Cambridge University Press.

Bentham, Jeremy. 1988. *The Principles of Morals and Legislation.* Amherst: Prometheus.

Broome, John. 1990. "Fairness." *Proceedings of the Aristotelean Society* 91:87–101.

Chang, Ruth. 2014. "Value Incomparability and Incommensurability." In *Oxford Handbook of Value Theory*, edited by Jonas Olson and Iwao Hirose. Oxford: Oxford University Press.

Davis, Michael. 1983. "How to Make Punishment Fit the Crime." *Ethics* 93(4):726–52.

Duff, Antony. 2001. *Punishment, Communication, and Community.* Oxford: Oxford University Press.

Duus-Otterström, Göran. 2013. "Why Retributivists Should Endorse Leniency in Punishment." *Law & Philosophy* 32(4):459–83.

Duus-Otterström, Göran. 2018. "Retributivism and Public Opinion: On the Context Sensitivity of Desert." *Criminal Law & Philosophy* 12(1):125–42.

Feinberg, Joel. 1974. "Noncomparative Justice." *Philosophical Review* 83(3):297–338.

Gordon-Solmon, Kerah. 2017. "Comparative Desert vs. Fairness." *Law and Philosophy* 36(4):367–87.

Hart, H. L. A. 2008. *Punishment and Responsibility*, 2nd ed. Oxford: Oxford University Press.

Hestevold, Scott. 1983. "Disjunctive Desert." *American Philosophical Quarterly* 20(4):357–63.

Hsieh, Nien-hê. 2016. "Incommensurable Values." *Stanford Encyclopedia of Philosophy*, edited by Edward N. Zalta. https://plato.stanford.edu/archives/spr2016/entries/value-incommensurable.

Husak, Douglas. 2010. *The Philosophy of Criminal Law*. Oxford: Oxford University Press.

Husak, Douglas. 2019. "The Metric of Punishment Severity: A Puzzle about the Principle of Proportionality." In *Of One-Eyed and Toothless Miscreants: Making the Punishment Fit the Crime?* edited by Michael Tonry. New York: Oxford University Press.

Kagan, Shelly. 2012. *The Geometry of Desert*. Oxford: Oxford University Press.

Kolber, Adam. 2009. "The Subjective Experience of Punishment." *Columbia Law Review* 109(1):182–236.

Matravers, Matt. 2014. "Proportionality Theory and Public Opinion." In *Popular Punishment*, edited by Jesper Ryberg and Julian Roberts. Oxford: Oxford University Press.

McLeod, Owen. 2003. "On the Comparative Element of Justice." In *Desert and Justice*, edited by Serena Olsaretti. Oxford: Oxford University Press.

Miller, David. 2003. "Comparative and Noncomparative Desert." In *Desert and Justice*, edited by Serena Olsaretti. Oxford: Oxford University Press.

Morris, Norval. 1974. *The Future of Imprisonment*. Chicago: University of Chicago Press.

Rachels, James. 1997. "Punishment and Desert." In *Ethics in Practice*, edited by Hugh LaFollette. Oxford: Blackwell.

Rawls, John. 1999. *A Theory of Justice*, rev. ed. Oxford: Oxford University Press.

Raz, Joseph. 1986. *The Morality of Freedom*. Oxford: Clarendon.

Reiman, Jeffrey. 1985. "Justice, Civilization, and the Death Penalty." *Philosophy & Public Affairs* 14(2):115–48.

Robinson, Paul. 2013. *Intuitions of Justice and the Utility of Desert*. Oxford: Oxford University Press.

Ryberg, Jesper. 2004. *The Ethics of Proportionate Punishment*. Dordrecht: Kluwer.

Ryberg, Jesper. 2019. "Proportionality and the Seriousness of Crimes." In *Of One-Eyed and Toothless Miscreants: Making the Punishment Fit the Crime?* edited by Michael Tonry. New York: Oxford University Press.

Steiner, Hillel. 2003. "Equality, Incommensurability, and Rights." In *Rights, Culture, and the Law: Themes from the Legal and Political Philosophy of Joseph Raz*, edited by Lukas Meyer, Stanley Paulson, and Thomas Pogge. Oxford: Oxford University Press.

Tadros, Victor. 2011. *The Ends of Harm*. Oxford: Oxford University Press.

Temkin, Larry. 2011. "Justice, Equality, Fairness, Desert, Responsibility, and Luck." In *Responsibility and Distributive Justice*, edited by Carl Knight and Zofia Stemplowska. Oxford: Oxford University Press.

Tonry, Michael. 2011. "Can Twenty-First Century Punishment Practice Be Justified in Principle?" In *Retributivism Has a Past. Has It a Future?* edited by Michael Tonry. Oxford: Oxford University Press.

Von Hirsch, Andreas [Andrew]. 1993. *Censure and Sanctions*. Oxford: Oxford University Press.

Von Hirsch, Andreas [Andrew]. 2011. "Punishment Futures." In *Retributivism Has a Past. Has It a Future?* edited by Michael Tonry. Oxford: Oxford University Press.

Von Hirsch, Andreas [Andrew], and Andrew Ashworth. 2005. *Proportionate Sentencing: Exploring the Principles*. Oxford: Oxford University Press.

Von Hirsch, Andreas [Andrew], Kay Knapp, and Michael Tonry. 1987. *The Sentencing Commission and Its Guidelines*. Boston: Northeastern University Press.

Waldron, Jeremy. 2003. "Security and Liberty: The Image of Balance." *Journal of Political Philosophy* 11(2):191–210.

Wringe, Bill. 2016. *An Expressive Theory of Punishment*. London: Palgrave Macmillan.

3

Proportionality and the Seriousness of Crimes

Jesper Ryberg

THE FACT THAT the principle of proportionality has come to play a significant role in modern penal theory is not surprising. First of all, in the modern
epoch of penal theory, there has been a shift of focus from having been concerned mainly with questions about the justification of punishment to dealing
with the various intricacies associated with the distribution of punishment.
As an influential theorist has put it, there has been a theoretical expansion
of focus from "why punish?" to "how much?" (von Hirsch 1991). Second, it
is an often-described fact that modern penal theory has been dominated by a
retributivist approach to punishment. Although some theorists have followed
in the footsteps of Jeremy Bentham by holding that the principle of proportionality can be justified on consequentialist grounds—a contention that at
the end of the day is an empirical issue—it has generally been held that the
idea of proportionality follows directly from a desert-theoretical approach
to the justification of punishment.[1] However, even though proportionality
today is defended by many as the plausible principle of penal distribution and
has (to some extent) been enacted in criminal law and penal practice, it is
nevertheless the case that the principle faces several theoretical challenges.

Jesper Ryberg is Professor of Ethics and Philosophy of Law at Roskilde University.

1. For retributivist justifications of the principle of proportionality, see, e.g., Kleinig (1973);
Davis (1992); Scheid (1997); von Hirsch (1993, 2017); von Hirsch and Ashworth (2005). For
an overview and critical discussion of the retributivist justifications, see Ryberg (2004).

The purpose of this essay is to present and discuss a set of challenges associated with the concept of the seriousness of crime.

It is obvious that the task of giving content to the concept of crime seriousness constitutes a sine qua non for the idea of proportionality. If it is not possible to make some sort of ranking of crimes in gravity, that is, if it is not possible to tell whether assault is a more serious crime than burglary or whether theft is more serious than reckless driving, then the whole idea of punishing offenders in proportion to the seriousness of their crime falls apart. However, although several theorists have engaged in systematic reflections of some of the factors that are held to determine seriousness, it is still the case that the idea of crime gravity faces a number of serious problems; at least, so it will be argued in the following sections.

The essay proceeds as follows. Section I briefly presents three challenges to the idea of the seriousness of crime. The first challenge concerns the specification of the concept of criminal harm. It is generally accepted among proportionalists that criminal harm constitutes the main factor in the determination of seriousness. This naturally gives rise to the question of what criminal harm consists of. Seminal work has been conducted by von Hirsch and Jareborg (1991) with regard to the content and measurement of criminal harm as caused to identifiable individuals. Other theorists have more recently expanded on the ideas of von Hirsch and Jareborg in order to develop theories for the measurement of criminal harm in relation to other types of crime (see, e.g., Greenfield and Paoli 2013).[2] However, as will be argued, there still exists a challenge when it comes to the delimitation of criminal harm. Briefly, the challenge concerns the fact that some crimes do not in any direct way involve harm, while others involve harm to an extent that, morally speaking, seems to reach far beyond what can plausibly be attributed to the criminal act that has caused it. The second challenge follows from the fact that it is generally agreed that the seriousness of a crime is determined not only on the ground of harm but also on the ground of the culpability of the offender. But this gives rise to the obvious challenge of how different degrees of harm and culpability should be combined in a nonarbitrary manner into an overall assessment of the seriousness of a crime. The third challenge concerns the simple fact that even if one has developed clear conceptions and methods for the measurement of the factors that determine the seriousness of crime, it may well be the case that certain types of crime affect victims very differently. Moreover, as

---

2. It should be mentioned that Greenfield and Paoli have presented their proposal not as part of considerations of proportionality but in relation to a policy of harm reduction.

will be suggested, there will usually also exist certain individual differences in the culpability of offenders who commit the same criminal act. However, altogether, this means that crimes of the same type—say, burglary or assault—may differ significantly with regard to the factors that determine the gravity of crime. The question, of course, is what this means for the possibility of ranking crimes in gravity and meting out proportionate punishments.

Having outlined the three challenges, I examine in section II three different approaches for how the challenges could be met. First, I consider whether it can plausibly be held that the challenges should be rejected as arising from a sort of overtheorization. Second, I consider whether a so-called subjectivist approach to criminal conduct may alleviate the force of the challenges. Third, I discuss whether the idea of drawing on standardization may constitute a proper answer to the challenges. It is argued that not only does none of the three possible approaches succeed in solving all the challenges—a fact that need not be worrying if they could somehow be combined into an overall solution—but they also do not succeed in delivering plausible solutions to any of the challenges.

This leads on to section III, in which I consider how serious the challenges are. Obviously, some theoretical challenges are more serious than others. However, it is argued that the three challenges constitute serious problems and that this is the case across the different interpretations that have been given of proportionality. Section IV is a summary and conclusion.

Before embarking on the considerations, a final initial comment. It might perhaps be objected that the ensuing discussion of the possibility of comparing crimes in seriousness is somewhat superfluous, in the sense that people already seem to have a pretty clear idea of the relative seriousness of crimes prior to any philosophical inquiry. In other words, it could seem that a theoretical discussion has little to offer if we already have the appropriate answers at hand (see Ryberg 2004, p. 60). This view might find support in the empirical work that has been conducted by social scientists to determine community views on crime gravity. The locus classicus is Sellin and Wolfgang's *The Measurement of Delinquency* (1978), in which the authors found that there exists considerable agreement on the relative seriousness of crimes among people from different countries, as well as among people from different social groups within the same country. This work has been followed up by many other studies. Furthermore, it has been emphasized that sentencing commissions that have constructed generic scales of crime have usually carried out their work without much dissension and without facing insuperable difficulties (von Hirsch, Knapp, and Tonry 1987; von Hirsch 2017). Thus, is it plausible to hold that theoretical discussion of the seriousness of crimes and the challenges associated with the ranking of crimes is basically to search for something that is already there?

The answer must be in the negative.[3] First of all, there is the simple problem that popular perceptions of the seriousness of crimes need not be well informed. For instance, they may be based on false perceptions of how different crimes affect the victims. More generally, the mere fact that people agree on how crimes should be ranked does not in itself establish that such a ranking should be morally accepted. This would require an independent normative argument. In this sense, the consideration of how crimes should be ranked is not different from other problems in criminal justice ethics (or ethics in general), which are solved not merely by carrying out polls or by surveying popular judgments but by engaging in reflections on values and underlying rationales. And this is precisely what adherents of the proportionality principle have done. Thus, even though the ensuing considerations are critical concerning the concept of crime gravity as employed within the retributivist idea of proportionality, the discussion takes place on the ground of a theoretical foundation that proportionalists themselves fully accept.

I. Three Challenges to the Ranking of Crimes in Seriousness

Despite the fact that there exists a theoretical discussion of the content of components that determine the seriousness of crime, the discussion of the ranking of crimes is still somewhat modest. Perhaps this is due to the above-mentioned feeling that there exists considerable agreement on the matter and that the task, therefore, seems straightforward enough. Moreover, some theorists have bypassed the question by holding that the construction of a crime scale is more of a technical question than a philosophical one (see, e.g., Primoratz 1984). However, as we shall now see, the computation of seriousness is not straightforward and is indeed an ethical issue.

A. The Harm Specification Challenge

The standard view among adherents of the proportionality principle is that crime seriousness is determined partly by the harmfulness of the criminal act.

---

3. See Ryberg (2004) and von Hirsch and Jareborg (1991). For a more general discussion of the normative significance of public opinion in relation to penal theory and practice, see Ryberg and Roberts (2014).

That is, more precisely, everything else being equal, a crime is more serious if it causes more harm. That this is a broadly accepted view is not surprising. The view is immediately appealing and accords well with more general ethical views on what determines the wrongfulness of an act. Given the central position that the concept of harm plays in ethics in general, it is not surprising that much discussion has been concerned with the content of this concept. Moreover, preliminary work has been conducted by von Hirsch and Jareborg and other theorists with regard to procedures for gauging criminal harm.[4] The purpose here, however, is not to enter into the broader conceptual discussion of harm or to engage in a narrower discussion of the von Hirsch and Jareborg procedure. Rather, what I will do is direct attention to what could be called the harm specification challenge, namely, the fact that there seem to be some crimes that cause too little harm and others that cause too much.[5]

The first part of the challenge consists in the fact that there are several crimes that do not—at least, not in any straightforward way—involve harmful conduct. An obvious example is the inchoate crime of attempt. A planned crime may fail simply because a person does not succeed in carrying out all the acts necessary to bring it about (incomplete attempts), or a person may perform all the intended acts but nevertheless fail in bringing about the desired result (complete attempt) (see, e.g., Ashworth 1999, pp. 460ff). In neither case is there a direct harm to victims. Another obvious example is an act that involves risk, for instance, driving hazardously on a crowded street or breaking speed limits. Even if an act is highly risky, it may be performed without causing any harm to victims.

It should be noted that what we are considering here is not whether such acts should be criminalized in the first place (few would hold that risks or attempts should never be criminalized). The problem is that if these acts do not involve any harm (or only a marginal amount of derivative harm), then the perpetrator should not be punished (or should receive only a very lenient punishment). An obvious response to this may be to hold that it is not only realized harms that count in the computation of seriousness but also risk-adjusted harms. In fact, this has explicitly been suggested by von Hirsch and

---

4. However, it is remarkable how little theoretical work has been conducted on the concept and measurement of criminal harm. For instance, Paoli and Greenfield (2013) note that a recent publication search in Criminal Justice Abstracts, using "harm" and "crime" as keywords, yielded only 11 hits (p. 363).

5. For a discussion of this challenge, see also Ryberg (2004, chap. 2).

Jareborg (1991), who have incorporated "risk judgments" in their guidelines for gauging harms. However, such a suggestion is far from unproblematic.

First, it should be noted that if what matters in the computation of seriousness is risk-adjusted harm (that is, harm times probability), it does not then make any difference whether a harm is actually caused by the criminal act. The risk-adjusted harm is the same independently of whether or not the harm is realized (e.g., if there is a 50 percent risk of killing someone if I drive hazardously on the street, then this is the case independently of whether I end up hitting someone). It seems incoherent to hold that a harm should be risk-adjusted when it is not realized but that it should not be risk-adjusted if it is realized. But this would have the noteworthy implication that harm should be risk-adjusted for all types of crime. Second, and more important, it is by no means a simple task to explain precisely what risk adjustment implies. Suppose that the police succeed in arresting me before I carry out a planned murder. How should we estimate the risk of this criminal act? Or, to take an instance of a complete attempt, what is the risk of harming a person I shoot at but fail to hit? A possibility suggested by Husak (1994) is to "calculate the percentage of attempted crimes that actually succeeds and then use . . . this ratio to discount the punishment for unsuccessful attempts" (p. 66). But it is not clear what this implies. Should such a risk be determined only on the ground of registered attempts or on the ground of estimates of all criminal attempts? Moreover, should the calculation be based on all or only some types of attempt? If I attempt to shoot someone, should the risk be determined on the ground of all sorts of attempts (including, say, attempted theft and attempted tax evasion) or only on the ground of attempted murder by shooting or perhaps on the ground of attempted murder by shooting with a gun of a certain caliber at a certain range? It is not clear what a nonarbitrary answer is with regard to how the statistics should be calculated (see Ryberg 2004, p. 64). More generally, it seems clear that resorting to risk adjustments does not constitute a simple answer to the computation of the gravity of harmless crimes.

The second and even more complex aspect of the specification challenge consists in almost the opposite problem, namely, that a criminal act may cause a wide range of harms. For instance, an assault will, of course, cause harm to the direct victim of the crime. However, the direct victim is often not the only one to be affected. Family and friends may grieve for what the victim has been through. People who witnessed the crime may suffer serious trauma. Others in a neighborhood may fear that they will become victims of a similar crime and may consequently change their behavior in various ways (e.g., by not going out in the evening or by installing extra locks on their front doors).

In fact, even people who are not aware that a particular crime has taken place may sometimes be affected (e.g., crimes may increase the cost of insurance or lower the prices of houses in a neighborhood). And a crime may even be said to be harmful to everyone by bringing about law-enforcement costs (see Greenfield and Paoli 2013). In short, a crime may not only have consequences for the direct victim but may ramify in such a way as to affect the lives of many other people for the worse. Moreover, cases involving more remote harms may occur even if one considers only those cases involving the direct victim of a crime. For instance, the simple theft of a mobile phone may result in the death of the victim (e.g., if this person has a coronary but is unable to call an ambulance). Needless to say, a crime may trigger chains of harm in many ways other than indicated by the examples presented here. The problem, of course, is how much of the harm that is caused by a crime should be attributed to the criminal act by figuring in the computation of the seriousness of the crime. The easy answer, to contend that all harms that follow from a crime should figure in the assessment of the seriousness of this crime, is hardly satisfactory. For instance, few would subscribe to the view that the thief should be held accountable for the death of the person with the coronary. But if it is not all the harm that is caused by an act that should figure in the computation of the gravity of this crime, then some sort of nonarbitrary delimitation principle is required. Whether such a delimitation rationale can be provided is something to which I will return shortly. For the present, it is sufficient to note that the ascription of harm to a crime is seriously complicated by the fact that while some crimes do not involve harm in any straightforward way, others may result in comprehensive amounts of harm. So much for the specification challenge.

B. The Weighing Challenge

One of the things that has often been initially underlined by modern adherents of the proportionality principle is that a plausible exposition of principle is very much not the same as adhering to the idea of harm-for-harm equivalence. Although several objections have been raised against a principle that implies that the harm of a crime should simply be reversed against the perpetrator, the main problem is usually held that such a principle ignores the fact that the seriousness of crimes is determined not only by criminal harm but also by the culpability of the offender. The role played by culpability is indicated by the Nozickian formula according to which crime gravity is determined on the ground of the product $H * C$, where H is the harm of the crime and C the culpability of the offender indicated by numerical values 0 to 1.[6] This nicely illustrates the widely accepted view that if an offender is not culpable at all, that is, if C = 0, then he or she does not deserve a punishment and, furthermore, that culpability is a matter of degree.

The idea of culpability is to draw attention to the intent, motive, or circumstances that determine the degree to which an offender should be held accountable for the harm caused by the criminal act. More precisely, a first aspect of culpability is mens rea, that is, the degree to which the offender was mentally directed to the harm that was caused. Standard mens rea distinctions, representing different degrees of culpability, are among intention, knowledge, recklessness, and (perhaps) negligence. A second aspect of culpability concerns what is standardly referred to as "excuse," "justification," and "mitigation" defenses instantiating an underlying view of the responsibility of the offender. Traditional considerations of this aspect concern, for instance, whether an offender acted under constraints from defects of knowledge or will. As one might expect, both mens rea and responsibility are concepts that have led to comprehensive, more detailed discussions that need not be entered into here. What matters in the present context is that if it is the case that crimes vary in the degree of harm they cause and if culpability is a matter of degree, then the question arises of how one should determine the relative seriousness of crimes varying in both respects. More precisely, how should a more harmful crime committed by a less culpable offender be ranked relative to a less harmful crime committed by a more culpable offender (e.g., is intentional assault more or less serious than reckless homicide, or is assault committed under duress or provocation more or less serious than robbery committed with no excuses)?[7] What I will refer to as the weighing challenge consists in providing a nonarbitrary answer to this question.

Despite the fact that the challenge arises straightforwardly enough when one holds that there are several factors determining the seriousness of crime and even though the acknowledgment of the challenge is not new—for instance, Hart (1968) clearly recognized the challenge when he asked whether "negligently causing the destruction of a city [is] worse than the intentional wounding of a single policemen" (p. 162)—it is remarkable how little has been said to meet the challenge. One of the few penal theorists to have commented

---

6. Nozick (1981) himself presents the formula as the product of harm and responsibility, where "responsibility" refers to the degree to which a person flouts correct values (p. 363).

7. For more examples, see Ryberg (2004, chap. 2).

on this is Scheid (1997), who holds that "some confusion on the topic could be avoided . . . if a distinction between the legislative and judicial tasks were kept in mind" (p. 484). His point is that the question of how harm and culpability should be combined "is not a concern for the legislative task," which merely deals with standard cases of crimes. It only arises in relation to the judicial task of meting out sentences for individual offenders. However, this is clearly not a genuine answer to the challenge. If the idea is that an offender should receive a sentence that is proportionate to the gravity of the crime, then it is necessary to know how harm and culpability affect the seriousness of the crime relative to the seriousness of other crimes. And this is so even if it is correct that the question arises only at the judicial level.

C. The Individualization Challenge

The final challenge to which attention should be directed consists in the fact that the factors determining the seriousness of a crime may vary significantly between two instances of the same crime. This is easily seen with regard to the harm dimension. Differences in the living conditions of two victims may imply that they are affected very differently by the same type of crime. For instance, while the theft of a car from a person who has another car may cause some inconvenience, such a theft may have more serious consequences for a victim who has only one car (and who perhaps subsequently loses his or her job because he or she can no longer drive to work). The rich victim may be affected much less by a theft than the poor person. And the psychologically more sensitive victim may suffer much more from an assault than one who is more resilient. Numerous examples, of course, can be given indicating that crimes that are the same in name may affect the lives of victims for the worse to a very different extent. In general terms, we can say that victims may be affected differently simply because some are physically, psychologically, or socially more vulnerable than others.[8] But does this imply that a proportionate sentence should be determined relative to the harmfulness of the individual criminal act? And does it make sense at all to talk of the proportionate punishment for a certain type of crime?

While it is easy to see that two instances of the same crime may cause different amounts of harm to different victims, it has less often been realized that an individualization challenge also arises in relation to the other dimension

---

8. For a parallel discussion in relation to the comparison of the severity of punishment, see Ryberg (2004, 2010) and Kolber (2009).

of seriousness, namely, culpability. As mentioned, one aspect of culpability is the degree to which an offender is responsible for the criminal act. According to a widely accepted view, responsibility depends on the degree to which certain cognitive and affective capacities have been developed in the offender (see, e.g., Hart 1968; Brink 2004; Vincent 2013). For instance, this constitutes the standard justification for why adolescent offenders should usually be treated more leniently by the criminal justice system than adult offenders. Adolescents should receive a "youth discount" simply because they are less mature; that is, the capacities that determine responsibility have not yet been developed to the same degree as in the adult (Feld 2007; Steinberg 2009). However, this idea has another implication that is relevant in the present context. It seems to imply that there may be individual differences between the degree to which ordinary adult criminals are responsible for having committed the same type of crime. Differences in the development of capacities vary not only between adolescents and adults but also between one individual adult and another. However, if that is the case, then it seems to follow that two offenders who have committed the same crime, say, burglary—which has caused precisely the same amount of harm—and who have acted with the same mens rea may nevertheless have committed crimes of a different degree of seriousness, simply because the first burglar happens to have more developed mental capacities than the second.

Thus, the individualization challenge consists in the fact that if one takes the suggested dimensions of crime gravity for granted, then it seems to follow that seriousness can only be determined of individual crimes, and talk of one crime being more serious than another (say, that theft is more serious than assault) only makes sense as a kind of morally irrelevant generalization.

II. How Could the Challenges Be Met?

That the construction of a scale of crimes in seriousness is not as straightforward a task as it might seem to be prima facie has not gone unnoticed. The time has come to consider to what extent theorists who have engaged in the theoretical discussion of a crime scaling have managed to solve the three challenges. The three answers that will be considered, respectively, consist in the contention that the challenges are the result of some sort of overtheorization, that they could be blocked on the ground of a subjectivist approach to crime, or that a solution follows by adopting a proper degree of standardization in the computation of seriousness. However, as will be argued, none of these approaches succeeds in delivering satisfactory solutions to the challenges.

A. The Overtheorization Response

A possible approach to the intricacies associated with a comparison of crimes in seriousness might be to hold that there are limits to what can plausibly be expected with regard to the theoretical underpinning of ethical positions. The job of philosophers consists in providing and assessing basic rationales. However, it is a well-known fact that there are limits to how far the demand of justification can take us. Therefore, could it be the case that a proper diagnosis of the alleged challenges is some sort of overtheorization? Should they be seen as arising from the excessive interest of philosophers in searching for well-argued rationales even in places where such rationales can no longer be provided and where the proper attitude would simply be to listen to what we feel?

What an answer along these lines more precisely amounts to obviously needs clarification. However, before considering this in more detail, it should be noted that it hardly constitutes a proper answer to all the presented challenges. The specification challenge, that some crimes do not seem to involve harm while others can trigger long chains of harms, cannot properly be seen as a result of overtheorization. Neither can the individualization challenge plausibly be rejected along these lines. However, the answer may be more apposite with regard to the weighing challenge. Is it not a matter of philosophical naiveté to expect that a strict and well-sustained metric can be developed for the weighing of harm and culpability in order to deliver precise judgments of crime gravity?

A view along these lines has been suggested by Ten (1987). In his view, the scaling of crimes is "a project that seems capable of being carried out," and he supports this contention by drawing attention to other manageable cases involving a balancing of values. What he suggests is that the problems related to the comparison of crimes in gravity are basically the same problems confronting teachers in the ranking of essays: "When tutors and teachers rank the essays of their students, they do not have only one relevant feature to look for. There are a number of different features—originality, understanding of the issues discussed, lucidity of presentation etc.—which each makes contribution to the quality of the essay. An essay may be strong in one dimension but weak in another, and yet it is possible to make an overall assessment of the essay as being better or worse than another" (p. 155). Ten's observation is correct. However, the question is what precisely it manages to establish with regard to crime gravity. Obviously, the point is not simply to suggest that it is in a strict sense possible to make judgments combining harm and culpability. Surely, one can suggest a certain ranking of crimes involving different degree of harm and culpability. In fact, to some extent, this is what legislators and judges already do. Thus, the point must be that it is somehow possible to make reasonable or at least partly justified assessments even in the absence of some sort of strictly justified metric or equation. Although this view (as well as the analogy) certainly has some appeal, I still believe there are reasons to be skeptical with regard to what it manages to establish (see also Ryberg 2004, p. 85).

First, it is obviously correct that one can imagine some sort of overall guiding principles governing cases in which different values have to be balanced and where no type of more strict equation exists for the way the balancing should be made. For instance, to stay within Ten's analogy, it may be regarded as crucial for the assessment of an essay that the assignment has, in fact, been answered, while less important that the punctuation is correct. However, when it comes to the combination of harm and different degrees of culpability, beyond the fact that harm is regarded as playing a significant role, very little has been said to guide the balancing.

Second, as mentioned, it might be held that at this point, all that can be done is to rely on some sort of intuitive judgment of what strikes us as a reasonable weighing. However, if this is the case, then what kind of intuition should one draw on? If it is an intuition with regard to how much the seriousness of a crime generally is reduced if the harm is caused recklessly rather than intentionally, then it is not obvious that we have this sort of intuition. Conversely, if what we are talking about are not general intuitions but rather those in specific cases of crime, then it is probably more likely that people have some intuitions. But in that case, is that all we should rely on? For instance, should there be no demand of some sort of consistency in how we assess the significance of recklessness in relation to different types of crime?

What these questions indicate is not that the overtheorization response should be rejected but, more modestly, that even if one accepts the response, it is still not very clear where this leaves the proportionalist with regard to the task of comparing crimes in gravity. Moreover, it seems that the response implies that one has at an important point almost renounced the idea of principled sentencing, which is not unproblematic if one believes that justificatory power constitutes a theoretical virtue. Thus, the conclusion must be that the response does not meet the harm specification and individualization challenges, that it is not clear where it leaves the proportionalist with regard to the weighing challenge, and that it seems to some extent to give up with regard to the justificatory power of the principle of proportionality.

B. The Subjectivist Response

Another response could be to draw on the idea of a so-called subjectivist approach to criminal justice. The distinction between objectivism and subjectivism reflects a traditional dispute with regard to what constitutes the true ground for criminal liability. The idea of subjectivism is that a defendant should be held accountable not for the actual result of a proscribed act but for the conduct as perceived by the offender himself or herself. The rationale behind subjectivism consists in a combination of the fact that an agent never has full control over the outcome of an act—outcomes may be the result of good or bad luck—and the view that it is unjust to hold an agent accountable for something that is beyond his or her control.[9] What the agent should be held accountable for, therefore, is his or her intention and his or her effort to implement it. For instance, Ashworth (1984) has defended a subjectivist position by subscribing to what he calls the "fully subjective principle," according to which a "defendant should be held responsible for what he intended to do, believed he was doing or believed he was risking" (p. 88). However, even though subjectivism concerns criminal liability and sentencing and, therefore, presupposes that the appropriate punishments for different crimes have already been determined, it might nevertheless be asked whether the idea of focusing on the mental attitudes of offenders could also be invoked at an earlier stage, namely, as the basis for the determination of crime gravity (in fact, it might perhaps even be held that this is actually what follows if one subscribes to the tenet of subjectivism).

For instance, as we have seen, determining seriousness on the ground of harm was challenged by the fact that some crimes do not cause any harm. However, in the comparison of attempted harm and a proscribed act that results in a harm, it could be held that these crimes could be regarded as equally serious if it is not the actual outcome that matters but rather what is intended or foreseen. Similarly, it could also be held that if criminal justice, so to speak, is harnessed to choice rather than chance, then it should make no difference whether a harm actually materializes when someone exposes others

---

9. For a presentation of the general discussion of the significance of moral luck, see, e.g., Nelkin (2013).

to a serious risk. Moreover, the fact that some crimes may initiate long causal chains of harm could perhaps be disregarded if it is not the actual outcome of a crime that matters. However, whether this is the case obviously depends on the crucial question of what precisely it is that constitutes the seriousness-determining factor if this is no longer the actual harm.

One possibility is to suggest that seriousness should be determined on the ground of intended harm. Although this view raises several questions concerning the more basic question of what is precisely meant by "intention," it seems that on a standard account, there are many crimes that do not involve the intention of harm. Stealing a wallet may involve an intention of performing a particular act or of reaching a particular goal (to get some money) but will usually not involve an intention of causing a particular harm (the offender might not care at all about whether the victim is harmed or might sometimes even wish that this was not the case).[10] The same is the case for numerous (probably most) other crimes that are not committed with the intention of harm. And this problem is even more obvious when it comes to the relative comparison of the seriousness of crimes. Even if harm is intended, it need not be the case that the offender intends a specific amount of harm, which would have to be the case in order to make relative comparison of crime gravity. Thus, all in all, intended harm is not a good candidate for the assessment of seriousness.

Another possibility is to modify the suggestion by holding instead that what matters is not intended harm but rather the harm that an offender expects or believes will follow in committing the criminal act. However, this suggestion also faces serious problems. First, there may be many cases in which an offender has not really considered how much harm will follow from an act. The offender usually knows that an act is criminal and may know that it causes harm, but this is not tantamount to having considered how harmful it would be (neither relative to other crimes nor in itself). Second, even if an offender has considered the harmfulness of a proscribed act, it does not follow that he or she has reached an answer. And in some cases, at least, it may be quite difficult to have clear expectations (e.g., how much harm do you think follows from a particular instance of tax evasion, bank robbery, computer hacking, or smuggling of cigarettes?). Moreover, even when it comes to crimes that more directly harm individuals, it may be difficult to form a precise idea of the harm involved, and this may be so for the simple reason

---

10. For a comprehensive discussion of intention as defined by which of one's beliefs about consequences explain one's acting in a certain way, see, e.g., Bennett (1995).

that one knows that a particular act may harm different individuals very differently. Third, the beliefs or expectations of offenders may be mistaken. In some cases, an offender may not believe at all that committing a proscribed act will cause any harm. For instance, in most cases where people exceed speed limits, they do not believe or expect any harm to follow (in fact, they may not even believe they have increased the risk of harm). Furthermore, there may be cases where an offender suspects an act to be harmful but significantly under- or overestimates the harm (e.g., an offender may fail to properly recognize the psychological side effects of a residential burglary). However, even if one believes that this is not a problem—but perhaps only a reasonable implication if one subscribes to the basic idea of subjectivism—the former problems indicate that the move from the actual harm of an act into the awareness of the offender prompts a series of problems that do not call for easy solutions.

To sum up, the idea of abandoning the focus on outcomes of a proscribed act by invoking the mental states of offenders does not provide a solution to the weighing challenge and the individualization challenge, and, more important, it does not even seem to provide an unproblematic solution to the harm specification challenge. Obviously, this does not settle the question with regard to the general dispute between subjectivism and objectivism. All we have seen is that the subjectivist approach to crime ranking does not seem to be an attractive option.

C. The Standardization Response

While the previous two responses have constituted attempts to meet the harm specification challenge and the weighing challenge, the time has now come to consider a response that directly addresses the individualization challenge but may also be held to have wider implications. In short, that crimes of a certain type may harm victims to a very different extent and that two offenders may be responsible for their conduct to a different extent even if there are no standard excuses related to the conduct imply that seriousness may differ significantly between two crimes that are the same in name. However, the obvious response, if one is not willing to give in and accept this implication, is to suggest that the measurement of seriousness should be based on standardization, which is precisely the procedure taken by several theorists. For instance, in the development of their living-standard account of harm— according to which it is not the well-being of victims that matters but the "means and capabilities" for achieving a certain quality of life—von Hirsch and Jareborg (1991) specifically underline that they are concerned with the "standard harm" involved in a given category of crime. Likewise, standardization is also an explicit element in the more recent framework developed by Greenfield and Paoli (2013). Moreover, and we shall return to this shortly, von Hirsch has also defended a type of standardization in relation to assessment of responsibility. By invoking standardization, it is clear that the complexity of comparing crimes in gravity seems to be resolved. And perhaps it is not only the individualization challenge that is met in this way but also part of the harm specification challenge. It might be suggested that the fact that a crime may sometimes cause long chains of harm could, at least to some extent, be ignored by focusing only on the standard harm of a crime. However, standardization gives rise to several questions: what should be standardized, how should it be done, and—most important—can it be justified?

In considering standardization in relation to the assessment of the harmfulness of a criminal act, two interpretations must be distinguished. One possibility is to hold that in order to make the proportionalist penal scheme work, it is necessary to construct a scaling of crimes in gravity and that this scaling should be based on standardized accounts of harm. This view, however, need not imply that a standardized judgment should be used in the sentencing of individual offenders. In individual cases of crime, it could still be held that it is the actual harm of the proscribed act that should count in the determination of the proper sentence. Thus, on this account, standardization is only used to construct the scale, not to determine the seriousness of individual crimes. Another possibility is that standardization should also figure in the imposition of sentences of individual offenders. Thus, on the first account, standardization works only as a technical tool in order to construct a scale that can be linked to a scale of punishment severity. This means that when it comes to individual sentences, two offenders who have committed the same crimes—say, theft—may nevertheless be sentenced very differently (if the first thief caused more harm to the victim than the second). On the second account, the two will receive the same sentence, because they have committed equally serious crimes (seen from a standardized point of view).

If one does not wish to cede and accept that the harmfulness of two instances of the same crime can vary significantly and that the proportionate sentence of two offenders may therefore also vary, even though they have committed the same type of crime, one will have to subscribe to the second account of standardization. But if that is so, how should the standard harm of a certain type of crime be determined? One possibility is to hold that the standard harm is the typical harm of a certain type of crime. But this raises the question of whether there really is a degree of harmfulness that is usually caused by a certain crime or whether the harmfulness is simply too diverse for it to make sense to talk of the typical harm. Another possibility is that the standard harm should be regarded as the average harm caused by instances of a particular type of crime. If this is what standardization implies, then the diversity is not a problem (the average harm could, in principle, be determined even if all instances of a certain crime cause different degrees of harm). However, no matter what constitutes the most plausible answer, we are still left with the crucial question of how standardization can be justified within a proportionalist penal scheme. Even though discussion of the justification is quite sparse, a few arguments have been presented.

A first possibility is to contend that it is simply not possible to determine the harm caused by individual instances of crime and, therefore, all one can do is rely on judgments of the standard harm. Perhaps this is what von Hirsch and Jareborg (1991) have in mind when they say that "particular criminal acts are too diverse to be rated on an individualized basis" (p. 4) or that precisely how much a crime victim "is injured by the loss of her particular vase would require a delving into her personal situation to a degree which the law cannot possibly undertake" (p. 5). Along the same lines, Greenfield and Paoli (2013) hold that "some standardization . . . seems unavoidable" (p. 867). However, there are several reasons to be skeptical regarding this argument.

First, it is not accurate that harm cannot to some extent be determined on an individualized basis. It is a fact that with regard to many types of crime, the criminal justice system is in contact with the crime victim(s), and to some extent, it would be possible to get an idea of the harm that has been caused. It is possible to ask the victim of a car theft how this has affected his or her life ("Do you have another car? Have you as a consequence of the theft lost your job?"). To contend that, strictly speaking, it is not possible to get a closer picture of the harm caused in individual cases than what is provided by a purely standardized account of the harm of type of crime is simply not correct. Moreover, it is worth noting that the claim that it is impossible to assess the harm in individual cases of crime would constitute a problem with regard to determining what constitutes the standard harm if this is understood as the typical harm or the average harm caused by a crime.

Second, even if it were the case that it is impossible to approximate the harm of individual crimes, this would not establish that relying on standardized harm is justified. Briefly put, suppose one holds that "Our moral theory presupposes that we can do A; however, A is impossible, therefore we do B." It seems obvious that the latter move to B does not in itself follow from the impossibility of A. Rather, the obvious inference seems to be that if our theory presupposes A, and if A is impossible, then our theory is seriously defective. Or that if we—in the light of the impossibility of A—decide to do B instead, then it has to be shown that B can actually be justified within the framework of the moral theory. In less abstract terms, the fact that it is impossible to determine the harm in individual cases of crime does not in itself establish that it is justified to rely on a standard account of harm. This will require an independent argument. Therefore, all in all, the impossibility argument is a poor one; it is based on a false premise and is logically defective.

However, perhaps there is a more reasonable interpretation of the argument. It might be suggested that the point is not to hold that it is, strictly speaking, impossible to get a more precise picture of individual harms than what is provided by relying on the standard harm of a crime. Rather, the point is that it would constitute an enormous task for the criminal justice system if it had to make thorough investigations of the harm in individual cases. In short, although this type of endeavor is not impossible, it would require too many resources. This argument has some appeal. However, on closer inspection, it is clear that it is flawed.

First, it is obvious that it is not only the inspection into the harm of individual crimes that requires resources. It also requires resources to determine which of the standard crimes a criminal has committed. Presumably, it would be much less time-consuming and thus require many fewer resources for the criminal justice system if the standard categories of crime were put into two or three overall broad categories, each of which had a fitting punishment. This shows that if one starts balancing justice and resources, then the argument that the determination of individual harms would require too many resources does not in itself establish that the proper balance is reached by relying on the standard harm of the typical categories of crime. This will require an independent argument. Second, and more important, it is far from obvious what the significance of resources should be within a retributively based penal system. If the basic idea is that the punishment should be determined on the ground of what an individual perpetrator deserves from having committed his or her misdeed and that this would require the determination of the harm caused by this particular act then—as we shall return to shortly—the idea of relying instead on a standard account of harm seems basically to be a way of compromising justice (the perpetrator will end up being punished either too severely or too leniently relative to the crime). But compromising or sidestepping justice because this will have desirable consequences (in terms of resources) is usually something that retributivists are not willing to accept. Therefore, the resource argument will require the development of a new theory of how to balance justice and resources. On this point, retributivists have had very little to say, and it seems obvious that it will be a theoretically demanding task.[11] Thus, the resources argument does not seem promising for the proportionalist.

In sum, none of the above arguments is persuasive, to the effect that it is neither possible nor desirable for the criminal justice system to try to determine criminal harm on an individual basis and that the system should therefore be based on a standard account of harm. As earlier noted, however, the considerations concerning individualization versus standardization are not only relevant in relation to the assessment of harm. The question also arises in relation to the culpability dimension of seriousness, more precisely in relation to judgments of criminal responsibility. If one believes that the responsibility of an offender depends (partly) on the development of cognitive capacities (the capacity to fully appreciate the consequences of a criminal act) and volitional capacities (such as impulse control and perhaps the capacity to resist peer pressure), then it seems obvious that different offenders, who are not otherwise excused for their behavior, may possess differing degrees of culpability, simply because it is a fact that the development of such capacities varies from one offender to another. Can one escape the obvious implication that the computation of the seriousness of a crime requires assessment of individual culpability through inspections of the degree to which such capacities have been developed in the individual offender?

Apparently, von Hirsch believes this to be the case. He presents his thoughts as part of his discussion of why there should be an age-based mitigation for juvenile offenders. The argument—also advanced by several other theorists—is that the capacities of juveniles are less developed than those of adults (see, e.g., Feld 1999; Fagan 2003; Steinberg 2009; Ryberg 2014). However, confronted with the fact that there are great variations in the degree to which these capacities are developed between juveniles at the same age level, von Hirsch (2001) suggests that what matters is not the actual development of the relevant capacities but rather the "normative expectations" we have of offenders (p. 225). In this view, the crime committed by the juvenile should result in a mitigation, because young individuals cannot be expected to have fully developed comprehension of the consequences of their criminal acts or fully developed control over how they behave. And this is so even where the relevant capacities are differently developed among juveniles of the

---

11. For a more extensive discussion of the problem of balancing retributive justice and resources, see Ryberg (2013).

same age. But this would also be the case with regard to adult offenders. If the judgment of culpability is based on "normative expectation," then it does not matter whether there exists a de facto difference in the degree to which these capacities are developed in various adult offenders. Thus, with regard to this particular aspect of culpability, individualization is rejected by employing the idea of normative expectations. Is this account of standardization in culpability judgments plausible?

A first problem facing the proposal is that it is not obvious why judgments of culpability should be based on general normative expectations (Ryberg 2015). Suppose that we know that a perpetrator has capacities less developed than those included in the general normative expectation with regard to these capacities. Why, then, should we hold the perpetrator culpable to an extent that is not possible for this person? In my view, it seems somewhat bizarre to expect something of a person when one knows that this person cannot live up to what is expected of him or her (in particular when we are considering something as serious as the imposition of punishment). At least, this seems to require a very good reason, which has not been provided by von Hirsch.

However, not only does it seem implausible to expect something of an offender's capacities that fail to reflect the actual capacities possessed by this person, but a more general problem is also involved in this sort of standardization, no matter whether we are considering the culpability dimension of seriousness or the harm dimension. The problem, briefly hinted at above, is that standardization does not seem to accord with a retributivist framework underlining the idea of proportionality. Consider a simple analogy. Suppose that I am about to move to a new apartment and that Peter has kindly helped, moving much of my furniture. In fact, he has done a tremendous job moving most of the heavy stuff. Moreover, suppose that in response to the help, I reason as follows: "Peter, it seems that you deserve a great dinner for all your assistance. However, a few days ago, Tim and Tom also helped me, and they both did a very poor job. Therefore, considering the average or typical assistance, it is clear that you do not deserve a dinner after all. A beer will do!" I take it that most would regard this piece of reasoning as implausible. It seems absurd that the poor job done by Tim and Tom should have any influence whatsoever on what Peter deserves. But the same seems to be the case if we turn to considerations of negative desert.

Retributivists believe that an offender deserves a punishment for his or her wrongdoing. It is often underlined that this is a way of respecting the perpetrator as a person who has decided to carry out the misdeed or a way of taking the person seriously as an autonomous individual. However, once one starts drawing on averages or on what is typical in the determination of crime gravity, it seems one is basically relying on the same sort of reasoning as in the example with Peter. If a perpetrator has committed an assault that was less harmful than the typical or average assault or if he or she (due to less developed capacities) is less culpable, then it seems dubious to hold that this perpetrator deserves a more serious punishment than that warranted by the seriousness of his or her crime (if seen in isolation) simply because other people have committed more serious assaults. The fact that other perpetrators have committed more serious acts of crime should not figure in the desert base of what the individual deserves. Needless to say, it may be much more practical for the criminal justice system to rely on averages or what is typical. However, one should not rely on something that is morally arbitrary simply because this is practically convenient. And it is precisely the lack of a strong argument for how standardization is compatible with the basic idea of individual desert that is hard to imagine and that, to my knowledge, has not been presented in the debate.

III. How Serious Are the Challenges?

The answers considered in the previous section were not satisfactory. None of the responses succeeded in meeting all the challenges, and, as argued, it was questionable whether they managed to solve any. Thus, the idea of combining the different answers in order to get around the challenges seems dubious. But in the absence of a satisfactory response, it is reasonable to ask, how serious are the challenges? Theoretical challenges may be of a very different nature. Some strike to the heart of theory, while others constitute theoretically more peripheral concerns. And, as is well known, all normative theories seem to face some sort of theoretical challenges. So how serious are the outlined challenges for the principle of proportionality?

In order to answer the question, it is important to recall what constitutes the theoretical preconditions for a full-fledged proportionalist penal scheme. To make the idea of proportionality operational, it is necessary to construct a scaling of crimes in seriousness, a scaling of punishments in severity, and a procedure for knitting these two scales (an anchor theory). But this means that a failure at one step in the procedure is sufficient to undermine the idea of proportionality. Even if a scale of punishment has been successfully constructed and an impeccable anchor theory developed, the principle of proportionality will still not be lifted off the ground if the ranking of crimes in gravity faces problems.

In this light, it is clear that the different challenges must be regarded as serious. If the harm specification challenge and the weighing challenge have not been properly answered, then there will be a lack of guidance with regard to how several crimes should be compared in terms of seriousness. To this, it may perhaps be objected that even if there are some crimes that are not easily comparable in gravity, this will not prevent construction of some scaling of comparable types of crime, and this crime scale—with a proper anchor theory and a scaling of punishments—can be used to determine proportionate punishments for some crimes. But if this is the case, it is still clear that if the individualization challenge has not been properly met, one will still face problems when it comes to the determination of proportionate sentences in individual cases of crime. Moreover, there is a further aspect in the task of crime ranking that adds to the problems.

Most proportionalists seem to agree that a mere ordinal ranking of crimes in seriousness is unsatisfactory as a basis for a proportional distribution of punishment (see, e.g., Kleinig 1973; Ten 1987; von Hirsch 1992; Scheid 1997). The reason behind this claim is easy to see. If we consider three crimes ranked in ascending order of seriousness, then it is not sufficient to contend that proportionality has been observed as long as the third crime is punished more severely than the second and the second more severely than the third. Rather, in a plausible account of proportionality, it also matters, for instance, whether the second crime is only slightly more serious than the first, while the third is considerably more serious than the second (such as would be the case if we compare the theft of $50, the theft of $1,000, and murder).[12] In other words, a purely ordinal ranking of crimes will not be plausible. Rather, as has been repeatedly underlined, a plausible ranking of crimes is one that indicates the relative differences in seriousness, and spacing is reflected in the way the crimes are being punished. However, an interval ranking of crimes in gravity is obviously much more demanding. But this means that the force of the three challenges increases. Even if some rough guidelines could help meet the weighing problem and the harm specification problem, they may not bring us as far as being able to make interval comparisons for different types of crime. And, most important, the lack of an answer to the individualization challenge certainly makes it an unsurmountable task to ensure that all individual sentences reflect interval differences in the gravity of the plethora of individual crimes dealt with by the criminal justice system.

---

12. For a more comprehensive discussion of the problems related to a purely ordinal matching of the scales of crime and punishment, see Scheid (1997) and Ryberg (2004).

Therefore, the result of the absence of satisfactory answers to the challenges seems to be that it will in many cases be left theoretically unclear how different crimes vary in terms of seriousness and, hence, unclear what constitutes proportionate punitive reaction. Also, one is left with several other collateral challenges (such as how many resources the criminal justice system should use to ensure that proportionality is observed) that do not invite easy answers. Finally, it should be noted that these problems arise independently of the type of moral constraints one believes to follow from the idea of proportionality; that is, independently of whether one subscribes to a positive proportionalist view, according to which perpetrators should receive no more and no less than the proportionate punishment, or to a negative proportionalist view, according to which proportionate punishments place only upper constraints on the punitive treatment of perpetrators.

IV. Conclusion

Despite the influence of retributivism in modern penal theory and the theoretical work that has been done in the elaboration of the various theoretical aspects of the principle of proportionality, it seems fair to hold that there still exist various theoretical lacunas in the theories that have been developed to sustain and guide the comparison of the seriousness of crimes. In this essay, I have directed attention to three challenges: the challenge concerning the specification of criminal harm, the challenge concerning the relative weight that should be ascribed to harm and culpability, and the challenge concerning the fact that harm and culpability seem to vary (perhaps even significantly) from one offense to another. Moreover, I have argued that none of the three possible responses to these challenges—respectively, that the challenges arise as a result of overtheorization, that one or more of the challenges can be met by adopting a subjectivist view on criminal offending, or that they can be met by basing the determination of seriousness of standardized judgments— provided satisfactory solutions. Finally, it has been argued that given a closer look at what a plausible proportionalist penal scheme requires, the three challenges cannot be regarded as trivial or as merely peripheral problems.

Where do these considerations lead us? To draw the conclusion that the outlined problems are devastating for the retributivist idea of proportionality would, in my view, be premature. First, it is clear that even if a challenge appears to be very hard to meet, this does not show that it is theoretically impossible (after all, dealing with challenges is precisely what the job of penal theorists is all about). Second, some of the problems that have been identified are not uniquely related to considerations of crime gravity within a proportionalist framework. For instance, the challenge of delimiting what should be regarded as morally relevant harm or of balancing different values may have a clear affinity with challenges that face other ethical theories (e.g., nonmonistic consequentialist theories). Thus, although I believe that the outlined challenges are serious, it seems reasonable not to draw too strong conclusions without ultimately engaging in considerations of the comparative merits of alternative theories of the distribution of punishment. Such an endeavor reaches far beyond the scope of this essay—and is, in fact, remarkably rare in modern penal theory.

References

Ashworth, Andrew. 1984. "Sharpening the Subjective Element in Criminal Liability." In *Philosophy and the Criminal Law*, edited by Antony R. Duff and Nigel Simmonds. Wiesbaden: Steiner Verlag.

Ashworth, Andrew. 1999. *Principles of Criminal Law*. Oxford: Oxford University Press.

Bennett, Jonathan. 1995. *The Act Itself*. Oxford: Clarendon.

Brink, David O. 2004. "Immaturity, Normative Competence, and Juveniles Transfer: How (Not) to Punish Minors for Major Crimes." Bepress Legal Series Working Paper 120. Berkeley: Bepress.

Davis, Michael. 1992. *To Make Punishment Fit the Crime*. Boulder, CO: West View.

Fagan, Jeffrey. 2003. "Atkins, Adolescence, and the Maturity Heuristic: Rationales for a Categorical Exemption for Juveniles from Capital Punishment." *New Mexico Law Review* 33:207–54.

Feld, Barry C. 1999. "The Honest Politician's Guide to Juvenile Justice in the Twenty-First Century." *Annals of the American Academy of Political and Social Science* 564:10–27.

Feld, Barry C. 2007. "Unmitigated Punishment: Adolescent Criminal Responsibility and LWOP Sentences." *Journal of Law and Family Studies* 10:11–82.

Greenfield, Victoria A., and Letizia Paoli. 2013. "A Framework to Assess the Harms of Crimes." *British Journal of Criminology* 53(5):864–85.

Hart, H. L. A. 1968. *Punishment and Responsibility: Essays in the Philosophy of Law*. New York: Oxford University Press.

Husak, Douglas. 1994. "Is Drunk Driving a Serious Offense?" *Philosophy and Public Affairs* 23:52–73.

Kleinig, John. 1973. *Punishment and Desert*. The Hague: Martinus Nijhoff.

Kolber, Adam. 2009. "The Subjective Experience of Punishment." *Columbia Law Review* 109:182–237.

Nelkin, Dana K. 2013. "Moral Luck." In *Stanford Encyclopedia of Philosophy*, edited by Edward Zalta. https://plato.stanford.edu/archives/win2013/entries/moral-luck.

Nozick, Robert. 1981. *Philosophical Explanations*. Cambridge: Harvard University Press.

Paoli, Letizia, and Victoria Greenfield. 2013. "Harm: A Neglected Concept in Criminology, a Necessary Benchmark for Crime-Control Policy." *European Journal of Crime, Criminal Law, and Criminal Justice* 21:359–77.

Primoratz, Igor. 1984. "On Retributivism and the Lex Talionis." *Rivista Internazionale di Filosofia del Diritto* 61:83–94.

Ryberg, Jesper. 2004. *Proportionate Punishment: A Critical Investigation*. New York: Kluwer Academic.

Ryberg, Jesper. 2010. "Punishment and the Measurement of Severity." In *Punishment and Ethics*, edited by Jesper Ryberg and J. Angelo Corlett. Basingstoke: Palgrave Macmillan.

Ryberg, Jesper. 2013. "Retributivism and Resources." *Utilitas* 25:66–79.

Ryberg, Jesper. 2014. "Punishing Adolescents: On Immaturity and Diminished Responsibility." *Neuroethics* 7:327–36.

Ryberg, Jesper. 2015. "Youth Discounts, Diminished Culpability, and Retributivism." *International Journal of Applied Philosophy* 29:253–69.

Ryberg, Jesper, and Julian V. Roberts, eds. 2014. *Popular Punishment: On the Normative Significance of Public Opinion*. New York: Oxford University Press.

Scheid, Don E. 1997. "Constructing a Theory of Punishment, Desert, and the Distribution of Punishments." *Canadian Journal of Law and Jurisprudence* 10:441–556.

Sellin, Thorsten, and Marvin E. Wolfgang. 1978. *The Measurement of Delinquency*. Montclair, NJ: Patterson Smith.

Steinberg, Laurence. 2009. "Should the Science of Adolescent Brain Development Inform Public Policy?" *American Psychologist* 64:739–50.

Ten, C. L. 1987. *Crime, Guilt, and Punishment*. Oxford: Clarendon.

Vincent, Nicole. 2013. "Enhancing Responsibility." In *Neuroscience and Legal Responsibility*, edited by Nicole Vincent. New York: Oxford University Press.

Von Hirsch, Andreas [Andrew]. 1991. "Proportionality in the Philosophy of Punishment: From 'Why Punish?' to 'How Much?'" *Israel Law Review* 25:259–81.

Von Hirsch, Andreas [Andrew]. 1992. "Proportionality in the Philosophy of Punishment." In *Crime and Justice: A Review of Research*, vol. 16, edited by Michael Tonry. Chicago: University of Chicago Press.

Von Hirsch, Andreas [Andrew]. 1993. *Censure and Sanctions*. Oxford: Oxford University Press.

Von Hirsch, Andreas [Andrew]. 2001. "Proportionate Sentences for Juveniles." *Punishment and Society* 3:221–36.

Von Hirsch, Andreas [Andrew]. 2017. *Deserved Criminal Sentences*. Oxford: Hart.

Von Hirsch, Andreas [Andrew], and Andrew Ashworth. 2005. *Proportionate Sentencing*. Oxford: Oxford University Press.

Von Hirsch, Andreas [Andrew], and Nils Jareborg. 1991. "Gauging Criminal Harm: A Living Standard Analysis." *Oxford Journal of Legal Studies* 11:1–38.

Von Hirsch, Andreas, Kay A. Knapp, and Michael Tonry. 1987. *The Sentencing Commission and Its Guidelines*. Boston: Northeastern University Press.

4

The Place of Proportionality
in Penal Theory

OR RETHINKING THINKING ABOUT PUNISHMENT

Matt Matravers

THE CLAIM THAT punishment ought to be proportionate has an undeniable intuitive appeal. However, stated just like that, it provides no guidance for what ought to be done, as it leaves open the question "Proportionate to what?" Various answers are possible, including, for example, proportionate to rehabilitative or therapeutic needs and effectiveness. That is, two offenders who have committed identical crimes may be very differently responsive to rehabilitation and postconviction regimes that recognize this can be proportionate given those differences.[1] More broadly, we can assess whether a given action or policy is proportionate only once we specify the purpose of that action or policy.

Matt Matravers is Professor of Law and Director of the Morrell Centre for Toleration at York Law School, University of York. I am grateful to all those who commented on a previous version of this essay that was presented at Worcester College, Oxford University, in 2018 and to Michael Tonry for extensive written comments. I am particularly grateful to Doug Husak, Julian Roberts, and Michael Tonry for organizing the workshop and to Su Smallen for administrative and editorial assistance.

1. The point here is familiar in discussions of equality. Equality requires that relevantly like cases are treated alike and relevantly dissimilar cases are treated dissimilarly. That leaves open the issue of relevance; a racist, of course, thinks that skin color is a relevant criterion.

For much of the last half century, following the pioneering work of Andreas von Hirsch (1976, 1985, 1992, 1993, 2017),[2] the most common account of proportionality has been in the service of theories of punishment in which the purposes of sentencing have been taken to be to impose censure and hard treatment in response to culpable criminal wrongdoing. That is, proportionality in punishment has been associated with the idea that the severity of punishment ought to be proportionate to the seriousness of the offense. As Douglas Husak (2019) puts it, "ceteris paribus, the severity of the punishment should be a function of the seriousness of the crime" (p. 97).

However, even within such an account, there is a great deal of work still to be done, and there are several reasons to be skeptical about the degree of practical guidance proportionality can provide. To see this, consider what is minimally needed to get the theory off the ground (further complications are introduced as the argument unfolds). First is a method of arraying crime seriousness on a scale. Second is a method of arraying sentence severity on a scale. Third is a method for relating seriousness and severity (von Hirsch 2017, p. 23). More formally, and following Duus-Otterström (2019, pp. 31–32)—with the small adaptation to reflect it being persons not crimes that are punished—what is required is:

- Parity: Persons convicted of equally serious crimes should get the same punishment.
- Difference: Persons convicted of unequally serious crimes should get different punishments.
- Positive slope: The more serious a crime, the more severe the punishment of the perpetrator should be.
- Spacing: Persons convicted of unequally serious crimes should get different punishments, and the difference in severity between punishments should correspond to the difference in seriousness between crimes.

With respect to crime seriousness, this is usually taken to be a composite of harmfulness (or endangerment, as not all crimes lead to actual harm) and culpability.[3] Although empirical evidence suggests that there is a surprising

---

2. The author was then known as Andrew von Hirsch, but is now Andreas von Hirsch.

3. Even this seemingly simple formula is fraught with difficulties, not the least of which is how the correct measures of harm and culpability are related. On one account, "harm" is equated with the actual harm done or threatened, and "culpability" is a matter of the blameworthiness of the agent (for example, whether he or she acted intentionally or only recklessly). However, it is not obvious why the harm that counts is not only that which was intended, foreseen, or recklessly disregarded (in which case, harm and culpability would not have independent weight).

degree of agreement in the ranking of core crimes (Robinson 2013), the expansion of criminal law, particularly into what Andrew Ashworth (2000) calls "regulatory offenses," and the need to combine more "objective" elements such as the harm done, or risked, and more "subjective" elements such as the intent or recklessness of the conduct pose a formidable challenge (cf. Ryberg 2019).

With respect to penal severity, the problems are no less difficult. One issue arises from the range of possible sanctions and the difficulty of comparing, say, exclusion from public office, community service, a fine, and incarceration. Moreover, in some jurisdictions, penal sanctions extend into medical and other corporal domains. How, for example, ought one to compare judicial caning as carried out in Singapore and Malaysia, the loss or reduction of sexual desire that follows so-called chemical castration, and the sanctions already mentioned?[4] A second problem, discussed at length by Husak (2019) is how to combine the purposes of imposing hard treatment ("deprivation" in Husak's terms) and of imposing censure with the aim—if it is an aim—of shaming the offender.[5] Third, the goal of subjecting the offender to hard treatment seems to invite issues of the felt experience of those punished and associated problems (Husak 2019; Kolber 2009; Lippke 2019).

Finally, even if we were successfully to solve those problems, we would still need an account of the ratio of offense seriousness and penalty severity. That is, we would need to solve the problem of "cardinal" (von Hirsch 2017, p. 59) or "absolute" (Duus-Otterström 2019) proportionality, of the overall appropriate level of severity. For reasons given elsewhere, proportionality theory lacks the resources to resolve this issue and so, at best, needs supplementing with other ideals (Matravers 2019).

In what follows, I do try not to solve these problems but rather to show that a proper understanding of the nature and justification of punishment can both help in thinking about them and reduce their significance. The argument proceeds as follows. Section I briefly considers various possible justifications

---

4. For example, in the Czech Republic, both surgical and chemical castration can be prescribed by the court. See Ryberg (2015); Stojanovski (2011).

5. Husak (2019) writes, "Arguably, in order for a sanction to qualify as a clear and uncontroversial instance of punishment, it not only must be imposed with the intention to censure, but it must also succeed in creating shame" (p. 112). I am not convinced this is right, but it is at least likely that an uncontroversial instance of punishment will feature sanctions that are broadly understood to be censuring and so likely to induce shame. However, discussion of this goes beyond the aims of this essay.

of criminal law and punishment before offering a positive account. Section II examines the implications of this account for crime seriousness and sentence severity. Section III looks briefly at questions of absolute proportionality. Section IV concludes.

I first argue that context matters—in particular, that not all failures of proportionality are best described as failures of justice. Second, I argue that the institutions of punishment are best understood as political institutions that contribute to the stability of society by establishing authoritative rules that, by having sanctions attached to their breach, both deter those who would free-ride and (re)assure those who comply. Third, I argue that this political theory of punishment resituates issues of crime seriousness and penal severity in a complex relationship between public beliefs about both and the empirical facts about what works. Finally, I suggest that making desert a matter of politics in this way helps in addressing both issues of how to understand proportionality and, by appealing to the liberal commitment to treat people as equals (as against treating people equally), issues of when and why a liberal society ought to take account of subjective differences between people (and so between offenders).

I. Why Purposes Matter

The demands of proportionality can only be known once the purpose(s) of the overall scheme are established. This issue is considered below, but first, it is worth pointing to another difference "purpose" makes to the argument: this is in determining the best, or most appropriate, way to capture nonproportionate outcomes. It is taken for granted in penal theory that to fail to adhere to the demands of proportionality is, other things equal, to act unjustly. And because justice is an important moral and political virtue, this implies that the stakes are high. However, it is not at all clear that matters of justice are always the most relevant in characterizing failures of proportionality. To see this, consider the case of grading students' work.

A. Grading

For simplicity's sake, assume that a class of students are assigned an examination paper of 100 questions where each question has a simple right or wrong answer, and each is assigned one mark per question. Clearly, students who get the same number of answers right ought to receive the same numerical mark (parity); those who get different numbers right ought to receive different marks (difference); there is a positive slope in that the more correct answers given, the more marks ought to be awarded; and differences in the numbers of correct answers ought to be reflected in the marking scale (spacing). In short, a student who gets 30 correct answers should get a mark of 30, and so on for students with 50 or 70 correct answers.

What kind of mistake is made if the examiner awards 100 to both Anna, who answers 100 questions correctly, and Beatrice, who answers only 90 correctly (and, in particular, does the examiner do either or both an injustice)? These marks clearly constitute some kind of mistake and violate relative proportionality (they also violate absolute proportionality given the marking scheme of one mark per question, but put that to one side for the moment). For Feinberg (1974) and McLeod (2003), among others, a situation such as Anna's and Beatrice's immediately engages issues of justice. Perhaps it does, but it is not at all obvious that this is so or that if it is some kind of mistake of justice, then the fact of its being an injustice is the most important aspect of what has gone wrong.

To understand what has happened—or what is most important about what has happened—to Anna and Beatrice, we need to know more about the purpose of the examination and its associated grading scheme. With respect to the purpose, consider two possibilities: *formative*, that the purpose is to allow the students and their instructor to gauge what the students know and where they need to improve, and *summative*, that the purpose is to test what the students know and to publish the results for the students and others to use in gauging what the students know (in relation, say, to deciding class ranking or whether to interview for a job). With respect to the grading scheme, I discuss below a scenario in which the students' marks are categorized as As, Bs, Cs, and so on, in accordance with a scheme that converts their numerical marks into letter grades.

1. *Formative Grading*. In his paper "Noncomparative Justice," Feinberg (1974) writes, "when the object of a grading system is simply to assess as accurately as possible the degree to which a person has some talent, knowledge, or other estimable quality, then the fairness or unfairness of a given grade assessment is of the noncomparative sort" (p. 306). This is right; to the degree that fairness is the issue, the fairness involved is noncomparative. But identifying the type of fairness involved is not the same as implying, as Feinberg does throughout the paper, that fairness or justice is obviously the most important issue that arises in such cases.

Imagine, for example, that I decide in my retirement to learn the names of all the capital cities of the states of the United States, and to help me with this,

I employ an American graduate student as my tutor. At the end of our sessions together, he administers a test and gives me 100 percent, although I have incorrectly identified New York and not Albany as the capital of New York State. He may do this intentionally, because he sees how excited I am and does not want me to be disappointed, or perhaps he does it maliciously, because he believes I am frivolously spending money that I could otherwise donate to Oxfam to save lives. As it happens, nothing more hinges on this—my desire to learn this particular set of facts is merely a hobby motivated by not having been able to do so when I was at school—and I never need the information I have learned.

It is possible to describe me as having been treated unfairly or unjustly. However, it would be both more natural and more relevant to say that I have been the object of a mistaken kindness or of malicious spite or perhaps that I have been deprived of the chance to achieve what I set out to achieve. There are a number of such "thick" moral judgments available with which the judgment that I have been treated unjustly competes (and, it seems to me, loses when it comes to what really matters).

Those of a Feinbergian bent could say, "Well, of course, human interactions can be characterized by many moral virtues and vices. The point is just that insofar as fairness or justice is involved in such a case, it is noncomparative." That is right, but it does not resolve the question of how important that description is relative to others, and in this case, my claim is that the language of justice or fairness does not capture the most important description of the case.

The contrast is clear if we return to Beatrice. On the one hand, the marks are only shared between the instructor and the individual students, so no one other than Beatrice knows that she was awarded 100 for a paper in which she only answered 90 questions correctly. Moreover, as it happens, the mistake makes no difference to her revision plans, and she goes on to get 100 on the subsequent final summative assessment.

On the other hand, we can imagine Beatrice's case going differently. Beatrice, convinced that she knows the subject, may prioritize other courses in preparing for her final assessments and, as a result, may get only 90 for this course, when she could have gotten 100 had she known that she needed to work on the 10 questions she answered incorrectly in her formative test. As a result, her final overall grade may drop, which, in turn, may make it harder for her to secure the graduate internship she was hoping to get. In addition, the instructor may publicize the grades, and the members of the class may then make evaluative judgments of one another (such as that Anna and Beatrice are equally clever or equally hard-working and that Clara, who received 50, must be stupid or lazy or both). In these cases, issues of fairness and justice come to the fore by virtue of the meaning or purpose of the assigned grades.[6]

2. *Summative Grading.* The comparative issues that arise above are often central to the meaning and purpose of summative tests. Assume that after a summative test, the marks are publicized and used as the basis for evaluation of the candidates. As a result of the mistake, Anna and Beatrice enter a competitive job market with equal grades, their peers speak of them as on a par, and so on.

In these cases, the language of justice seems fitting. Anna is treated unjustly by virtue of the failure of the examiner to award marks that meet the requirement of relative proportionality. Anna's performance was better than Beatrice's, by 10, and the appropriate marks would have seen Anna receive 100 and Beatrice 90 (with the consequences that would have for the kinds of evaluative judgments mentioned above). Here, the point of grading is in large part to allow for such comparative judgments, and so it matters that the marks are wrong.

Before moving on to issues of punishment, I want to introduce a final wrinkle in the argument: the issue of classification. Suppose, for example, that the school Anna and Beatrice attend converts numerical marks into alphabetical grades and that marks of 90 and above receive an A. In this case, there is no inaccuracy in Anna and Beatrice both receiving an A, even if Beatrice's paper is marked correctly, and this is true in both the formative and summative contexts. It is clear that the instructor does not make a mistake or treat either unjustly in awarding both an A. If any issues of injustice—or other failing—arise, they arise with respect to the design of the system that converts fine-grained numerical marks into coarser alphabetical ones.

B. The Purpose(s) of Punishment

The purpose of the scheme in which the principle of proportionality is nested is important, then, not only in answering the question "Proportionate to what?" but also in determining what is most at stake when it comes to failures of proportionality. When it comes to criminal law and punishment,

---

6. Compare Feinberg (1974): "Indeed, the grade itself can be taken to express a *judgment* (or assessment, or appraisal) of a person, and thus is fair or unfair to him in precisely the same manner as other judgments. When grades come to be used as the basis for subsequent job assignments, opportunities, competitive honors, and other benefits, then an undeservedly low grade can cause a *further* injustice of a comparative kind" (p. 306, emphasis in original).

the debate over its purposes, nature, and justification is well established, and this is not the place to try to resolve it. Nevertheless, it is worth canvassing the options, although the argument then proceeds on the basis of a presumption that the criminal justice system is a public institution whose rules are authoritative for citizens committed to living together on terms that can be justified to each.

1. *Moralism.* For a subset of moral retributivists, the purposes of criminal law and punishment are as follows: to specify rules that mirror a certain subset of moral rules (primarily prohibitions); to censure those who culpably violate those rules; and to express that censure in the form of a proportionate sanction (on some accounts, a sanction that delivers what the condemned person deserves). If the system of rules did not exist, we would have a good reason to create it to ensure that people get the appropriate censure (and sanction) for certain kinds of conduct.[7]

There are a number of reasons to be skeptical of this account.[8] As traditional opponents of retributivism have pointed out, the nature of the desert claim remains "a mysterious piece of moral alchemy in which the combination of the two evils of moral wickedness and suffering are transmuted into good" (Hart 2008, pp. 234–35). This is perhaps not true of the communicative version of retributivism espoused by Antony Duff—the claim that moral wickedness deserves censure being less mysterious than the claim that it deserves suffering—but in that case, the challenge is to establish a necessary connection between the expression of censure and the need for hard treatment. No compelling argument for such a connection has been made (Matravers 2011*a*). Moreover, the moralist account seems to miss something significant about *legal* punishment, which is that it is a political institution that serves political ends. To claim that we have good reason to bring institutions of criminal justice into existence solely to ensure that the wicked receive punishment (sanctions or censure) strikes me as just as implausible as the claim that we have a good reason to create the 100-meter race solely to ensure that the fastest runner over that distance receives praise and reward.

2. *Instrumentalism.* On the other side of the traditional debate lies instrumentalism, which holds that what justifies the state adopting a set of rules prohibiting certain conduct and attaching the threat of imposed hard

---

7. See, e.g., Moore (1987, 1997) and Duff (2001, 2007). For Moore, punishment imposes morally deserved suffering. For Duff, it expresses morally deserved censure.

8. For developed critiques of the retributive position, see Matravers (2000) and Tadros (2011).

treatment for the breach of such rules is that it has desirable effects (in the main, crime reduction). It does this—or fails to do it (as the verdict is out on some of these)—through:

- Norm-defining and norm-reinforcing effects.[9]
- General deterrence.
- Special deterrence.
- Incapacitation.
- Rehabilitation of the offender.

There are important empirical questions about the effectiveness of criminal law and punishment in delivering these consequences, but the main, and very familiar, problem with grounding the justification of punishment solely in the consequences it delivers is that it falls afoul of general objections to instrumental arguments that revolve around the need to respect the rights and claims of individual persons. Reducing crime by incapacitation, for example, might be best achieved by imposing an evening and nighttime curfew on all men between the ages of 16 and 24, but no one seriously argues that the state would thus be justified in enacting such a policy.[10]

3. *A Mixed Systemic Theory.* The position that underpins the rest of the argument is instrumentalist in one sense, in that it holds that good consequences in terms of crime reduction, rehabilitation, and so on—to the degree that they can be effectively achieved by criminal law and punishment—provide reasons to adopt a set of rules prohibiting certain conduct and attaching the threat of censure and imposed hard treatment for the breach of such rules. However, the account is not solely instrumental. A liberal society is a contingent and fragile cooperative endeavor. In coming together to cooperate on the basis of authoritative rules, participants have good reason to adopt those rules only if they can be assured that sufficient others do so, too. The status of rules as authoritative and, thus, other things equal, of those who break those rules as at

---

9. It is worth emphasizing that instrumental goals do not need to be reduced only to crime reduction. There may be significant advantages to norm-defining and norm-reinforcing other than compliance. Indeed, a society in which important norms are acknowledged and used in structuring interactions is likely to be able to enjoy the many and various benefits of, among other things, "arts, letters, and society" that Hobbes ([1668] 1994, p. 76) identified as unavailable in the state of nature.

10. There are numerous powerful critiques of consequentialism in general and of its application to punishment in particular. For a flavor, see Matravers (2000), McCloskey (1968), Rawls (1971), and Williams (1973).

fault (and so properly the object of criticism) is constitutive. In the language I used above, norm construction and norm reinforcing are intrinsic parts of there being shared authoritative norms.

This is what Vincent Chiao (2019) calls "a political theory of punishment" (p. xiii).[11] On this account, the criminal justice system is one of a number of institutions that sustain liberal society. It does this by making public the appropriate rules and threatening condemnation and sanctions for those who culpably break them. In so doing, it contributes to the stability of the society by assuring those who do cooperate that they are not making some kind of mistake in treating the rules as authoritative, rather than themselves free-riding, and it gives those tempted to free-ride a reason not to do so.[12]

In practice, this is a "mixed theory" in which those who culpably break the rules are condemned for their past conduct, and through that system of condemnation, the traditional instrumental effects of punishment are realized. In particular—although the verdict is out on the effectiveness of some of these—this is through the mechanisms of norm-defining and norm-reinforcing effects, general deterrence, special deterrence, incapacitation, and the rehabilitation of offenders. It is "mixed" because these instrumental ends are achieved—and thus constrained—by traditional criminal justice values such as publicly identifying criminal justice rules and censuring and punishing only those who culpably break those norms.

Finally, it is important to note that there is an empirical dimension at the very heart of this account. We can imagine societies—perhaps small communities in which there is widespread belief in a supernatural being that both sustains community cohesion and threatens "punishments" and "rewards" in the afterlife—in which the overall level of rule breaking is so small as not to threaten social stability. In such a case, there may be no need, and there would be no justification, for a criminal justice system of the kind

---

11. Chiao contrasts moralistic and individualistic accounts of punishment (as found, for example, in Moore 1997 and Duff 2001, 2007) with political accounts, including my book *Justice and Punishment* (Matravers 2000), that treat the criminal justice system as political institutions designed to foster cooperation (in part by providing assurance to those who do cooperate) and, in Chiao's case, to secure people's effective access to a range of central capabilities.

12. This is, of course, a very brief statement of a very complex account (it leaves unanswered, for example, the question of which rules ought to be part of criminal regulation and which ought to be part of other forms of social control). A fuller account can be found in Matravers (2000, pp. 205–68).

being discussed here.[13] Conversely, as Jonathan Jacobs has suggested in relation to the United States, a society in which traditional forms of social order,
civic trust, and civility have broken down or are in retreat may have greater
need of institutions of criminal justice to secure stability.[14]

II. Crime Seriousness and Sentence Severity

If we think of the institutions of criminal justice as part of the regulative ap-
paratus of the state designed to secure a cooperative society, what follows for
the principle of proportionality and for the metrics of crime seriousness and
sentence severity?

A. The Principle of Proportionality

The political theory of punishment offered above has a place for the principle
of proportionality in the general sense offered by Husak. This is because the
function of criminal law and punishment is, in part, to announce what ought
not to be done (or, more rarely, what ought to be done) and in punishing
to censure the offender for his or her failure to comply with the authoritative rules on which the cooperative enterprise relies and to communicate to
those who do comply that they are not deceived in aligning their self-interest
with the cooperative whole. To achieve this, the scheme must include ways of
indicating the relative seriousness of offenses and of reassuring cooperators of
others' general compliance. However, quite what this means and how deter-
minative it is depend on what can be said about each element: crime seriousness, sentence severity, and absolute proportionality.

---

13. A version of this claim can be found in those otherwise implacable philosophical antagonists,
G. W. F. Hegel and Friedrich Nietzsche:

> The ... magnitude [of the crime] varies, however, according to the condition of civil so-
> ciety, and this is the justification both for attaching the death penalty to a theft of a few
> pence or of a turnip, and for imposing a lenient punishment for a theft of a hundred and
> more times these amounts. (Hegel [1821] 1952, §218R, see also §18, §18A)

> The "creditor" always becomes more humane to the extent that he has grown
> richer. . . . It is not unthinkable that a society might attain such a consciousness of power
> that it could allow itself the noblest luxury possible to it—letting those who harm it go
> unpunished. What are my parasites to me? It might say. May they live and prosper: I am
> strong enough for that! (Nietzsche 1956, p. 72)

14. Note that this does not provide a *justification* for greater use of criminal justice (and Jacobs
certainly does not mean it to do so). There may be more effective and less harmful policies that
could be implemented to restore civility (Jacobs 2017).

B. Crime Seriousness

In one sense, the political account of punishment sketched above makes the issue of crime seriousness more complex. This is because the advantage that the account makes it easier to understand why crimes are "public"—they are attacks on the authoritative rules of the cooperative scheme—means that crime seriousness becomes a function of the harm done or threatened to the overall scheme, as well as that done or threatened to the individual victim, and, finally of the culpability of the offender.

As of now, it is not clear (at least, to me) how the political account can respond to the issues identified above when it comes to arraying crimes on scale with any precision. Moreover, the assurance aspect of the theory allows (possibly problematically in the eyes of some retributivists) factors such as prevalence of particular offenses to influence measures of crime seriousness. However, there are three reasons to believe that the account may be better situated than traditional retributivism in attempting to address these issues.

First, given that one critical function of criminal law and punishment on this account is to reassure those who would cooperate and to sustain the legitimacy of the system, there are good reasons for the system not to drift too far from what Robinson (2013) calls "empirical desert." Robinson argues that popular commitment to, and cooperation with, the criminal justice system is dependent on the system reflecting, or at least staying roughly true to, popular beliefs about both crime seriousness and penal severity. Robinson's argument has been criticized (Slobogin 2014). Generally, questions of the relation of public beliefs about punishment and state criminal justice institutions are fiendishly complex (see, e.g., Dzur 2012; Matravers 2014; Roberts and Keijser 2014). However, to the degree that the political account given here relies in part on solving the assurance problem, it cannot but require a relationship between beliefs about justice and the efficacy of criminal justice practices (even if this relationship is yet to be established).

One issue with empirical desert is that people's beliefs tend to be less clear in "marginal" cases, such as, for example, regulative or complex financial crimes. However, that brings me neatly to the second reason to think the political account may make crime seriousness simpler than it first appears. This is that the justification of deploying criminal law and punishment in response to threats depends on its being effective when compared with other tools of public policy. It is only a conjecture, but that may mean that the scope of criminal law—at least, compared with the current situation in the United Kingdom and United States—will be restricted. In particular, many noncore offenses could, and should, be moved to what Ashworth (2000) calls systems of "civil violations" or "administrative offenses."

Third, criminal law addresses cooperators primarily as citizens rather than as moral agents. It lays down rules that enable cooperation and sets standards for compliance. In so doing, it also specifies different degrees of noncompliance. Thus, the substantive criminal law includes specifications of fault—intention and recklessness, for example, and, less often, negligence. These inform both theoretical and empirical judgments of seriousness and rightly so.

C. Sentence Severity

Above, three problems were identified in trying to determine a scale of sentence severity: the comparability of different kinds of sanctions, the issue of how to combine in one sentence the purposes of imposing hard treatment and imposing censure, and the "objective/subjective" debate that surrounds gauging penal severity. As with crime seriousness, I am not in a position to try to answer these questions, but it is possible to say something about how one might think about them.

With respect to the comparability problem, a smaller and more "core" criminal law may help. If violating electoral spending laws were not a crime (but some other kind of regulatory offense), then we might not need to fit a sanction such as exclusion from public office into the sentencing scheme. However, this does little to address the central issue of comparability. The direction in which the answer to this, and to the second issue around censure, lies in partially decoupling the expression of censure, the details of the sanction, and the empirical consequences of the announced sanction for stable cooperation. That is, we can think of three elements to the sentencing stage of a criminal trial: the declaration of guilt, the labeling, and the verbal censuring of the offender; the "headline" sentence; and the details and manner of the sentence as served.

In the past, I have tentatively suggested entirely decoupling these and tying censure only to the pronouncement of guilt, leaving sanctions to play only an instrumental role (Matravers 2016, 2019). However, for a number of reasons, I now think this is an overstatement. First, language only allows a limited number of ways in which censure can be expressed and "graded." There is some scope for emphasis between "I say, that's a bit much" and "I condemn you as an utterly wicked being" but not enough, and not with enough nuance, to capture what is needed in punishment. To some degree, then, the degree of censure will have to be reflected in the sentence imposed. Second, as noted above, the account gives a central place to reassurance and to sustaining the cooperative scheme, and given current beliefs about the (dis)incentives needed to ensure compliance, mere verbal censure is unlikely to be sufficient. Nevertheless, there are reasons to think that there is space between the headline expressions of censure and the sanctions (if any are imposed), space that can be exploited in addressing, in some part, the comparability issue.

Consider, first, the expressive and communicative aspects of criminal law and punishment. The state announces that certain things must not be done and attaches to these announcements the threat of censure and sanctions for those who do them. However, in the vast majority of cases, those who break the law are not apprehended and prosecuted. That is, no one is censured or has imposed on him or her some deprivation for the vast majority of offenses.[15] In short, in large part, the grading function of criminal law—in terms of expressing the relative seriousness of different offenses—is given by the sentencing scheme, not by the prosecution of convicted offenders. As with the discussion of crime seriousness and public norms above, this grading function interacts with existing social norms. Thus, the argument appeals to the Durkheimian (or Scandinavian [positive]) account of general prevention and to a complex and potentially fragile two-way relation between the law's grading of crimes and social norms about comparative seriousness (Lappi-Seppälä 2019). One way to mitigate this complexity is for "headline" sentencing schemes to operate with a limited "currency" of community service, fines, and incarceration, thus simplifying—though not solving—the problem of commensurability.[16]

This argument assumes that degrees of hard treatment are a mechanism for expressing degrees of censure. Husak (2019) takes issue with this approach for three reasons. First, he argues that state censure, to be successful, must be appreciated as such by society and by the offender (in the form of "shame"). Second, he argues that contemporary forms of punishment shy away from the expression of public censure. Third, he argues that while the deprivations of penal hard treatment are in most cases temporary, the censure and shame

15. The percentage of crimes that end in a charge is difficult to determine, but, for example, the UK Home Office (2018) estimates that for the year ending March 2018, "The proportion of crimes which resulted in a charge/summons fell by two percentage points, from 11% to 9%." This, of course, threatens the stability and legitimacy of the cooperative system, but it seems that such systems are relatively resilient (up to some tipping point).

16. I am grateful to Michael Tonry for his suggestions on this particular point. For a general overview of Durkheim and the Scandinavian positivists, see Matravers (2011c).

associated with offending can extend far into the future in the form of criminal record checks, restrictions on access to public welfare, and so on.

Husak's third claim points to an important issue: the collateral effects of punishment. However, we need to be careful to distinguish among intended continuing deprivations, such as disenfranchisement, denial of access to welfare and social housing, and so on; foreseeable effects, such as the loss of employment and the breakdown of marriages; and other forms of interpersonal stigmatization, such as withdrawal of goodwill. With respect to intended deprivations, these need to be either included in the scale of penalties or eliminated (Hoskins 2019). To return to the example of being barred from holding public office: if imposed, that is punishment, not some extra dimension of censure or attempt to elicit shame on the part of the offender. With respect to foreseeable effects, collateral effects that can derail both the offender's reentry into society and the lives of his or her family and dependents, these are not part of punishment or of censure, and they place on the punishing authorities a moral burden to design systems that minimize these effects. With respect to other stigmatization, this is not the state's business. Of course, those who behave badly and who are discovered may suffer from a loss of goodwill from former friends, neighbors, and associates. However, that is not any part of the scheme of state punishment.

Husak's first two points rest on his attraction to subjectivism. That is, he worries that state censure may be ineffective for a given individual—he cites Henry David Thoreau, for whom imprisonment was a source of pride—and similarly that the forms of punishment inflicted in contemporary societies fail to instantiate public censure (in the ways that, for example, branding and the stocks were both public). However, this is to miss the point. On a political theory of criminal law and punishment, the state holds to account those offenders it tries and on conviction censures them for their conduct. It does so by both the fact of conviction and through the penalty it imposes. The function of the latter is to signal seriousness—to grade—and while, of course, the state intends the offender to understand and to feel censured, that is not a necessary condition for its successful expression. Public stigma and shaming have no part in this theory whatsoever.

That said, if the imposed penalty were subject to widespread mockery, then it could not convey censure, but it also could not fulfill its function as part of a scheme of criminal law designed to sustain the cooperative endeavor of the liberal state. In that sense, the penalty would have failed both as part of the overall scheme and as a mechanism of conveying censure, which is what one would expect given the link between the two.

This takes us to the heart of the debate between subjectivists and objectivists. For the former, the measure of imposed deprivation inflicted as penal hard treatment must take into account the lived experience of the offender, and if this is right, it would render arraying penal severity on a single scale impracticable.

The intuitive pull of the subjectivist position is perhaps best captured by the example of two offenders who are 5 and 7 feet tall, respectively, and each is confined to a 6-foot-high cell. Surely, here, it is said, the tall offender suffers a great deal more than the shorter man, and that difference in suffering is relevant in assessing where each falls on the scale of penal severity (Kolber 2009). If so, it seems a short step to differential sentences for the prison-hardened and the sensitive, and so on. Or, to quote Husak (2019): "Suppose 6-year-old twin brothers Billy and Bobby continuously fight each other, and their parent decides to discipline them. If Billy loves video games and Bobby loathes them, it would be ludicrous to think they are punished equally if their father bans video games for both. Even children would understand they had been punished unequally" (p. 109). It is important to note the contrast being proposed here: a subjectivist would take into account the differences between the experiences of the tall and short offenders and of Billy and Bobby, whereas the objectivist insists on identical treatment.

However, this is a mistake. As Ronald Dworkin (1977) pointed out nearly half a century ago (and as cited by Husak), there is a difference between "equal treatment" and "treatment as an equal" (p. 227). Billy and Bobby's father fails to notice this distinction, and in subjecting them both to identical (equal) treatment, he fails to treat them as equals (that is, "with the same respect and concern" [Dworkin 1977, p. 227]). Similarly, a prison system that disregards the height of its inmates—or, indeed, whether some are in wheelchairs, deaf, or blind—may treat all equally, but it fails to treat its inmates as equals.

The critical point is that treating as equals does not necessarily require making reference to the subjective lived experience of the people concerned. "Cells ought to be built to accommodate all heights," "cells ought to be distributed relative to height," and "Billy and Bobby are both required to forgo their favorite games for a week" are claims that implicitly refer to the existence of differences between people but without reference to the interior mental states of those people.

The same point applies to Husak's favored day fines. These, as Husak (2019) says, are relativized "to the income or wealth of the particular offender" (p. 109), but that does not make them subjective in the relevant sense. A sanction of 10 percent of income will result in an absolute fine that is relativized to each offender, and so offenders with different incomes will pay different absolute sums, but again, this can be done without asking whether it so happens that this or that offender loves money more than any other.

Dworkin's move does not resolve all questions of distribution, as it leaves open the question of which features of human beings are relevant, and which are not, in deciding what constitutes treatment as an equal. Famously, Dworkin argued that someone who had cultivated expensive tastes such that he could not enjoy cheap food and wine had no claim on extra resources even where those tastes had been inculcated in him by his parents. This and similar arguments gave rise to a significant dispute with G. A. Cohen over whether identical treatment would be mandatory in a world without free will (Dworkin 2000; Matravers 2002; Cohen 2004). Thus—again—the argument is not conclusive but suggestive. It is understood as part of a political theory of liberalism; we still need to decide how and why to deviate from equality when treating others as equals, but this has nothing to do with, and so avoids the "quagmire" (Husak 2019, p. 101) of, subjective assessments of individuals' lived experiences.

III. Absolute Proportionality

The question of absolute proportionality concerns the overall scales of punishment. As noted above, and as I have argued at length elsewhere, proportionality theory in itself does not have the resources to set its own anchoring points (Matravers 2011b, 2014, 2019). At the core of the political theory of punishment sketched here are two claims: (1) that authoritative rules and the threat of punishment are needed to ensure the continuing existence of fragile and contingent liberal schemes of cooperation, but (2) that their effectiveness compared with other means of sustaining the cooperative scheme is central to their justification. Punishment does terrible harm not only to the punished but also to the innocent (and, perhaps, to all of us in whose name it is done). My suspicion is that we can achieve the ends of punishment with far less of it and by paying far greater attention to other aspects of public policy, such as education and economic inequality. However, sustaining cooperation is also a matter of providing assurance and meeting the demands of perceived legitimacy. These factors are also empirical and put a constraint on any radical change but perhaps not on decremental policies of decriminalization and reduced punishments. For the moment, then, absolute proportionality is both context-sensitive and likely to be a matter of trial and error.

IV. Conclusion

The problems of determining metrics for crime seriousness and sentence severity, and of fixing the scales of punishment, that have motivated this volume are real and significant. Given that, they pose a serious challenge to the principle of proportionality that has been a mainstay of the dominant punishment paradigm of the last half century. In this essay, I have not solved any of the problems. Rather, I have suggested that the focus on an individualistic, moralized, account of criminal law exacerbates the issues by both making proportionality central and making the metrics harder to determine. In the place of such an account, I have sketched a picture of criminal law and punishment as an institution of public policy addressed to the need to sustain the fragile achievement of the modern liberal democratic state. The main aim of the essay, then, has been to try to show how the questions of metrics and of absolute proportionality appear in such a political theory and to suggest that they do so in ways more amenable to solutions.

In concluding, I return to the example of grading student papers. As anyone who has graded papers in legal theory—and many other domains—knows, it is a rough and ready business in which one seeks for rough equivalence and not precise differences. It is for this reason that the conversion of precise individual marks into, for example, alphabetical marking schemes—or the knowledge that one's mark is only one in a series that will be converted into a single score—is often a solace. We can, and of course do, look at the overall schemes to check that they are still functional and effective and to ask if another scheme might be better, and in so doing, we are—or ought to be—aware of the damage that the current scheme has done to individuals. Of course, the stakes are much higher in criminal justice, and so our pursuit of better schemes should be more urgent, but they will always fall far short of perfection, and individuals will suffer unjustly as a result.

Finally, as with different kinds of grading, the criminal justice system (at least as currently constituted in many countries) responds to different demands and purposes. A scheme that is designed around punishment severity that is proportionate to crime seriousness meets the demands of proportionality even if it allows the diverting of a chronic drug addict from prison to rehabilitation. Such a diversion need not be unjust if a way can be found that precludes comparative judgments of the relative blameworthiness of this individual based on the sentence, but rather it locates the intervention in the realm of noncomparative need. Where such need is the norm, we surely have reason to doubt that we have met the justificatory condition of the use of criminal law and punishment, that is, of its being more effective (in terms of outcomes and the marginal costs in resources and other values of those outcomes) than any alternative public policy intervention.

References

Ashworth, Andrew. 2000. "Is the Criminal Law a Lost Cause?" *Law Quarterly Review* 116:225–56.

Chiao, Vincent. 2019. *Criminal Law in the Administrative State*. New York: Oxford University Press.

Cohen, G. A. 2004. "Expensive Taste Rides Again." In *Dworkin and His Critics: With Replies by Dworkin*, edited by Justine Burley. Oxford: Blackwell.

Duff, Antony. 2001. *Punishment, Communication, and Community*. Oxford: Oxford University Press.

Duff, Antony. 2007. *Answering for Crime: Responsibility and Liability in the Criminal Law*. Oxford: Hart.

Duus-Otterström, Göran. 2019. "Weighing Relative and Absolute Proportionality in Punishment." In *Of One-Eyed and Toothless Miscreants: Making the Punishment Fit the Crime?* edited by Michael Tonry. New York: Oxford University Press.

Dworkin, Ronald. 1977. "Taking Rights Seriously." In *Taking Rights Seriously*, edited by Ronald Dworkin. Cambridge: Harvard University Press.

Dworkin, Ronald. 2000. *Sovereign Virtue: The Theory and Practice of Equality*. Cambridge: Harvard University Press.

Dzur, Albert. 2012. *Punishment, Participatory Democracy, and the Jury*. New York: Oxford University Press.

Feinberg, Joel. 1974. "Noncomparative Justice." *Philosophical Review* 83:297–338.

Hart, H. L. A. 2008. *Punishment and Responsibility: Essays in the Philosophy of Law*. Oxford: Oxford University Press.

Hegel, G. W. F. 1952. *Philosophy of Right*. Oxford: Oxford University Press. (Originally published in 1821.)

Hobbes, Thomas. 1994. *Leviathan*, edited by Edwin Curley. Indianapolis: Hackett. (Originally published in 1668.)

Hoskins, Zachary. 2019. *Beyond Punishment: A Normative Account of the Collateral Legal Consequences of Conviction*. New York: Oxford University Press.

Husak, Doug. 2019. "The Metric of Punishment Severity: A Puzzle about the Principle of Proportionality." In *Of One-Eyed and Toothless Miscreants: Making the Punishment Fit the Crime?* edited by Michael Tonry. New York: Oxford University Press.

Jacobs, Jonathan Aaron. 2017. "Civics, Policy, and Demoralization." *Criminal Justice Ethics* 361:25–44.

Kolber, Adam. 2009. "The Subjective Experience of Punishment." *Columbia Law Review* 109:182–236.

Lappi-Seppälä, Tapio. 2019. "Humane Neoclassicism: Proportionality and Other Values in Nordic Sentencing." In *Of One-Eyed and Toothless Miscreants: Making the Punishment Fit the Crime?* edited by Michael Tonry. New York: Oxford University Press.

Lippke, Richard L. 2019. "Penal Severity and the Modern State." In *Of One-Eyed and Toothless Miscreants: Making the Punishment Fit the Crime?* edited by Michael Tonry. New York: Oxford University Press.

Matravers, Matt. 2000. *Justice and Punishment: The Rationale of Coercion.* Oxford: Oxford University Press.

Matravers, Matt. 2002. "Responsibility, Luck, and the 'Equality of What?' Debate." *Political Studies* 503:558–72.

Matravers, Matt. 2011a. "Duff on Hard Treatment." In *Crime, Punishment, and Responsibility*, edited by R. Cruft, M. Kramer and M. Reiff. Oxford: Oxford University Press.

Matravers, Matt. 2011b. "Is Twenty-First Century Punishment Post-Desert?" In *Retributivism Has a Past: Has It a Future?* edited by Michael Tonry. New York: Oxford University Press.

Matravers, Matt. 2011c. "Reassurance, Reinforcement, and Legitimacy." In *The Oxford Handbook of Crime and Criminal Justice*, edited by Michael Tonry. New York: Oxford University Press.

Matravers, Matt. 2014. "Proportionality Theory and Popular Opinion." In *Popular Punishment: On the Normative Significance of Public Opinion for Penal Theory*, edited by Jesper Ryberg. Oxford: Oxford University Press.

Matravers, Matt. 2016. "Punishment, Suffering and Justice." In *Justice and Penal Policy*, edited by S. Farrall, B. Goldson, I. Loader, and A. Dockley. London: Routledge.

Matravers, Matt. 2019. "Rootless Desert and Unanchored Censure." In *Penal Censure: Engagements within and beyond Desert Theory*, edited by Antje du Bois-Pedain and Anthony Bottoms. Oxford: Hart/Bloomsbury.

McCloskey, H. J. 1968. "A Non-Utilitarian Approach to Punishment." In *Contemporary Utilitarianism*, edited by M. Bayles. New York: Doubleday.

McLeod, Owen. 2003. "On the Comparative Element of Justice." In *Desert and Justice*, edited by S. Olsaretti. Oxford: Clarendon.

Moore, Michael. 1987. "The Moral Worth of Retribution." In *Responsibility, Character and the Emotions*, edited by F. Schoemann. New York: Cambridge University Press.

Moore, Michael. 1997. *Placing Blame: A General Theory of the Criminal Law.* Oxford: Oxford University Press.

Nietzsche, Friedrich Wilhelm. 1956. *On the Genealogy of Morals.* New York: Doubleday.

Rawls, John. 1971. *A Theory of Justice.* Cambridge: Harvard University Press.

Roberts, Julian V., and Jan de Keijser. 2014. "Democratising Punishment: Sentencing, Community Views and Values." *Punishment and Society* 16:474–98.

Robinson, Paul. 2013. *Intuitions of Justice and the Utility of Desert.* Oxford: Oxford University Press.

Ryberg, Jesper. 2015. "Is Coercive Treatment of Offenders Morally Acceptable? On the Deficiency of the Debate." *Criminal Law and Philosophy* 9:619–31.

Ryberg, Jesper. 2019. "Proportionality and the Seriousness of Crimes." In *Of One-Eyed and Toothless Miscreants: Making the Punishment Fit the Crime?* edited by Michael Tonry. New York: Oxford University Press.

Slobogin, Christopher. 2014. "Empirical Desert and Preventative Justice: A Comment." *New Criminal Law Review* 17:376–403

Stojanovski, Voislav. 2011. "Surgical Castration of Sex Offenders and Its Legality: The Case of the Czech Republic." *Journal on Legal and Economic Issues of Central Europe* 2:2043–85.

Tadros, Victor. 2011. *The Ends of Harm: The Moral Foundations of Criminal Law.* Oxford: Oxford University Press.

UK Home Office. 2018. *Crime Outcomes in England and Wales: Year Ending March 2018.* London: Crown Copyright.

Von Hirsch, Andreas [Andrew]. 1976. *Doing Justice: The Choice of Punishments. Report of the Committee for the Study of Incarceration.* New York: Hill and Wang.

Von Hirsch, Andreas [Andrew]. 1985. *Past or Future Crimes: Deservedness and Dangerousness in the Sentencing of Criminals.* New Brunswick, NJ: Rutgers University Press.

Von Hirsch, Andreas [Andrew]. 1992. "Proportionality in the Philosophy of Punishment." In *Crime and Justice: A Review of Research*, vol. 16, edited by Michael Tonry. Chicago: University of Chicago Press.

Von Hirsch, Andreas [Andrew]. 1993. *Censure and Sanctions.* Oxford: Oxford University Press.

Von Hirsch, Andreas [Andrew]. 2017. *Deserved Criminal Sentences.* Oxford: Hart/Bloomsbury.

Williams, Bernard. 1973. "A Critique of Utilitarianism." In *Utilitarianism: For and Against*, edited by John Jamieson, Carswell Smart, and Bernard Williams. Cambridge: Cambridge University Press.

5

The Metric of Punishment Severity

A PUZZLE ABOUT THE PRINCIPLE
OF PROPORTIONALITY

Douglas Husak

I START WITH three admittedly controversial assumptions: first, retributivism is a plausible (and, I think, correct) theory of the justification of state punishment and sentencing; second, desert is essential to any respectable retributive theory; and third, sentencing according to the principle of proportionality is crucial if the state is to treat offenders as they deserve. Therefore, it is of the utmost importance that philosophers in the retributivist tradition offer a detailed and attractive explication of the principle of proportionality.[1] Although many distinct formulations of this principle have been advanced, my preferred version states that ceteris paribus, the severity of the punishment should be a function of the seriousness of the crime. In what follows, I struggle (with only modest success) to provide content to this principle as so construed.

I do not examine (and barely mention) any number of questions that must be answered before this principle can be applied in the real world. Some of

---

Douglas Husak is Professor of Philosophy at Rutgers, the State University of New Jersey, New Brunswick.

1. I take retributive theories of punishment to be those that afford a central and indispensable role to desert. Elsewhere, I have argued that a host of familiar problems in the philosophy of punishment can be avoided by contrasting two questions: first, what punishment p is deserved; and second, whether the state should actually impose p. I believe the significance of judgments of desert in sentencing is not especially great; more weight should be placed on consequentialist considerations when we turn to the second question.

these topics are familiar; others are less often discussed. The following are four examples of issues I do not explore. First, what makes one crime more serious than another? Since some crimes are wrong because of the harms they cause and others are wrong for other reasons, is there a single scale along which the seriousness of all crimes can be ranked? Are violent crimes, for example, generally more serious than those that are nonviolent? Second, what is the function that relates the seriousness of crime to the severity of punishment? Is it linear, or does it have a more complex shape? Third, how is the punishment system anchored so that cardinal proportionality can be established? What role, if any, do social conventions play in the answer? Fourth, what issues does the "ceteris paribus" clause preclude from consideration under the scope of proportionality? How much does this clause preclude? Can it be explicated in a way that does not beg questions against arguments that purport to reject proportionality?

Instead of addressing the above topics, I mostly focus on a single problem, a problem generally thought to be easier than any of the foregoing. Rather than solving the problem I identify, however, I am at best able only to minimize its significance in a theory of punishment. But I do not regard my lack of success as a powerful reason to abandon proportionality and retributivism altogether. After all, nearly all penal theorists, including consequentialists, accept these principles in some guise or another (Farrell 2010). Instead, I construe my failure as an invitation to legal theorists to try to meet the challenges I present.

The primary issue I discuss is that of specifying the metric of punishment severity—that is, the currency with which to express whether one punishment is more or less severe than another. In other words, by what common denominator are the punishments imposed on, say, Peter and Paul equal or unequal in severity? An (admittedly imperfect) analogy might be helpful to understand this problem. Suppose we are interested in losing weight. We know, for example, whether a bowl of ice cream contains more food than a bowl of pasta because we can express the amount of each in terms of caloric content. We can make this determination even though calories are not defined as food or identical to it; they are the common measure by which different quantities of food can be compared. Now, suppose we are interested in punishing two offenders according to their desert. What unit plays the role in gauging punishment severity that calories play in comparing the quantity of foods? Unless we have a tolerably clear idea of "in virtue of what" the sanction imposed on Peter is more severe than that imposed on Paul, I see no prospects for applying the principle of proportionality beyond cases that are intuitively obvious. No one would contest, for example, that a lifetime sentence of imprisonment without parole is more severe than a period of probation. Any such example, however, conceals the difficulty of my topic, inasmuch as we are unlikely to be forced to explain exactly what it is that makes the first sentence so clearly more severe than the second. Although we can muddle along without a metric, how could we hope to persuade someone of our judgment that Peter had been punished less severely than Paul, for example, if we were unable to say why?

Unfortunately, I may not succeed in identifying my own candidate for a single metric with which to express the severity of a punishment. The problem might well be insoluble. All we might be able to say is that a given instance of punishment is more severe along one dimension and less severe along another, with no clear means to specify which is more or less severe, all things considered. But my position is not entirely negative. I indicate why this problem is so difficult and describe the hard decisions that must be made before any progress can be expected. I also indicate how a retributive theory might be salvaged despite the enormous problems applying proportionality in the absence of a single metric with which units of punishment severity can be expressed.

I. Earlier Efforts and Some Problems They Face

It may be surprising that contemporary theorists do not agree about how to answer my question and all too often proceed as though it need not be answered at all (Husak 2018). The issue has not always been neglected, however. Theorists once exerted a fair amount of effort to assess whether two instances of punishment were equally severe. The scholarly occasion was the need to decide when alternative sanctions—different modes of punishment, such as fines and probation—were equally severe or could be made equivalent to terms of confinement. Perhaps the two most well-known such attempts were undertaken by Paul Robinson and Andreas von Hirsch. Robinson (1987) painstakingly described a sentencing scheme that employs "sanction units" to decide whether two modes of punishment are interchangeable. He proposed that a sanction of one unit, for example, might be expressed either in 2 weeks' imprisonment or in 160 hours of community service. He admitted, however, that the "preliminary empirical research on the proper assignment of sanction values to particular sanctioning methods" has so far "resulted in mere informed speculation" (p. 54). What further "empirical research" could Robinson have had in mind that would have resolved this problem? If it is amenable to an empirical solution at all, perhaps we could solicit the preferences of individual defendants through questionnaires (May and Wood 2010). Or these preferences could be idealized, correcting for the inevitable mistakes of fact committed by respondents. If two offenders are indifferent between undergoing alternative m or n—as when they are offered a choice between, say, "10 lashes or a fine of \$1,000"—then m and n should be equated as comparably severe.

Note that this method can be employed to measure the relative severity of punishments even without a clear metric with which units are expressed. After all, we can decide whether 100 Israeli shekels is more or less than 25 British pounds because they are traded on a market, even though there is no single currency to which each can be reduced. If this empirical device were employed, perhaps we could apply the principle of proportionality without identifying the metric I seek. But can the metric of severity really remain unspecified simply by relying on personal preferences to move from one mode of punishment to another? Doesn't the question resurface in the inevitable situation in which one offender prefers m to n and the other prefers n to m—or when their preferences between suffering m as opposed to n shift from one time to another?

Rather than evade this issue, let us confront it head-on. Exactly what is a "sanction unit" a unit of? Of course, it is a unit of punishment severity. But what is that? By what common denominator can we express the severity of different tokens of punitive sanctions, whether or not they involve different types? The answer proposed by von Hirsch is more helpful. He proposed that two instances of punishment should be deemed equally severe by reference to much the same measure used to assess the seriousness of two different crimes. I suspect that a viable means to gauge crime seriousness is every bit as problematic as a device to measure punishment severity (see, e.g., Ryberg 2019). Von Hirsch, however, famously contended that one offense is as serious as another when each intrudes equally on the interests victims typically need to lead a good life (von Hirsch and Jareborg 1991). Analogously, then, one punishment is as severe as another when each has a comparable impact on the living standards of offenders (von Hirsch 1993, p. 60). More particularly, he thought we should rank the severity of punishments "according to the degree to which they typically affect the punished person's freedom of movement, earning ability, and so forth" (von Hirsch 1998, p. 189).[2] Von Hirsch hastened to admit, however, that "such an analysis, examining the living-standard

---

2. The "and so forth" clause reveals the imprecision in this standard.

impacts of various intermediate sanctions, has yet to be undertaken," thus leading him to explicitly retreat to "the aid of common sense" (1993, p. 60). But even common sense, I am afraid, offers little guidance on this matter (Bronsteen, Buccafusco, and Masur 2009).

John Rawls (1955) also seemed to favor an objective metric. He wrote, "A person is said to suffer punishment whenever he is legally deprived of some of the normal rights of a citizen" (p. 10). Pursuant to this suggestion, we simply identify "normal rights" and quantify the extent of a deprivation by determining how many of them a defendant has lost. Actually, it is unclear whether Rawls's view is designed merely to identify what a punishment is or to gauge punishment severity. If the latter, we must somehow decide whether the loss of, say, freedom of religion is more or less severe than the loss of the right to freedom of speech. In any event, I regard these objectivist measures of severity as orthodox among philosophers of sentencing, although they rarely are explicit about the matter. I suspect a great part of the appeal of objectivist metrics is the desire to avoid the deep quagmire into which we would be plunged if the units we adopt are even partly subjective.

This issue is conceptually formidable partly because of the lack of consensus about the nature of punishment itself. Unless we agree on what punishment is and why it has proved so hard to justify, we are unlikely to concur about what makes one instance more or less severe—and thus more or less difficult to justify—than another. I contend without much argument that any response we should countenance as a form of punishment involves an intentional deprivation intended to express censure. We should not characterize a response as punitive unless it constitutes a deprivation or (in terms I will use interchangeably) hard treatment. In addition, according to my definition, a response is not punitive unless it expresses condemnation. As Joel Feinberg (1970) famously observed, a punishment is "a conventional device for the expression of attitudes of resentment and indignation, and of judgments of disapproval and reprobation" (p. 98). In the absence of this latter feature, an account of punishment would be overinclusive. We could not distinguish a tax (which surely is a deprivation but rarely is punitive) from a genuine punishment unless the latter were used to censure the person on whom it is imposed. Finally, it is important to stress that a response does not amount to a punishment because it happens to deprive and to censure. Real punishments are intended to have these effects.[3] A genuine punishment necessarily contains these essential features, each of which must be taken into account when assessing its severity.

---

3. The difficulty of discerning the intentions of sentencing authorities—or even of knowing

The measurements of hardship and censure both turn out to raise distinct conceptual and normative problems. Even when both components are taken into account, however, the full significance of the difficulty of justifying punishment may escape our notice. All too often, philosophers focus solely on what punishers are permitted to do (or to intend to do). The normative challenge, according to this train of thought, is to decide whether and under what circumstances legal officials are permitted to harm offenders—to deliberately deprive and censure them. But this way of conceptualizing the problem threatens to neglect the perspective of the persons who are harmed. As one commentator indicates, "One natural way of understanding the amount of punishment we inflict is to consider the amount of suffering our punishments cause" (Kolber 2018, p. 23.) Punishment has proved so hard to justify partly because of what it does to offenders and not merely because of what officials are permitted to intend to do to them. In gauging the severity of a punishment, should we adopt the point of view of the punisher or that of the individual who is punished or some combination of each? To phrase the issue differently, we must decide whether the units used to express the severity of a punishment are wholly objective, making no essential reference to the psychological or phenomenological state of the person who is punished, or are at least partly subjective, requiring such a reference.[4] Determinations of whether and to what extent a particular offender has been punished can differ radically depending on which of these perspectives we take.

The various collateral consequences of conviction provide a dramatic example of how these two perspectives can diverge. Countless commentators have noted that offenders bear not only the hardship and censure sentencing officials intend to impose but also a host of harms resulting from decisions by other state actors as well as by private persons. Offenders can be denied any number of benefits, such as student loans, employment opportunities, the right to vote or own a gun, and a great many more (Hoskins 2018). I believe it is futile to ask whether any or all of these collateral consequences should be conceptualized within the ambit of punishment itself (Mayson 2015). The best reply may be that they are not a part of punishment if we adopt the perspective of the punisher but are a part of punishment if we adopt the

---

whose intentions are relevant—helps to explain why so many cases of sanctions are borderline, difficult to categorize as punitive or nonpunitive.

4. This way of expressing the debate is admittedly clumsy, since psychological states—intentions—are essential to either perspective. The issue, then, is not whether mental states matter but whose and which such states matter.

perspective of the person who is punished. If we focus not merely on what punishers intend but also on what happens to offenders as a result, these collateral consequences must be included in any attempt to answer the justificatory questions philosophers of law have posed about punishment since the time of Plato (Kolber 2012).

To be sure, selecting the appropriate perspective hardly settles the question of what metric to use. But this decision advances the inquiry by indicating what we are looking for. If objective matters such as Rawls's are employed, we would need a political theory that identifies our rights and liberties and ranks them by degree of importance. Moral philosophers might also be consulted inasmuch as they have struggled to defend objective theories about what is important or valuable in a life. If subjective aspects are also important, however, the foregoing political and moral theories must be supplemented by a psychological or phenomenological theory about how given stimuli are felt and experienced. Some small progress on this matter has been made.[5] Healthcare professionals, for example, sometimes ask patients to rank the severity of their pain on a scale of 1 to 10. Although such devices are obviously crude and imperfect, they are probably better than nothing. More to the point, they would be completely irrelevant to the present inquiry if the units to express severity were wholly objective and indifferent to their actual effects on individuals.

Different metrics are needed when different perspectives are taken. But regardless of the perspective we choose, we might need different metrics to express the severity of hard treatment and censure, the two components of punishment I have mentioned. I discuss each of these two elements separately. I begin with the first, turning to special problems involving the censuring component of penal sanctions in section III.

II. Measuring Deprivation

Efforts to quantify the relative extent of a given deprivation or imposition of hard treatment would appear to be the easier of the two problems to solve. Still, questions arise immediately. I have already introduced the most basic decision that must be made before we can identify the relevant units: whether to adopt the perspective of the punisher or that of the person who is punished. Return to the earlier efforts to assess severity that I described in section

---

5. For example, moral philosophers (Temkin 1985, esp. chap. 2) have tried to assess whether persons have a complaint about how they are treated and how the strength of their complaint might be measured.

I. Impact on a typical living standard would seem to be wholly objective in that it is indifferent to phenomenological differences among particular offenders. Presumably, my living standard could erode without my noticing or caring. Should we really represent two tokens of hard treatment as equally severe by a metric that is completely objective in this sense, that is, that does not consider their impact on the mental states of the individuals on whom they are imposed? Jeremy Bentham, as I construe him, is clear on this matter. He famously contended that punishments necessarily involve an evil that could be justified only by the prevention of a greater evil. All evils, in turn, involve disutility, by which Bentham himself meant pain or unhappiness. Thus, Bentham would not have recognized a response as a punishment unless it caused pain or unhappiness for the person on whom it was inflicted. Pain and unhappiness are paradigm examples of psychological states; we feel unhappy and experience pain. As a result, he would rank one deprivation as more severe than another when it caused more of these negative states. Bentham would not have conceptualized a state response as a punishment if the offender neither knew nor cared about whether it had been inflicted.

I regard H. L. A. Hart as more evasive about whether the units of severity are objective or partly subjective.[6] In the first clause of his celebrated definition, Hart (1968) indicated that "standard cases" of punishment "must involve pain or other consequences normally considered unpleasant" (pp. 4–5). The first disjunct of this clause ("pain") is clearly subjective; the second ("other consequence normally considered unpleasant") is not. Hart himself did not elaborate on why a consequence should count as hard treatment because it is "normally considered" unpleasant, even when it is not regarded as such by the particular person on whom it is imposed. One might suppose that the imposition of a sanction "normally considered" unpleasant to which a given offender is indifferent should be treated as a failed attempt to punish rather than as a successful instance of it. In any event, I suspect that Hart is ambivalent about whether the units with which to express the quanta of a deprivation are wholly objective or at least partly subjective.

Even if we decide not to countenance a response as a mode of punishment unless it produces a negative psychological state, we still would need to specify which psychological state(s) should count. Given deprivations may cause pain, discomfort, boredom, regret, anguish, and a plethora of other effects. How might these subjective states be represented on a common

---

6. Hart's definition seems to neglect censure and focuses solely on the deprivation or hard treatment aspect of punishment.

scale? It is tempting to fudge this matter by expressing each as an instance of *disutility*. But I prefer a term in ordinary English that is understood by nonphilosophers. Although no obvious solution comes to mind, I propose *unhappiness* or *suffering* as the best candidates.

Whatever term we select, we must grant that persons have radically different subjective reactions to whatever treatments qualify as "objectively similar" deprivations (Raaijmakers 2018). Adam Kolber, a tireless champion of the view that subjective experience should be relevant in assessments of punishment severity, presents a wealth of examples to illustrate this point; I summarize only two (Kolber 2009*b*). Suppose two offenders vary significantly in height. The first is 7 feet tall; the second is 5 feet tall. No one would doubt these two offenders would experience different quanta of unhappiness, disutility, pain, or suffering if each was confined to the same 6-foot-high cell. Or suppose two offenders differ radically in weight and have different needs for food. A similar diet of 1,200 calories a day for each would have a markedly different impact on their respective levels of subjective utility. In light of their distinct psychological responses, would anyone insist that these individuals would suffer the same quanta of deprivation if their sentences were calculated objectively?[7]

How should sentencing authorities accommodate this uncontestable point? As I have indicated, Hart's reference to what is "normally considered unpleasant" represents something of a compromise on this issue. I regard Robinson's response similarly. Obviously, different defendants would offer different answers to whether 10 lashes are more or less severe than a $1,000 fine. Some would suffer more disutility from the former, others from the latter. Robinson implicitly proposes to compile an average from the responses of all (possible or actual?) offenders. But what is the argument for using an average rather than assessing the impact on the particular defendant? Von Hirsch (1998), in turn, contends that the "living standard" analysis used to gauge the severity of punishments "refers to the means and capabilities that *ordinarily* assist persons in achieving a good life," even though the offender himself may be indifferent about them (p. 189). I regard these objectivist measures of severity as orthodox among philosophers of sentencing, although they rarely are explicit about the matter. I suspect a great part of the appeal of objectivist metrics is the desire to avoid the deep quagmire into which we would be plunged if the units we adopt are even partly subjective. But why

---

7. In the context of equality, Ronald Dworkin (1977, pp. 226–29) has long pointed out that a right to treatment as an equal is distinct from a right to equal treatment.

should we decide how severely a given deprivation punishes a particular offender because of its effects on a typical or standard offender? In most other contexts, our system of criminal justice goes to enormous lengths to do justice in individual cases without recourse to objective standards.[8] I take these efforts to point to an ideal to which institutions of penal justice should aspire.

What, then, is the bridging premise that connects the severity of what a given defendant receives to what is received by the average, ordinary, or typical offender? Is this generalization embraced for principled or pragmatic reasons? Legal philosophers should always strive to distinguish what is an ideal from what is a necessary but regrettable retreat from an ideal. Admittedly, pragmatic difficulties in utilizing a subjective metric can be astronomical; efforts to calibrate particular tokens of punishment to the sensibilities of individual offenders would encounter a host of practical problems. They may be too costly, violate privacy, fail to give offenders adequate notice, encourage deceit, or lead to unjust discrimination on the basis of wealth and privilege (Kolber 2009b). In addition, if punishment severity is to be fixed ex ante, when a sentence is pronounced, it cannot be too sensitive to its actual impact without requiring constant recalibration. Although each of these obstacles is formidable in the real world, we need not even attempt to overcome them without good reason to do so. If we have a principled basis for making the extent of a deprivation sensitive to phenomenological differences between particular offenders but practical problems prevent us from succeeding, we should at least be candid that our sentencing practices involve a compromise with an ideal. Thus, I pose the philosophical question that must be answered before confronting these real-world problems: should we aspire to ensure as best we can that any mode of deprivation or hard treatment produces whatever quantum of negative psychological response our best theory of proportionate sentencing tells us to impose?

Unlike Kolber, I believe that retributivism provides the better theory of sentencing with which this question should be addressed. Thus, I ask whether we should aspire to ensure that any mode of deprivation or hard treatment produces whatever amount of negative psychological reaction is deserved. Kolber himself believes that a retributive framework is especially ill suited to accommodate subjective differences among offenders. He reaches this

---

8. I regard the rarity of criminal liability for negligence as well as holdings about the unconstitutionality of various presumptions (e.g., defendants intend the natural and probable consequences of their conduct) to demonstrate a commitment to subjective standards in individual cases.

conclusion because he thinks (correctly) that retributivists have a special commitment to a principle of proportionality. He seemingly believes that proportionality is impossible to preserve while taking account of the extent to which a given deprivation causes different psychological responses among offenders (Kolber 2009*a*). The decision to build a higher cell for the tall offender than the one for the short offender has nothing to do with the seriousness of their respective crimes, which, we can stipulate, are identical. Thus, Kolber concludes that retributivists must disregard proportionality if they hope to accommodate the fact that individual offenders have different psychological responses to given deprivations. As a result, retributivists must depart from what is foundational to their theory. Since consequentialists have little or no attachment to the principle of proportionality in the first place, Kolber believes they can abandon it without theoretical inconsistency.

Hence, Kolber believes he has provided a powerful reason to prefer a consequentialist theory of punishment to its retributivist counterpart. Is he correct to invoke his commitment to subjective differences between offenders as a reason to reject proportionality and thereby resist retributivism? I think not, even though I share much of his skepticism about our ability to apply the principle of proportionality as I have formulated it. One flaw in his reasoning is his failure to understand that the principle of proportionality contains a ceteris paribus clause. My formulation makes the severity of the punishment a function of the seriousness of the offense only when all other relevant variables are held equal. If two offenders differ in the ways Kolber describes— in their height or caloric need, for example—we should not assume that the principle of proportionality requires that they be treated identically. But an even greater flaw, it seems to me, is the metric to which Kolber seems curiously committed when gauging punishment severity. If a psychological state such as suffering is used to measure severity, Peter is punished more than Paul when he experiences more suffering. Thus, two offenders who commit the same crime but suffer to different degrees when sentenced to the same term of imprisonment are punished unequally rather than equally. If the metric of severity is partly subjective, as Kolber himself believes it to be, the principle of proportionality supports rather than undermines his claim that subjective experience matters.

This latter point merits further emphasis, for it corrects a misunderstanding to which even the most astute critics (and, indeed, Kolber himself) are susceptible. Ken Simmons (2009), for example, construes those who favor a subjective metric to claim that the sensitive should be punished less than the insensitive or that the rich should be punished more than the poor. He writes: "Suppose

'Sensitive' is claustrophobic, while 'Insensitive' suffers less distress from punishment than most people. Under the subjectivist theory, Sensitive should be punished less than the typical offender, while Insensitive should be punished more" (p. 1). Once we appreciate that the contested issue involves the metric by which the relative severity of punishments are measured, however, it should be clear that subjectivists are not making this outlandish claim. Their point, instead, is that a longer term of imprisonment need not involve more punishment. Thus, Sensitive is punished more severely than Insensitive when each is sentenced to comparable periods of confinement. If the metric of punishment severity is suffering rather than, say, length of imprisonment, imposing equally lengthy prison sentences on persons who suffer to different degrees is to punish them unequally, not equally. On objective accounts, of course, these phenomenological differences turn out to be quite beside the point.

How, then, should we decide whether the units of deprivation severity ultimately refer to a psychological state of individuals or to something that can be characterized wholly objectively? To my mind, no single argument is likely to settle the matter. Both objectivists and subjectivists contend that their side has intuitive support; they marshal examples in which respondents are likely to concur with their judgments (Katz 1996). Some cases involve deprivations that are objectively severe but cause no subjective effect. Suppose, for example, that a defendant is sentenced to a term of house arrest for the duration of her life. Her doors are locked, and her whereabouts are monitored. But she is unaware that she has been confined, is delighted to remain at home, and never makes an attempt to leave.[9] Other cases involve deprivations that are objectively lenient but cause substantial negative subjective reactions. The example of the 7-foot-tall defendant confined in the 6-foot-high cell is illustrative. Although reasonable minds may disagree, I suspect most respondents would concur that the subjective rather than the objective dimension is more significant when assessing the severity of these deprivations. But intuitions about other cases tug in the opposite direction. Suppose one prisoner manages to spend much more time asleep than another and experiences far less distress throughout her incarceration as a result. Is the extent of her deprivation less than that of the latter? Presumably not (Gray 2010). Perhaps we can defend plausible positions about whether the metric of punishment is wholly objective or partly subjective while explaining why we should not be overly troubled by the foregoing alleged counterexamples to whatever answer we provide. To

---

9. Such cases resemble "Frankfurt-type" counterexamples to the principle of alternative possibilities in the literature about free will and responsibility.

my mind, however, these examples serve to demonstrate our ambivalence and uncertainty about the matter.

At least one other set of considerations favors a subjective metric. Consider a situation in which the punishing authority knows perfectly well that the persons to be punished react differently to the objectively same sanction. This scenario is believable when parents punish children—a nonlegal context from which I think philosophers of law have much to learn. Suppose 6-year-old twin brothers Billy and Bobby continuously fight each other, and their parent decides to discipline them. If Billy loves video games and Bobby loathes them, it would be ludicrous to think they are punished equally if their father bans video games for both. Even children would understand they had been punished unequally. Why would adults reach a different conclusion when punishments are administered by the state?

III. Subjective Metrics and Day Fines

On principled grounds, I tend to prefer partly subjective metrics to gauge the severity of a given deprivation. Someone is punished to the extent that he or she experiences suffering or unhappiness. In this section, I point out that a commitment to a wholly objective metric unduly constricts our efforts to decide which modes of deprivation to employ. The unchallenged assumption that the severity of hard treatment can be expressed only by an objective unit has blinded reformers to the very real possibility of alleviating the epidemic of mass incarceration by making more use of monetary fines than of imprisonment. Perhaps the most telling objection to the greater use of monetary fines is that they are inadequate. If amounts are set too high, poor defendants are unable to pay them. If they are set too low, wealthy defendants are insufficiently deterred, because they can regard them as a cost of living or of doing business. But this problem is not intractable. The best solution is to implement a system of day fines, capitalizing on familiar ideas about the diminishing marginal value of money by relativizing the amount of the payment to the income or wealth of the particular offender. Day fines, of course, take a substantial step away from construing the metric of a deprivation objectively. They do not resort directly to statistical averages or typical cases but seek to measure the severity of a deprivation by reference to its impact on the welfare of the particular offender in question.[10]

---

10. My appreciation of the advantages of day fines is largely due to my supervision of Daisy Lee, a Rutgers undergraduate (Lee 2017).

A system of day fines does not exclusively involve subjective experience, however, inasmuch as its administration involves two steps (McDonald, Greene, and Worzella 1992). First, a day-fine "unit" is assigned to an offender depending on the seriousness of his or her offense. This unit is independent of the person's income. The unit-rate system, or a system of "benchmark scales," is invoked to determine the number of units appropriate for each offense. Hence, the same number of day-fine units is applied for each instance of the same offense. The second step identifies the value of the day-fine unit for the particular defendant. This calculation takes into account the offender's personal income or wealth. The total amount is then calculated by multiplying the number of day-fine units by the value of the unit. To be sure, no efforts are made to assess whether a given fine affects a particular defendant more or less than another with the same wealth or income. Even a rich person may care more about a dollar than a poor person; generalizations are made about the probable impact of a fine on the population of similarly situated offenders. As a result, day fines seemingly involve a hybrid of objective and subjective elements.

It is unfortunate that day fines are not employed more frequently in light of their many advantages. Traditional systems of fixed fines have proved disappointing. Monetary penalties with some prospects of deterring members of the middle class are often beyond the ability of the poor to pay. As a result, a great many fixed fines are uncollected, requiring a device to ensure that some mode of hard treatment is actually imposed. All too often, this device involves incarceration. Moving to a system of day fines would increase state revenue, reduce the need for imprisonment, and lessen the differential impact of a deprivation on the rich and the poor. Thus, this system should appeal both to retributive and to consequentialist schools of penal thought. If I am correct, the outstanding question is why the United States rarely implements systems of day fines rather than fixed fines or incarceration. One possible answer is the unexamined commitment to an objective metric of deprivation severity.

The replacement of fixed fines by day fines is probably the most promising innovation if we agree that the metric of the severity of a deprivation should be partly subjective. But the possibilities for replacing one mode of deprivation with another are endless if we continue down this path. To my knowledge, however, few theorists have seriously proposed that two offenders who commit the same crime should be sentenced to different amounts of time in prison because the hardships of incarceration are likely to be greater for one than for the other. Why is this idea so rarely entertained if the rationale for day fines is so powerful? A theory of the diminishing marginal utility of money appears to have a rough counterpart when other deprivations are examined. I can only speculate that day fines are seen as especially attractive because their implementation would benefit the poor and the disadvantaged, classes of people who have most often been treated unfairly by the criminal justice system. By contrast, a plan to reduce a prison term for offenders who are predicted to suffer disproportionately is more likely to benefit the rich and powerful, the very persons who already receive favorable treatment by the criminal justice system.

Still, why do those legal philosophers who hold a partly subjective metric of the severity of a deprivation not express more enthusiasm for day fines as a replacement for incarceration? The most respectable answer, I believe, is that a more extensive use of day fines would not adequately censure those defendants who commit serious crimes (Kahan 1996). It is to this second aspect of punishment that I now turn.

IV. Measuring Censure Subjectively

The hard treatment or deprivation component is only one of the two dimensions along which the severity of a punishment must be measured. Whatever difficulties are encountered in deciding whether to construe this feature objectively or subjectively are replicated (and probably magnified) when we turn to the censuring aspect of punishment. This part of punishment has always been the more elusive, receiving less scrutiny from philosophers of criminal law than its counterpart, hard treatment. Still, it is significant for purposes of applying the principle of proportionality. Feinberg (1970) goes so far as to contend that "it is social disapproval and its appropriate expression that should fit the crime, and not hard treatment (pain) as such" (p. 118). I regard this comment as an exaggeration; I think both aspects are equally important when assessing whether the principle of proportionality is satisfied. The point I wish to stress, however, is that Feinberg's contention is barely intelligible unless censure is quantifiable. If we are to make meaningful judgments that one defendant has been censured more or less than another, we must be able to explain what these judgments mean. Since even the terminology used to describe this dimension of punishment is nonstandard, I begin with what may or may not be a stipulation. I take censure to be a judgment expressed by a sentencing authority and shame to be an effect felt by someone who is censured (Hadjimatheou 2016). I use *condemnation* when I want to be deliberately evasive about whether I am referring to censure or shame.

I begin with some difficult questions that must be addressed if the principle of proportionality is to be applied to this dimension of punishment. If a response must be intentional to qualify as a punishment and if an expression of censure is an essential component of punishment, it, too, must be intentional. Thus, we must decide whose intentions should be taken as decisive in categorizing an expression as an instance of censure (McAdams 2015). Should we focus on the intentions of legal officials, the beliefs of the person to whom the expression is directed, the public at large, or some other agent(s) altogether? Even if we restrict our attention to the expressions of legal officials—probably the most common answer—we must decide what to say when their intentions diverge. The problem is not simply that of locating a single intention in a legislative body composed of several individuals. Even if this familiar difficulty could be surmounted, the intentions of the legislature and those of a judge (not to mention those of other legal officials) might well differ in a particular case. For example, if a legislator enacts a drug statute because he or she believes that users deserve condemnation, but a judge with the authority to place the offender on probation sends the offender to prison because he or she believes the offender is an addict with the disease of addiction who needs the treatment that is available there, has the offender been censured?

I do not mean to minimize these difficulties, but I put them aside in order to focus on the topic at hand. What possible units can be used to describe whether one instance of condemnation (censure or shame) is greater than another? To answer this question, we must again decide whether to evaluate the quantum of this dimension of punishment by adopting the perspective of the punisher or that of the person punished. In other words, is the amount of censure intended by the punisher decisive, or must we also consider the degree of shame experienced by the person to whom it is directed? The difficulty of answering this question mirrors that examined in the context of deprivations: identical expressions of censure do not shame all recipients equally and may not succeed in shaming a given person at all. No one doubts that offenders vary greatly in whether and to what extent they experience shame when censured. Some are racked with guilt and remorse and driven to the brink of suicide; others are unfazed. How should we deal with this fact? Arguably, in order for a sanction to qualify as a clear and uncontroversial instance of punishment, it not only must be imposed with the intention to censure, but it must also succeed in creating shame. If this assumption is correct, new difficulties in categorizing a sanction as punitive—and in gauging the extent of its severity—are presented. Consider an example. If an authority believes a shaved head is a badge of disgrace but a person whose head is shaved regards it with indifference or pride, does this mode of treatment satisfy this definitional component of punishment? This question does not simply involve persons with unconventional or idiosyncratic beliefs. Efforts to generalize over a diverse population are not especially meaningful when applied to individual cases—even less so, I believe, than in the case of deprivations in which variations among persons are probably less extreme. Although the relevant authorities may have a punitive intent, entire groups within a single jurisdiction may not regard given kinds of treatment as especially shameful.

As before with hard treatment, this problem can be bypassed by embracing an objectivist conception of this component. Thus, the actual attitudes or reactions of those who are censured would again turn out to be irrelevant in measuring the severity of this aspect of punishment. If the particular offender reacts with a shrug and feels no shame whatsoever, he or she has been punished as long as the relevant authorities hold whatever intentions are needed and treat him or her in a way that would typically be regarded as condemnatory. Even if the stern pronouncements rendered by sentencing judges fail to produce the intended reaction, objective accounts entail that the offender has been censured and thus punished. I suspect the majority of legal philosophers probably regard this requirement of punishment as satisfied when offenders are censured, irrespective of how these expressions are received.

An objective focus, however, again threatens to neglect an aspect of punishment that makes it especially hard to justify: its impact on the person punished. Restricting attention to the intentions of legal officials in order to gauge whether and to what extent this feature of punishment is present encounters all of the foregoing difficulties in addition to a problem not replicated in the parallel question about deprivation: there is only so much the state can do to ensure that a given mode of treatment produces shame. In fact, shame itself rarely results solely from the pronouncements of legal officials or even from state action more generally. The state can deprive an offender of one or more rights and inflict pain, but whether and to what extent a particular mode of treatment causes shame is not comparably within the power of the government to control. It can change the conditions of confinement to make them more or less pleasant, but the state has a limited ability to ensure that these effects will be experienced as shameful. For better or worse, shame cannot be created so easily.

It is not hard to devise alternatives to imprisonment that impose an appropriate amount of hardship. The greater challenge, however, is to identify alternatives that express the requisite degree of condemnation. Options are limited. The familiar alternative of community service, for example, is frequently deemed inadequate as a punishment, because it is not perceived as a mode of censure. After all, most persons are praised for community service; it is unclear how or why this activity becomes a source of shame simply because an individual is "sentenced" to perform it. And once alternative modes of punishment are available, by what criteria do offenders become eligible to participate in them? The most plausible means to distinguish those to be imprisoned from those to be punished by alternative means is that the former should be reserved for offenders whose crimes are serious or violent. But if shame less often results from the alternative sentences for which nonviolent offenders will qualify, it becomes difficult to successfully punish them. Day fines, to cite another example, are of limited use, because the public perceives them as inadequately condemnatory for the most serious offenses (Kahan 1998). Possible solutions to this problem are limited by the requirement that deprivations not be "degrading to human dignity." Liberal states can and do recognize strict limits on what can be done to ensure that offenders are shamed when they are censured (Duff 2001). If shame could be manufactured at will, as is more or less the case with deprivation, these problems could be solved far more easily.

It should be clear that the question of whether a particular form of treatment produces shame is dependent on social conventions in a way that the question of whether a particular mode of treatment imposes a hardship or deprivation is not. Whether and to what extent a sanction is shameful is largely a function of the relationship between the offender and the community in whose name the sentencing authority acts. Some legal philosophers go as far as to suggest that it is impossible to punish persons who are totally outside of a given community. Andrew Oldenquist (1988) writes, "It is impossible to punish some people, for if they are completely alien or sufficiently alienated, they cannot be disgraced, and they welcome rather than fear ostracism" (p. 469). But one need not be totally alienated from a community to fail to regard traditional modes of deprivations as causing shame. History is replete with examples of persons who, for one reason or another, felt no shame from attempts to punish them. Henry David Thoreau (1968) famously maintained that "under a government which imprisons any unjustly, the true place for a just man is also in prison. . . . The only house in a slave State in which a free man can abide with honor" (pp. 370–71). According to this train of thought, imprisonment in an unjust state, or even when imposed for an unjust law, is simply not to be construed as a punishment; it is a source of pride rather than shame. If Thoreau chose to adopt this perspective about his sentence, it is hard to see how the state could succeed in persuading him that his offense was, in fact, deserving of shame.

Since shame is not created by the state in quite the same way as it imposes hard treatment but depends more on social conventions that may or may not be shared, legal philosophers must pay more attention to the social conventions from which it derives. Following this suggestion will yield important insights. For example, I suspect that many discussions of collateral consequences among legal philosophers will turn out to be incomplete or misplaced. Instead of the narrow preoccupation with whether and to what extent non-state actors are justified in imposing deprivations on offenders, philosophers should also be attentive to the myriad ways in which non-state actors are a source of shame. This is a neglected but important worry raised by the increased use of collateral consequences.

Until we decide whether to measure condemnation as censure (what is intentionally expressed by the state) as opposed to shame (what is experienced by the offender who is censured), attempts to quantify this second aspect of punishment do not even get off the ground. We have little idea how to proceed, even though proportionality determinations require (ceteris paribus) the severity of this component of punishment to be a function of the seriousness of the offense.

V. *The Interplay between Deprivation and Shame*

Despite the foregoing perplexities, the greatest challenge in applying the principle of proportionality may lie ahead. To describe it, imagine that the above difficulties have been solved. Imagine, that is, that we somehow succeed in specifying a metric to represent the severity of a deprivation (d) and condemnation (c). How should these units be combined in a single measure of the all-things-considered severity of a punishment? No possible solution to this problem turns out to be unproblematic. Although each could be construed as an independent contributor to overall suffering or unhappiness, it might be better to disaggregate them. But at what theoretical price? At worst, no single measure of punishment severity would exist. Instead, all we could conclude is that a given instance of punishment is more severe along one dimension (d) and less severe along another (c), with no clear means to specify which is more or less severe simpliciter. This conclusion has potentially unsettling implications for the adequacy of any theory of sentencing but may present a special challenge to a retributive theory that takes desert and proportionality to be central.

I gather that these two analytically distinct definitional components of punishment—deprivation d and condemnation c—can be disentangled for purposes of gauging the overall severity of a punishment. That is, it is conceptually possible for a given sanction to impose a substantial deprivation but only to express a relatively small amount of censure. The converse is possible as well: a sentence can express enormous condemnation but inflict only a minor hardship. Both scenarios are coherent, although it would be convenient to pretend they are conceptual impossibilities. The most straightforward way to deny their coherence is to adopt a simplifying hypothesis: the imposition of the deprivation is just the means by which censure is expressed and offenders are made to feel shame. Although they are rarely explicit about the matter, many philosophers of punishment apparently take this hypothesis to be correct (Feinberg 1970, p. 118; Duff 2001, p. 132).

For three reasons, I find this simplifying hypothesis to be inaccurate and unhelpful. First, even if it were true in the case of censure, it is false in the case of shame. Once we include the perspective of the person who is punished, shame may or may not result from the expression of censure and the imposition of a deprivation. Thoreau is hardly the only example in which conventional deprivations fail to create shame and instead are a source of pride. Some gang members seemingly regard a prison sentence as a rite of passage and a badge of recognition. Second, when understood in its historical context, contemporary modes of punishment, less public than in previous eras, almost seem designed to divorce hard treatment from shame. Defendants are not required to wear scarlet letters or comparable badges of infamy, and the use of such practices as branding and other visible mutilations or of such devices as the stocks and pillory, have long been rejected as barbaric and unconstitutional. A third and final ground to doubt that either censure or shame is created by the same means as the deprivations that are imposed is that the former can and do survive long after the hardship has ended. In case there is doubt, one need only consider the long-standing use of criminal records exhaustively documented by Jim Jacobs (2015). As he explains, online permanent registries exist or have been proposed for sex offenses, persons convicted of drug trafficking, domestic violence, hate crimes, arson, and animal abuse. As a result of such efforts, the shame experienced by many offenders is destined to persist throughout the course of their lives. This effect is a deliberate or foreseeable consequence of the way criminal records are kept and used, at least in the United States.

The contempt to which some persons are subjected after having committed a criminal offense often qualifies as an important source of the shame that, from their perspective, makes up part of their punishment. Since persons who commit certain kinds of offenses, such as rape and child molestation, are ostracized so frequently and systematically, the issue of whether sentencing should be influenced by the shame caused by private parties arises more often than the parallel issue of whether sentencing should be influenced by the hard treatment imposed by non-state actors. After all, the state has some power to reduce the likelihood that offenders will be subjected to deprivations at the hands of persons who lack lawful authority. Still, I have speculated elsewhere about how the severity of a sentence should be affected by a case in which the state was unable to prevent private parties from imposing hard treatment upon an offender for an offense (Husak 2010). Consider an example in which a convicted criminal who deserves two years' imprisonment is abducted by vigilantes before he can be sentenced. To prevent what they fear will be an injustice, the vigilantes "sentence" the offender to a lifetime of solitary confinement in a makeshift "prison" of their own construction. Suppose that after two years, the police discover and release this victim of "vigilante justice." Surely, this person would be expected to plead that he had been "already punished enough" if he were finally brought before the appropriate legal authorities for sentencing. It seems callous to reply that the defendant's ordeal cannot be allowed to reduce the severity of his sentence because it had not been imposed by the state. Civil remedies against the vigilantes for the tort of false imprisonment do little to comfort the offender if he is subsequently required by the state to serve the full term of his deserved sentence as though he had not already suffered a hardship for his crime.

Clearly, states make substantial efforts to prevent persons from exacting these acts of vigilante justice. If so, one might be puzzled about whether the state should exercise a comparable power to ensure that offenders are not subjected to excessive ostracism at the hands of persons who lack authority. If the shame that results from ridicule is to be construed as part of punishment and the principle of proportionality limits the amount of shame that a given defendant should experience, it seems to follow that the state may occasionally have reason to intervene to limit the extent to which a defendant is ridiculed. In the absence of state action to protect criminal defendants, our society can hardly count on self-imposed restraint to ensure that individuals are not ostracized well beyond their deserts. To be sure, it is hard to imagine a liberal state using its police power to silence tasteless and vindictive comedians. Still, excessive condemnation at the hands of private persons might well provide a basis for reducing the severity of what is imposed by the state. If shame is a necessary part of punishment and is rarely created solely by the state but depends on social convention, it must be true that what is not imposed solely by the state can be punishment—at least, when judged from the perspective of the offender (Husak 2016). The shame experienced by many offenders should not be deemed immaterial to their sentences simply because it is not a product of state action. In such cases, shame emanates from the very source that is most effective in producing it.

Suppose, then, that the foregoing scenarios are conceptually possible. If so, legal philosophers who try to apply a principle of proportionality to particular cases must confront an enormous challenge. If the deprivation d_1 imposed on Peter is great but the condemnation c_1 (censure or shame) is trivial, and the deprivation d_2 imposed on Paul is small but the condemnation c_2 is significant, has Peter been punished more or less severely than Paul overall? That is, on what common scale are different amounts of deprivation and condemnation weighed to form a single judgment of the all-things-considered severity of a punishment? Although deprivation and condemnation could both be expressed as sources of unhappiness or suffering, the problem on which I am focusing would be concealed by lumping them together.

On the assumption that an offender deserves a quantum of deprivation d as well as a quantum of condemnation c, can the excessive amount of one component ever be a good reason to reduce the other below what would otherwise be deserved? The answer to this question depends in part on which of two theories is used to describe the relationship between the condemnation and hard treatment components of punishment. According to the first approach, these two components are independent: the fact that an offender receives more or less of one component of punishment than he or she deserves is not a good reason to adjust the amount of the remaining component. According to the second approach, these two components are dependent: the fact that an offender receives more or less of one component of punishment than he or she deserves is a good reason to adjust the amount of the remaining component. Suppose a defendant deserves d and c, which somehow have been quantified. If the independent theory is accepted, any increase in d or c beyond what she deserves is not a good reason to reduce the amount of the remaining component, so no offender should be heard to complain that the excessive amount of humiliation he or she has endured is a good reason to reduce his or her hard treatment below what would ordinarily be deserved. If the dependent theory is accepted, however, the contrary would be true.

Is the independent or the dependent theory preferable? Intuitions probably pull in both directions, but at least two arguments favor the dependent theory. First, if the shame a defendant suffers is less than he or she deserves, there may be no adequate means by which the state can compensate for this fact without increasing the hard treatment above that which he or she deserves and should otherwise receive. The dependence theory allows the state to make whatever adjustments in either component are needed to ensure that the overall quantum of punishment satisfies our judgments of proportionality. A second reason to hold that the two components of punishment are dependent is as follows. The principle of proportionality requires the severity of punishment to increase with the seriousness of the crime. Ideally, both the hardship component d and the condemnation component c would increase as crimes become more serious. Unfortunately, this generalization has any number of exceptions. Persons who commit a few kinds of offense are likely to suffer extraordinary shame, even though their crimes are not especially serious and do not merit very severe punishments. Some kinds of minor sexual offenses provide the best examples of this phenomenon. In our society, a defendant who is convicted of indecent exposure is likely to feel shame to a greater degree than a defendant who commits the more serious offense of burglary. How should sentencing policy respond to this fact, given the inability of the state to effectively regulate the extent to which offenders experience shame? On the independence theory, sentencing judges should not take this disparity into account in deciding on the amount of hard treatment that should be inflicted. Arguably, the sentence to be imposed on this defendant would not differ from the sentence that would be imposed were the degree of condemnation an accurate reflection of its real seriousness. As a result of this approach, the total quantum of punishment $(d + c)$ to be imposed on this offender is likely to exceed his or her desert. The best way to avoid the resulting injustice is to treat the two components of punishment as dependent, so that the undue shame provides a good reason to decrease the amount of deprivation that is otherwise deserved.

In principle, the amount of either d or c may be greater than that deserved by the defendant, but I suspect the latter is a more likely possibility than the former. As described above, the state is usually in a better position to limit the amount of hardship visited upon an offender to ensure that it is kept within the boundaries required by proportionality. But it is more probable that the degree to which an offender is ashamed will exceed the quantum he or she deserves. When defendants are shamed beyond their desert, the dependence theory provides a good rationale for reducing the amount of hardship that should otherwise be imposed.

To complicate matters further, the precise nature of the relationship between the condemnation and hard treatment components of punishment is probably more complex than is suggested by the simple labels *dependence* or *independence*. It may be reasonable to cap the extent to which increases beyond what is deserved in one component of punishment should offset decreases in the other. Perhaps the proper punishment for a serious crime should involve a minimum amount of deprivation regardless of whether the offender has been condemned beyond his or her desert. The important point, however, is to understand the appeal of treating these two dimensions of punishment dependently.

VI. A Deflationary Role for Proportionality

If most or all of the foregoing arguments are sound, the difficulties in applying the principle of proportionality are enormous. We should probably conceptualize the metric of severity as partly subjective, although it is hardly obvious how to do so. Moreover, we have little idea how punishments imposed in excess of desert along one dimension should affect applications of proportionality generally. How should philosophers of criminal law respond if they are persuaded of these difficulties and unable to overcome them? No answer is straightforward, and I advance the following solution with some trepidation. The most radical option would be to jettison the principle of proportionality as entirely unworkable in a scheme of sentencing (Lacey and Pickard 2015). I grudgingly take this alternative seriously. Indeed, as we have seen, problems similar to those I have raised are sometimes cited as a basis for rejecting theories that afford a central place to desert. Nonetheless, I believe we should prefer a less drastic response. If a difficulty cannot be solved, we should make efforts to limit the damage it inflicts.

The above problems loom large to the extent that sentencing policy is governed by desert. I am skeptical, however, that any scheme of sentencing can pretend to be shaped solely or even primarily by this consideration. Thus, we might adopt what might be called a deflationary account of the role of proportionality in sentencing theory. That is, we can continue to accept this principle despite its shortcomings by restricting its strength in our theory of sentencing. As I construe it, proportionality is a principle of desert, requiring offenders to be punished according to the seriousness of their offense. But this requirement does not entail that defendants must be punished according to their desert, all things considered. After all, my formulation of the principle of proportionality includes a ceteris paribus clause. Clearly, "other things" almost never are equal. The application of any given desert principle competes with other desert principles, as well as with principles that have nothing to do with desert. The latter are of special significance in this context. Even without abandoning retributivism and proportionality altogether, non-desert factors should permit substantial deviations from the elusive requirements of proportionality.

In determining whether a given sentence should be imposed, proportionality considerations provide only part of the answer. We must also consider the impact of the sentence on other parties who are affected. In cases of personal self-defense, for example, maiming a villain who threatens only to slap the face of an innocent victim is disproportionate and thereby unjustified. By contrast, maiming a villain who attempts to kill is proportionate. But even though the amount of force used by the innocent victim is proportionate to whatever harm is threatened by the wrongful attacker, it may still be unjustified because its infliction would cause more harm than it would avert overall. Suppose, for example, that the use of proportionate force against the wrongful attacker would cause his several dependent children to suffer enormously. The imposition of proportionate force might well produce more harm than good, and thus be unjustified, all things considered (McMahan 2008).

The same phenomenon I have mentioned in the context of personal self-defense is also present in the context of penal sentencing. Variables that are hard to reconcile with the desert of the offender have always been invoked to justify punishments less severe than the principle of proportionality would seem to permit. Reasonable minds can and do differ about what non-desert factors should play this role. But different criminal histories provide the most familiar reason to impose different punishments on such persons. Few theorists contest the intuition that first-time and repeat offenders should be punished with unequal severity, although the nearly universal policy that reflects this intuition has proved difficult to justify (Roberts and von Hirsch 2010). I doubt that this policy can be justified in terms of desert at all, but it may be justifiable nonetheless (Ryberg 2018). In any event, factors even more clearly irrelevant to desert than criminal history are routinely invoked to justify departures from proportionality.[11] Suppose an offender is terminally ill, for example, or old and infirm. Or suppose the offender has been seriously injured and permanently incapacitated in the very crime he or she perpetrated.

---

11. The US Sentencing Guidelines explicitly indicate that a number of factors, such as "lack of guidance as a youth," cannot be invoked to justify a departure from the sentence required by the Guidelines. See §5H1.12 in the US Sentencing Commission's Departure and Variance Primer. (http://www.ussc.gov/sites/default/files/pdf/training/primers/2014_Primer_Departure_Variance.pdf).

Or suppose the offender has evaded capture for decades and has shown himself or herself to be able to live respectably. It may be overly formalistic to insist that these factors must be immaterial to sentencing just because they cannot be reconciled with desert.

Recognizing these exceptions does not require that we reject the principle of proportionality as I have construed it. A different strategy is advisable: we should preserve the principle but weaken its strength. The weight of a principle, as I understand it, is a function of how easy or difficult it is to outweigh when it competes with other principles (Lord and Maguire 2016). I take the above discussion to show that the principle of proportionality is not especially weighty. We can maintain what we roughly believe proportionality requires while allowing exceptions, as long as we find a good rationale to do so. If the force of proportionality can be outweighed without too much difficulty, it turns out to have fewer implications for the severity of the punishment to actually be imposed than many retributivists appear to believe. If we have a good reason to inflict different quanta of punishment on two offenders who have committed the same crime with the same amount of culpability, we should not be overly worried that one sentence or the other does not implement proportionality. If I am correct, sentencing officials can appeal to all kinds of non-desert or consequentialist factors with little opposition from retributivists (Kolber 2013).

Again, my point is that the desert considerations represented by proportionality should play a relatively small role in overall judgments of punishment severity. This conclusion is not equivalent to holding that proportionality plays only a limiting role. Desert does not merely set an upper and lower bound or range within which other considerations operate. Even if we somehow were able to make accurate proportionality calculations, we still would have a great many other grounds for departing from the sentence it would require. My point is that our inability to make precise proportionality determinations is less worrisome to the extent that instrumentalist concerns play a larger role in overall judgments of sentencing severity. Hence, imprecision in the principle of proportionality is not a cause for panic. The weakness of this principle supplies the best explanation of how sentencing authorities are able to get by in the real world despite their inability to solve the many problems I have identified. There is no urgency to solve these problems with any precision, because desert plays only a minor role in sentencing.

Recent history in sentencing drug offenders illustrates the general view I have in mind. Since the introduction of drug courts, quite a few defendants have been diverted to treatment programs, while others have not. At one point, I questioned how this disparity could be justifiable. The treatment program mandated by a drug court and the punishment imposed by a traditional court are almost certain to differ in their severity (Husak 2011). How can both sentences possibly implement proportionality? Drug court enthusiasts have been sensitive to this difficulty and have long felt pressure to ensure that treatment regimens are onerous so that they do not deviate from proportionality (Nolan 2001). But a different response to this phenomenon is not to increase the severity of treatment regimes but to acknowledge the weakness of the principle of proportionality. Even when two offenders have committed the same crime with the same amount of culpability, evidence that each is likely to respond favorably to different sanctions may be sufficient to warrant a deviation from proportionality and desert.

If I am correct that desert plays a relatively small a role in all-things-considered sentencing determinations, why not punish in excess of desert when consequentialist goods can be attained? Have I not opened the door to mandatory minimums, three-strike laws, and other draconian measures? In reply, I doubt that desert plays a single, simple role in a theory of sentencing. I rely on the familiar belief that too much punishment is a far worse injustice than too little. Thus, we would need to be supremely confident of the efficacy of any punitive measure that exceeds the offender's desert. The foregoing innovations in sentencing policy clearly fail to meet this exacting standard. A punishment that is more severe than what is deserved is very hard to justify; a punishment that is less than what is deserved is not.

I hope my attempt to salvage a role for proportionality is not entirely ad hoc. The weight of proportionality is weak because proportionality is a principle of desert, and the weight of desert is weak in our all-things-considered judgments about how persons (offenders or otherwise) should be treated. Elsewhere, I have argued that a host of familiar problems in the philosophy of punishment can be avoided by contrasting two questions: first, what punishment p is deserved, and second, should the state actually impose p (Husak 2010)? I believe the significance of judgments of desert in sentencing is not especially great; more weight should be placed on consequentialist considerations when we turn to the second of these questions. Thus, we should be willing to accept a deflationary role for proportionality if we regard it as part of a general theory of desert (Hoskins 2018). I encourage retributivists to try to solve the problems I have presented. But they can stumble along tolerably well in the meanwhile, accepting a less central role for proportionality and desert without abandoning their relevance in a theory of sentencing.

VII. Conclusion

Identifying the metric of punishment severity involves a host of quagmires. What do these enormous difficulties entail about the fate of proportionality and a retributive theory of punishment? If the weight of the principle of proportionality is not especially great, is it nonetheless true that desert figures centrally in the justification of punishment, which I hold to be the defining mark of a retributivist theory? No definitive answer can be given unless we know how central desert must be in order for a theory to qualify as a version of retributivism. We should probably understand a commitment to retributivism to admit of degrees, so that some theorists turn out to be more retributivist than others. One theory is more retributive than another not because it recommends harsher punishments across the spectrum of offenses but rather because it affords a more central role to desert in sentencing philosophy. This way to conceptualize retributivism strikes me as all but inevitable once we admit that not everything of importance about the justification of punishment should be derived from considerations of desert. As I believe the arguments in this essay indicate, much that is important about the justification of sentencing cannot be derived from principles of desert.

References

Bronsteen, John, Christopher Buccafusco, and Jonathan Masur. 2009. "Happiness and Punishment." *University of Chicago Law Review* 76:1037–81.

Duff, R. A. 2001. *Punishment, Communication, and Community*. Oxford: Oxford University Press.

Dworkin, Ronald. 1977. "Taking Rights Seriously." In *Taking Rights Seriously*, edited by Ronald Dworkin. Cambridge: Harvard University Press.

Farrell, Ian P. 2010. "Gilbert & Sullivan and Scalia: Philosophy, Proportionality, and the Eighth Amendment." *Villanova Law Review* 55:321–68.

Feinberg, Joel. 1970. "The Expressive Function of Punishment." In *Doing and Deserving*, edited by Joel Feinberg. Princeton: Princeton University Press.

Gray, David. 2010. "Punishment as Suffering." *Vanderbilt Law Review* 63:1619–93.

Hadjimatheou, Katerina. 2016. "Criminal Labelling, Publicity and Punishment." *Law and Philosophy* 35:567–93.

Hart, H. L. A. 1968. *Punishment and Responsibility: Essays in the Philosophy of Law*. Oxford: Oxford University Press.

Hoskins, Zachary. 2018. "Multiple-Offense Sentencing Discounts: Score One for Hybrid Accounts of Punishment." In *Sentencing Multiple Crimes*, edited by Jesper Ryberg, Julian V. Roberts, and Jan W. De Keijser. Oxford: Oxford University Press.

Husak, Douglas. 2010. "Already Punished Enough." In *The Philosophy of Criminal Law*, edited by Douglas Husak. Oxford: Oxford University Press.

Husak, Douglas. 2011. "Retributivism, Proportionality, and the Challenge of the Drug Court Movement." In *Retributivism Has a Past. Has It a Future?* edited by Michael Tonry. Oxford: Oxford University Press.

Husak, Douglas. 2016. "Does the State Have a Monopoly to Punish Crime?" In *The New Philosophy of Criminal Law*, edited by Chad Flanders and Zachary Hoskins. New York: Rowman & Littlefield.

Husak, Douglas. 2018. "Modes of Punishment." In *Essays on the Influence of Larry Alexander*, edited by Heidi Hurd. Cambridge: Cambridge University Press.

Jacobs, James B. 2015. *The Eternal Criminal Record*. Cambridge: Harvard University Press.

Kahan, Dan. 1996. "What Do Alternative Sanctions Mean?" *University of Chicago Law Review* 63:591–653.

Kahan, Dan. 1998. "Punishment Incommensurability." *Buffalo Journal of Criminal Law* 1:691–708.

Katz, Leo. 1996. *Ill-Gotten Gains: Evasion, Blackmail, Fraud, and Kindred Puzzles of the Law*. Chicago: University of Chicago Press.

Kolber, Adam J. 2009a. "The Comparative Nature of Punishment." *Boston University Law Review* 89:1565–608.

Kolber, Adam J. 2009b. "The Subjective Experience of Punishment." *Columbia Law Review* 109:182–236.

Kolber, Adam J. 2012. "Unintentional Punishment." *Legal Theory* 18:1–29.

Kolber, Adam J. 2013. "Against Proportional Punishment." *Vanderbilt Law Review* 66:1141–79.

Kolber, Adam J. 2018. "Punishment and Moral Risk." *University of Illinois Law Review* 2018:487–532.

Lacey, Nicola, and Hanna Pickard. 2015. "The Chimera of Proportionality: Instituti onalising Limits on Punishment in Contemporary Social and Political Systems." *Modern Law Review* 78(2):216–40.

Lee, Daisy. 2017. "Day Fining: Its Justifications, Effects, and Place in a Democratic Society." Unpublished manuscript, Rutgers University, Department of Philosophy.

Lord, Errol, and Barry Maguire, eds. 2016. *Weighing Reasons*. Oxford: Oxford University Press.

May, David C., and Peter B. Wood. 2010. *Ranking Correctional Punishments: Views from Offenders, Practitioners, and the Public*. Durham: Carolina Academic Press.

Mayson, Sandra G. 2015. "Collateral Consequences and the Preventive State." *Notre Dame Law Review* 91:301–61.

McAdams, Richard H. 2015. *The Expressive Powers of Law*. Cambridge: Harvard University Press.

McDonald, Douglas C., Judith Greene, and Charles Worzella. 1992. *Day Fines in American Courts: The Staten Island and Milwaukee Experiments*. Washington, DC: National Institute of Justice, Department of Justice.

McMahan, Jeff. 2008. *Killing in War*. Oxford: Oxford University Press.

Nolan, James L. 2001. *Reinventing Justice: The American Drug Court Movement*. Princeton: Princeton University Press.

Oldenquist, Andrew. 1988. "An Explanation of Retribution." *Journal of Philosophy* 85:468–78.

Raaijmakers, E.A.C. 2017. "The Subjectively Experienced Severity of Imprisonment: Determinants and Consequences." PhD dissertation, Meijers Research Institute and Graduate School of the Leiden Law School.

Rawls, John. 1955. "Two Concepts of Rules." *Philosophical Review* 64:3–32.

Roberts, Julian V., and Andreas [Andrew] von Hirsch, eds. 2010. *Previous Convictions at Sentencing*. Oxford: Hart.

Robinson, Paul. 1987. "A Sentencing Scheme for the 21st Century." *Texas Law Review* 66:1–61.

Ryberg, Jesper. 2018. "Retributivism, Multiple Offending, and Overall Proportionality." In *Sentencing Multiple Crimes*, edited by Jesper Ryberg, Julian V. Roberts, and Jan W. De Keijser. Oxford: Oxford University Press.

Ryberg, Jesper. 2019. "Proportionality and the Seriousness of Crimes." In *Of One-Eyed and Toothless Miscreants: Making the Punishment Fit the Crime?* edited by Michael Tonry. New York: Oxford University Press.

Simmons, Kenneth W. 2009. "Retributivists Need Not and Should Not Endorse the Subjectivist Account of Punishment." *Columbia Law Review* 109:1–10.

Temkin, Larry S. 1985. *Inequality*. New York: Oxford University Press.

Thoreau, Henry David. 1968. "Civil Disobedience." In *The Writings of Henry David Thoreau*. New York: AMS.

Von Hirsch, Andreas [Andrew]. 1993. *Censure and Sanctions*. Oxford: Clarendon.

Von Hirsch, Andreas [Andrew]. 1998. "Seriousness, Severity, and the Living Standard." In *Principled Sentencing*, 2nd ed., edited by Andreas [Andrew] von Hirsch and Andrew Ashworth. Oxford: Hart.

Von Hirsch, Andreas [Andrew], and Nils Jareborg. 1991. "Gauging Criminal Harm: A Living-Standard Analysis." *Oxford Journal of Legal Studies* 11:1–38.

6

Penal Severity and the Modern State

Richard L. Lippke

IF WE SUBSCRIBE to the proposition that criminal offenders ought to be punished proportionately with the seriousness of their crimes, we will need to devise accounts of the seriousness of criminal offenses and the severity of penal sanctions. We will then need to explain how we should go about linking the crime seriousness and penal severity rankings, a challenge that Andreas von Hirsch (1993) has referred to as finding the "anchoring points" of a sentencing scheme (p. 19). In developing an account of crime severity, the notions of harm and culpability figure prominently. Crimes vary considerably in the damage they do, threaten, or attempt, and offending agents vary in the responsibility they have for acting in ways to cause or risk this damage. This much is familiar territory in the scholarly literature on criminal law and penal theory (Gross 1979; Feinberg 1984; von Hirsch and Jareborg 1991; Alexander and Ferzan 2009). Less familiar is how we should construct an account of penal severity. Should criminal sanctions be gauged by the amount of suffering they inflict on offenders—difficult as that might be to ascertain or measure—or by some proxy for suffering, such as dollar amounts of fines or the days, months, or years spent in custody? Put differently, how should we conceive of the currency of penal hard treatment so that we can grasp whether we have apportioned enough of it, or too much of it, to the criminal offenders under the state's purview?

Richard Lippke is Professor of Criminal Justice at Indiana University.

In section I of this essay, I develop an account of penal severity in the modern state. Among the varied tasks of the modern state, one stands out: it is charged with securing the basic moral rights of its citizens. What those basic rights consist of is, as we will see, a matter of some controversy. But there is less controversy about the agency tasked with seeing to their provision. The enforcement of conduct prohibitions of various kinds, in the form of criminal law, figures prominently in the state fulfilling its responsibilities. Yet as the state secures the basic rights of individuals, it must also respect them. It might be possible for the state to justify abridging those rights in some cases, but it should not be easy to do so if rights are to be accorded their proper weight. The state should have to demonstrate that the penal sanctions it employs advance legitimate purposes. Arguably, it should also have to show that they are proportionate to the seriousness of crimes and nondegrading. I contend that right abridgment can satisfy these conditions, and thus, it makes sense to conceive of penal severity in terms of the extent and duration of such abridgment. Other kinds of measures the state might employ, and historically has employed, will undoubtedly make punishment more awful but are not among the defensible weapons in the state's penal arsenal.

In section II, I take up various objections to the account of penal severity developed in section I. In one way or another, all of these objections hold that an account focused on right abridgment is inadequate because it does not take seriously the subjective experiences of the individuals being punished. In responding to these objections, I elaborate the right-abridgment approach. I grant that like offenders will experience proportionate punishments differently. But unless these differences in subjective experience are apt to produce deterioration in their capacities for responsiveness to moral considerations, I argue that they were risked by offenders when they acted in ways that they had both moral and prudential reasons to avoid. I also suggest that it is preferable for the state to keep its distance from efforts to manipulate the interior lives of citizens, including those of criminal offenders.

In section III, I discuss some hard cases for my own account. These are cases that seem to suggest that in some circumstances, or in limited ways, we should admit a role for subjective experience in our understanding of penal severity. I resist this suggestion, offering alternative solutions to the problems such cases raise.

Section IV concludes.

I. Penal Severity in the Modern State

Political theorists of a wide variety of stripes assign the modern state the task of securing the basic moral rights of its citizens. Disagreements among such theorists consist of varying accounts of the ground or basis of such rights, as well as the specific rights to be guaranteed by the state. The former disagreements concern whether rights secure certain vital interests or capacities of persons, help them meet their needs, promote the conditions of their agency, or do something else.[1] The latter disagreements concern whether the modern state should focus solely on protecting the liberty of persons or go beyond this to ensure some material equality for all citizens, including equality of input into the governance of their common affairs. Whatever their other differences, contemporary political theorists conceive of persons as beings who are equally entitled, within limits, to reflect on and carve out lives of their own choosing.[2] One common way of capturing all of this is to speak of the dignity of persons and the moral urgency of respecting and protecting it.[3] It is a short step from this notion to the familiar features of modern criminal law with its prohibitions on killing, violence, assault, and predation in all its forms.

It is important to note that basic moral rights are not the kinds of things that are supposed to be easy for the state to justify infringing (Waldron 1993). Although political theorists disagree about how to conceive of such rights and their demands on us, they generally agree that these rights and demands furnish weighty reasons against the state coercively interfering in the lives of individuals. Indeed, it is not uncommon to see the central problem of punishment theory cast in terms of the necessity of providing a persuasive account of how the state acts appropriately in depriving citizens of things to which they are usually believed to be entitled (Berman 2008; Wellman 2017). Not only must punishment be shown to serve defensible state purposes—the prevention of future crime or the allocation to offenders of their just deserts are the two dominant rationales—but the state must also bear the burden of proving,

---

1. For a useful overview of the current state of play in the foundations of human rights, see the essays in part 1 of Cruft, Liao, and Renzo (2015).

2. John Braithwaite and Philip Pettit (1990) capture something akin to this with their notion of dominion. They claim that it is an uncontroversial target for the criminal law. However, in characterizing dominion in terms of the assurance of citizens that they possess and can enjoy certain negative liberties, Braithwaite and Pettit reveal their libertarian leanings with respect to what constitutes the basic moral rights of persons.

3. Although commonly invoked, the notion of dignity or human dignity is not without controversy. See, among others, Waldron (2012), Kateb (2011), Rosen (2012), and Beitz (2013).

beyond a reasonable doubt, that those it has accused of crimes are guilty of them before it acts to intrude upon their rights.

Beyond this, it has been argued that such intrusions should not exceed those necessary to serve legitimate penal purposes (Morris 1982; Tonry 1992; Frase 2013), they must be kept proportionate both comparatively and absolutely with the seriousness of criminal offenses (von Hirsch 1993), and they must not be permitted to degrade offenders (Lippke 2014). The first constraint on penal sanctions, known as the principle of parsimony, can be defended by both crime reductionists and retributivists, although it is perhaps more often associated with the former. The idea that legal sanctions should be kept to the minimum necessary in order to serve appropriate penal purposes makes sense within a human-rights framework that takes the abridgment of rights to be a morally fraught enterprise. If it is difficult to justify depriving individuals of their rights, then arguably, the state must proceed with caution and circumspection in doing so, taking no more from those convicted of crimes than is necessary to serve defensible penal purposes.

The proportionality constraint is more closely associated with retributive accounts of legal punishment, although consequentialist versions of it can be defended (Frase 2013, p. 62). We can make sense of it within a rights framework by invoking the notion that the state, if it is to respect individuals, must treat them according to their choices with regard to criminal law. Criminal offenses vary considerably in their gravity; and the state, if it is to take seriously differences among offenders and the choices they have made in exceeding their rights, must key penal sanctions to their offenses. Simply put—too simply, in fact, because some crimes lack victims, and offender culpability must be taken into account in devising and assigning penal sanctions—if the state overpunishes offenders, it takes more from them than they took from their victims and thus treats offenders unjustly (Lippke 2012). If it underpunishes offenders, it demeans their victims by making the crimes against them seem less serious than they were (Hampton 1991).

The third constraint on penal sanctions, the requirement that they not degrade offenders, depends on a view about the appropriate subjects of punishment that is most closely associated with retributive theories of its justification. Such theories assume that the appropriate subjects of legal punishment are what some have termed *moral-reasons responsive* (Wallace 1996; Fischer and Ravizza 2000). To say that someone is moral-reasons responsive is to say that he or she is capable of understanding the moral reasons for abiding by the criminal law and conforming his or her conduct to those reasons. In the absence of such responsiveness, moral blame for criminal conduct makes little sense. It is for that reason, according to retributivists, that we should not punish infants, the insane, or the mentally disabled. Of course, many individuals are less than fully responsive to the moral reasons they have to abide by the criminal law. They are weak-willed or overcome by anger or temptation and thus commit crimes. But absent a narrowly tailored set of liability-excusing conditions recognized by criminal law, most adults are presumed capable of controlling their conduct so as to respect the rights of other citizens.

What bearing does this have on our thinking about appropriate penal sanctions? Arguably, it should lead us to rule out forms of hard treatment that degrade persons either quickly and more or less inexorably (for instance, torture or starvation) or more slowly and, perhaps, more contingently (for instance, isolation) (Lippke 2014). Here I use the term *degradation* to refer to the tendency of certain kinds of penal hard treatment to destroy or diminish the moral-reasons responsiveness of offenders. Such sanctions are at odds with a theory that deems legal punishment to make sense only for beings capable of moral responsibility.[4] Note also that offenders who are degraded will be unlikely to abide by moral constraints on their conduct once they have served their sentences, a point that crime reductionists could readily acknowledge.

Putting all of this together, we get an account of the modern state as one for which the currency of penal hard treatment consists of justifiably imposed departures from the normative standard of equal citizenship, where that standard is understood in terms of state guarantees of certain basic moral rights. Since basic moral rights are presumptively weighty, the state should abridge the rights of proven criminal offenders no more than is necessary to punish them proportionately to the seriousness of their crimes. Further, in inflicting justified losses or deprivations on offenders, the state must assiduously avoid forms of penal hard treatment that are degrading.

In opposition to the preceding analysis, some penal theorists have suggested that criminal offenders should be understood as having forfeited all or some of their moral rights or as having them suspended for the duration of their sentences (Morris 1991; McDermott 2001). However, full forfeiture or suspension views are deeply problematic (Quinn 1985; Lippke 2007).

---

4. It is tempting to trace the nondegradation constraint to Immanuel Kant (1991), who famously held that while murderers ought to be executed, doing so "must still be freed from any mistreatment that could make the humanity in the person suffering it into something abominable" (p. 141). However, immediately preceding his announcement of this apparent constraint on punishment, Kant endorses solitary confinement and forced labor for some offenders.

They imply that state officials, or even private citizens, can treat offenders as if they no longer have any rights. This would permit officials, with more or less complete moral impunity, to impose all manner of losses or deprivations on offenders. Partial forfeiture or suspension views are more plausible, although even they suggest that serious offenders lose the relevant rights in their entirety rather than having them substantially curtailed. I doubt that we should say of prison inmates, for instance, that they retain no liberty right to move about in their cells as they see fit or within the prison as long as they abide by defensible conduct rules. Could prison officials, for instance, justifiably order inmates to continually walk in circles within their cells or to ask permission to move within them? I suspect that we would not want to go that far in characterizing what the state permissibly may do to imprisoned offenders.

A more plausible view holds that legal punishment in the modern state consists of justified infringements of the basic moral rights of individuals or, in the case of more serious crimes, the justified and perhaps quite substantial curtailment of such rights. A survey of the kinds of sanctions typically employed in modern political states seems to confirm this. Fines, probation, and community service represent the mild end of the penal spectrum. Individuals who are assigned such sanctions can usually absorb them and still go about their lives. Large fines might impede the abilities of persons to do so, unless provisions are made to permit individuals to pay them off in installments. Nonetheless, a crimp in one's lifestyle is only that, not a major impediment to the pursuit of one's projects or the realization of one's interests. Intensive forms of probation, electronic monitoring, or home confinement are more severe sanctions because they impose more substantial deviations from the normative standard of equal rights to which all persons are entitled. The abilities of persons assigned such sanctions to live as they choose will be stunted somewhat for the duration of their sentences. However, it is still preferable to be free to move about in civil society, subject to certain restrictions or reporting requirements, or to be confined to one's own residence, than to be confined in a custodial institution. That much seems clear and explains why such intermediate sanctions are deemed less severe than assignment to a jail or prison. However, intermediate sanctions can be combined in ways that make them almost as onerous to offenders as brief stays in custodial institutions (Tonry and Lynch 1996). By onerous, I refer to the tendency of such combined sanctions to impose limitations on the abilities of offenders to move about freely in society or to choose activities to their liking for the duration of their sentences.

Imprisonment is a harsher sanction because it does more than impose on the free choices of individuals; it also curtails them significantly for a period of time. In the Scandinavian countries, so-called open prisons curtail liberty less drastically, since inmates can come and go freely from them, at least during the daytime (Pratt 2008). Closed prisons, by contrast, more fully curtail liberty and, because liberty is needed to enjoy and exercise other rights, impinge upon them as well. Yet even closed prisons vary to some extent. Consider the contrast between super-maximum-security prisons, which leave inmates with sparse opportunities to exercise their agency, and the more humane closed prisons in some of the northern European countries or the minimum-security prisons in the United States and elsewhere.[5]

It seems clear that right-abridgment accounts of penal severity, according to which criminal sanctions are more severe to the extent and for the time that they limit enjoyment or exercise of the rights of offenders, align with the dominant crime-reduction and retributive justifications of legal punishment. The prospect of right abridgment should generally deter would-be offenders and might especially deter recidivism. Such abridgments will predictably have greater deterrent effects the more, or the longer, they threaten to disrupt the lives of offenders or would-be offenders. Also, right abridgment will incapacitate offenders, especially as we move toward the more severe end of the sanction range with its employment of custodial sentences. Right abridgment alone might not rehabilitate offenders, but in combination with educational programs, drug treatment, work training, and the like, it could be made to do so. More serious offenders might be in need of more interruption in their abilities to carry on with their lives if they are to be successfully rehabilitated. Custodial sanctions provide that interruption, although again, penal confinement, all by itself, seems ill suited to reforming offenders (Haney 2006; Lippke 2007).

Conceiving of penal severity in terms of right abridgment also coheres with the logic of retributive accounts of legal punishment. Depriving offenders of things to which they are normally entitled as citizens censures them and their misconduct, and the more so the greater the deprivations imposed and their duration (von Hirsch 1993). In doing so, it also symbolically represents the value of any victims' lives and interests (Hampton 1991). Right abridgment also can be understood as depriving offenders of the unfair advantages they have gained over their fellow citizens in ignoring the justified limits of criminal law (Murphy 1973; Sadurski 1985; Sher 1987). Finally, if deserved punishment

---

5. For a description of super-maximum security prisons and their effects on inmates, see Haney (2003). A strong case can be made that such prisons degrade offenders. For an account of prisons in Germany, see Lazarus (2004).

is an intrinsic good, there seems to be no reason it could not take the form of state-imposed abridgment of the rights that individuals are usually entitled to exercise and enjoy, which abridgment should vary in its extent and duration depending on the seriousness of the crimes to be punished (Moore 1997).

One complication with the right-abridgment account of penal severity that I have described is the divide among political theorists concerning which basic moral rights individuals possess. Simplifying a great deal, at one extreme are libertarian or minimal-state views, which afford individuals a modest set of basic rights (typically, to life, liberty, and property), which are usually construed negatively, that is, as rights against interferences of certain kinds (Nozick 1974; Lomasky 1987; Narveson 1988; Barnett 1998). At the other extreme are egalitarian views according to which individuals have many more basic rights—to high social-welfare floors, meaningful democratic participation in all institutions and practices affecting their lives, and robust forms of political and economic equality (Nielsen 1985; Sen 1995; Roemer 2000; Cohen 2008). In between are welfare-liberal accounts, which go beyond minimal-state theories in ascribing rights to individuals to social-welfare minima (of varying degrees and kinds). Such theories also support market regulatory measures designed to facilitate work and protect individuals from unbridled economic competition (Rawls 1971; Ackerman 1980; von Parijs 1995; Dworkin 2000). Each of these accounts of the basic moral rights of persons will yield a different normative baseline against which penal losses and deprivations might be measured. This raises the question of whether we must accept plural accounts of penal severity or sidestep this theoretical dissensus and defend a single account.

Fortunately, there might be enough overlap among the competing conceptions of basic moral rights to yield some commonality in their respective scales of penal severity. All the plausible competing theories value the liberty of individuals and, with it, the right of individuals to carve out lives of their own reflective choosing. All defend freedom of speech and conscience and the right of persons to use their resources, including personal property, as they see fit (though within limits). Granted, the competing theories articulate and defend different limits to such self-shaping, but these differences are apt to be at the margins.[6] Thus, liberty abridgment should resonate as a means of constraining hard treatment within all accounts of the moral rights of persons. Similarly, fines, which deprive persons of some of their personal

---

6. For instance, theorists might disagree about whether things such as hate speech ought to be protected or whether certain forms of self-harming behavior (e.g., the use of drugs) should be.

property, should function as an appropriate sanction across theories that assign different limits to the acquisition and use of property.[7]

To be clear, the suggestion that there might be sufficient overlap among the competing theories of human rights to yield a consensus account of penal severity does not mean that no disagreements will remain. Consider closed prison confinement and the ways in which the curtailment of liberty will limit the exercise and enjoyment of other rights—to freedom of association, labor, religious exercise, and privacy. It is possible for the state to take steps to ameliorate the ways in which liberty curtailment impinges on the exercise and enjoyment of these other rights. Indeed, a strong case for its doing so can be made by invoking the principle of parsimony and the nondegradation constraint (Tonry 2004; Lippke 2007). For instance, the state could facilitate the labor of inmates by developing prison industries or entering into contracts with private corporations that would employ inmates and pay them wages for their work (Lippke 2007). Welfare liberals and egalitarians might support the facilitation of prison labor, believing it to be the state's obligation to provide inmates with opportunities to work. Failure by the state to do so might be seen by them as increasing the severity of the sanctions suffered by offenders, who would experience more of their rights abridged in its absence. Libertarians, by contrast, might believe it is up to inmates to somehow cobble together access to paid labor (Lee and Wollin 1985). Alternatively, and perhaps more realistically, libertarians might think it appropriate to seek reimbursement from inmates for any work facilitated by the state. Libertarians might also be more inclined to charge inmates for some or all of the costs of their confinement, rather than treating them as wards of the state. It is important that libertarians might not view required inmate contributions to work facilitation or to room and board as increasing the severity of offenders' sentences. No one, they might say, is entitled to a "free lunch," and those who have committed serious crimes are not entitled to have the state help them gain access to work or provide for their needs.

In spite of this, my sense is that the areas of agreement about penal severity among competing accounts of the basic moral rights of persons will outnumber the areas of disagreement. For all such accounts, confinement in a closed prison is more rights-restricting than confinement in an open prison, which is worse than home confinement, intensive probation, and so on down

---

7. It is worth noting that although there are different conceptions among countries concerning the human rights that their citizens possess, the range of criminal sanctions employed are remarkably similar. Fines, forms of probation, and custodial sanctions are ubiquitous.

the line. Also, the longer the duration of penal sanctions of whatever kind, the more they infringe on or curtail rights, and thus, the more severe they will turn out to be.

Two further points might be made in anticipation of some arguments that focusing on the subjective experience of punishment, rather than on state abridgment of basic rights, gives a better measure of penal severity. The modern state is not conceived to be responsible for micromanaging the lives of its citizens or entitled to do so. Instead, the state secures certain basic capacities of persons, along with opportunities for their exercise and enjoyment, then stands back and lets individuals run their own lives, for better or worse. If individuals do poor jobs of choosing their careers, hobbies, and pursuits or their spouses, friends, and associates, the state is not conceived of as responsible for stepping in and helping them do better. Granted, some theorists defend limited forms of legal paternalism, but respect for the autonomous choices of competent adults is a powerful regulatory ideal in modern political thought (Feinberg 1986, 1990). As long as individuals faithfully observe the limits of criminal law, the modern state is supposed to keep its distance from the lives of its citizens.

There is considerable variation in the extent to which persons choose to exercise or enjoy some of their basic moral rights. Some individuals may use their liberty to travel far, widely, and often. Others rarely leave their homes or local communities. Likewise, some individuals may exercise rights to freedom of speech or the free exercise of religion frequently and vigorously. Others seldom, if ever, do so. Yet there is little support among political theorists for the proposition that the state ought to expand or enhance the basic rights of citizens who often exercise or enjoy them or to contract the rights of persons who rarely do so. Instead, the state's role is standardly conceived of as ensuring the equal rights of citizens regardless of variations in the extent to which citizens put those rights to use.

II. The Subjective Experience of Punishment

Penal theorists who urge us to pay more attention to the subjective experience of legal punishment in evaluating its severity offer a number of arguments (Kolber 2009a, 2009b; Masur, Bronsteen, and Buccafusco 2009; Hayes 2016). Adam Kolber is the most insistent advocate of taking subjective experience into account, but others concur with him in holding that an exclusive focus on right abridgment will not suffice to yield a defensible understanding of penal severity.

One argument advanced by Kolber and others is that the subjective experience of the punished must matter at least to the extent that they are aware that they are being punished (Kolber 2009*b*; Husak 2019). Kolber asks us to imagine someone who is sentenced to home confinement but who, due to a series of miscommunications, does not realize that his sentence has commenced or that a guard is stationed outside his front door (2009*b*, p. 204). By the time he decides to leave his home a week later, his sentence is served, and the guard has left. Though the offender's rights have been curtailed, he has surely not been punished, since he was entirely unaware of his confinement.

As Kolber seems to recognize, this argument does not advance us very far down the road toward having to take the subjective experience of punishment into account when constructing a defensible account of penal severity. I would agree that in order to be punished, offenders must understand that they are being made to endure some abridgment of their rights. Fortunately, the overwhelming majority of persons punished will easily satisfy this requirement, assuming they are not deranged, comatose, infants, or severely mentally disabled and thus unsuitable candidates for legal punishment to begin with. Individuals who have endured arrest, arraignment, pretrial detention, trial or plea negotiations, judicial sentencing, and transport to prison facilities if they have been assigned custodial sanctions will very likely realize that they are in the state's grasp. Indeed, competent adult offenders who do not realize they are being punished are almost entirely fanciful creatures. In any case, ensuring that they understand what is happening to them will not require state officials to inquire very far into how much or in what specific ways offenders are suffering.

A second argument that Kolber advances involves a sadistic warden who surreptitiously introduces a chemical into the drinking water of prison inmates that renders them fearful and anxious (2009*b*, p. 197). Kolber thinks it obvious that the increased suffering caused by the warden's actions makes the punishment of the prison inmates worse. This suggests that the subjective experience of punishment must be taken into account in gauging penal severity. That the warden's actions will make the subjective experience of punishment worse cannot be denied. Of course, the same would be true if the warden ordered inmates to be beaten, tortured, starved, deprived of sleep, and a host of other things. Yet none of these is a justifiable form of state punishment, for two identifiable reasons. First, they are neither necessary to advance defensible penal aims nor apt to do so. Right abridgment will serve such aims and can be kept free of abuses that will devastate offenders' lives, rendering them more apt to commit further crimes. Second, almost all of the aforementioned

horrific penal measures will destroy or diminish the moral-reasons responsiveness of offenders, thus running afoul of the nondegradation constraint.
Granted, there are lots of ghastly things that state officials have employed or
might employ to reduce offenders to mere shadows of human beings, but they
are not among the legitimate tools of legal punishment at the beck and call of
the modern state. Kolber's argument for taking the subjective experience into
account in determining its severity is, in this instance, convincing only if we
are prepared to permit the state to resort to penal measures with very dubious
credentials.

Kolber also contends that failure to take the subjective experience of
offenders into account will produce disproportionality in punishment, something that retributivists, in particular, will strongly wish to avoid. He contrasts
"sensitive" with "less sensitive" offenders (2009b, p. 187). The former, if
assigned custodial sentences, will suffer in ways and to a degree that the latter
will not, even if both kinds of offenders committed identical crimes. For instance, an offender from the middle or upper classes, who is used to creature
comforts, will presumably suffer more from prison confinement than a homeless offender who is used to sleeping on the streets and scrounging for food.
If suffering is the measure of just punishment, as Kolber contends it is for
most retributivists, then failure to shorten or otherwise adjust the sentences
of sensitive offenders will inevitably result in their not being punished com-
mensurately with their less sensitive counterparts, in violation of ordinal proportionality requirements.

The problem with this argument is that it assumes that an account of proportionality in punishment that focuses on the ways in which penal sanctions
abridge basic moral rights is implausible or unworkable. Again, such an account posits that the severity of penal sanctions should be measured by the
types and duration of penal impositions on the basic rights of offenders. Fines
impose modest burdens on the rights of offenders. Probation, home confinement, and custody in closed prisons impose more substantial burdens—and
the more so the longer they persist. Punishment of offenders will be proportional, in the sense that like offenders will be treated alike, as long as penal
impositions are keyed to the offenses in question, perhaps along with being
keyed to other relevant sentencing factors (e.g., criminal history). If two otherwise similar drug offenders receive roughly the same sentences, then they
are treated alike. How their similar sentences affect their subjective experience of punishment is a different matter and, arguably, of little relevance
to those who hold that right abridgment is the most defensible currency of
penal severity in the modern state. Kolber cannot assert that because we are

ignoring differences in the two offenders' subjective experience of punishment, they are not being treated alike without begging the question against such accounts. That such accounts have some plausibility would be hard to deny. An offender who receives a 5-year prison sentence suffers more losses (to liberty and perhaps to other right-protected interests) and for longer than an offender who receives a 2-year sentence to a similar facility. The former is, in a straightforward sense, punished more than the latter.

The right-abridgment account seems to square with at least some of our intuitions about perceived injustices in punishment outcomes. There is in the United States disturbing evidence that black drug offenders are punished more harshly than white drug offenders, holding other factors constant (Davis 2007; Alexander 2012). Black drug offenders are more often sentenced to prison than similarly charged white drug offenders or are given longer prison sentences. Yet such concerns about disparate sentencing can be explicated by citing the differences in the objective right deprivations assigned to the two kinds of offenders. We need not, and, I suspect, typically do not, concern ourselves with how the two kinds of offenders subjectively experience their punishment.

Kolber is likely, at this point, to fall back on the claim that retributivists believe that offenders deserve to suffer for their crimes (2009*b*, p. 199). If he is correct about this, then the case for taking differences in the subjective experience of punishment into account will be hard for retributivists to resist. However, there is reason to doubt that retributivists must subscribe to the deserved-suffering view (see Gray 2010). And Kolber admits that some retributivists focus on more objective penal losses or deprivations such as abridging liberty or property rights. Kolber directs numerous arguments against such accounts. He claims that when people think about imprisonment, for instance, what they find worrisome about it is contemplation of the suffering they will experience if confined (2009*b*, p. 203). But it seems equally plausible to claim that what many find aversive about imprisonment is contemplation of the lost liberty to choose and act as they wish, to associate with anyone they please, and to work at jobs or careers they find rewarding or meaningful. All of these are losses that can be comprehended without having much understanding of precisely how much or in what ways they cause suffering.

Kolber also argues that if we focus on liberty deprivation as the primary mode of hard treatment, we will have to decide which liberties to deprive offenders of. If we take away the wrong ones, offenders might not find punishment aversive (2009*b*, pp. 204–5). This objection seems strained.

Imprisonment is fairly sweeping in its liberty-deprivation effects. Almost all offenders, no matter what their more specific aims and interests, will find that it drastically limits what they want to do; we can be pretty certain of that. Probation will likewise impose burdens on offenders regardless of their more specific interests, and more so the more intensive the forms it takes. Granted, some offenders will find penal burdens to be more difficult than other offenders, depending on their interests and pursuits or on what they have become accustomed to by way of their material living conditions. But it is not clear why we should have to cater to the sensitivities of such offenders. Surely, individuals who choose to commit crimes should be understood as bearing some responsibility for what they will have to endure if they are caught and convicted. This seems especially true if they were given fair notice of the likely sanctions they would encounter if they committed crimes, sanctions are kept proportionate (or not disproportionate) and nondegrading, offenders have clear and powerful moral reasons against committing crimes, and they have self-interested reasons against committing them. For all of these reasons, retributivists tend to be less moved by claims about the suffering of offenders than are consequentialists such as Kolber. Some hardships, losses, or sufferings are deserved, especially when individuals choose to offend despite the abundant reasons they have against doing so and despite their foreknowledge of the losses they will justifiably incur if the state catches and convicts them.[8]

Finally, Kolber argues that a liberty-deprivation account of penal severity will not work because some people have more liberty than others to begin with, usually because they have more income or wealth that enables them to go more places and do more things (2009a, pp. 27–33; 2009b, p. 207). Retributivists, he argues, will have to take these different baselines into account, or else penal hard treatment will, once again, run the risk of imposing dissimilar losses on like offenders. However, this argument rests on a deeply contentious view about what the state's responsibility is in relation to the liberty rights of its citizens. Numerous theories of rights permit significant inequalities in the income or wealth of citizens, although they insist that citizens must be guaranteed equal liberty rights (Rawls 1971; Nozick 1974). Only strongly egalitarian theories of human rights say that individuals' liberty

---

8. Kolber criticizes what he terms the "forewarned is forearmed" argument, claiming that it would license the use of disproportionate sanctions (2009b, pp. 210–11). But no clear-thinking retributivist would say that as long as we warn would-be offenders about the disproportionate (or degrading) sanctions we will inflict on them if they commit crimes and are convicted of them, we can go ahead and employ such sanctions. For a similar response to Kolber, see Markel and Flanders (2010, p. 962).

rights must be equalized by strictly limiting differences in the resources on which individuals can call in exercising them. On other conceptions of basic rights, individuals have equal liberty rights as long as the state protects them against violence and predation and against interferences with such things as their speech, religion, or conscience. By doing so, the state carves out areas of autonomy for all citizens in which they can live and act as they choose. State punishment of proven offenders, when it occurs, reduces this provision of autonomy in some manner or to some degree. This treats like offenders alike as long as the reductions reflect the gravity of the offenses they have committed.

Although Kolber urges us to pay more attention to the subjective experience of punishment, he does not claim that it should be the sole measure of punishment severity. Still, how far he would have us go in taking subjective experience into account is unclear. The only limits he seems to recognize on modifying penal sanctions in response to variations in the subjective experience of them depend on the likely negative consequences of our efforts to do so. For instance, he admits that it might produce more bad than good consequences to punish rich, sensitive offenders less harshly than their like-offending poor, insensitive counterparts, although the subjective experiences of punishment of the former will be significantly worse (2009*b*, p. 230). Likewise, he would presumably resist the suggestion that offenders who accept their punishment as just and fair and who thus cheerfully attempt to make the best of it should be punished with longer sentences than offenders who resist and resent their punishment and who are thus made miserable by it. Perhaps there will be convincing consequentialist reasons to discourage the state from going down such a path, along with a host of others somewhat like it. The problem is that once we are persuaded to go down such paths very far at all, we would be tempted to go farther. We will have to hope that consequentialist considerations convince us of the folly of doing so in each case. It might be better to insist on a more categorical or principled hesitancy on the part of the state to delve into the minds of the individuals it punishes and thus to attempt to manipulate their punishment experiences according to what its officials think is best or appropriate (Markel and Flanders 2010, pp. 982–84). Indeed, there is a rich vein of retributive thinking that counsels against state efforts to shape or mold the minds of offenders so that they adopt what state officials believe are appropriate attitudes toward or experiences of legal punishment (Hampton 1984, p. 232; Duff 1986, p. 254). The human dignity of offenders precludes such official meddling. Offenders should be left to their own devices in deciding how to respond to the sanctions that their crimes merit and in coping with them.

III. Hard Cases

To this point, I have taken an unyielding line against those who would urge the state to take the subjective experience of offenders into account in gauging the severity of criminal sanctions. However, in a few cases, I admit to some hesitation about this unyielding line.

Two examples that Kolber raises do give me pause. One of them involves an offender who suffers from claustrophobia (2009*b*, p. 190). If claustrophobes are assigned to a closed prison, even one that is respectful of the retained rights of serious offenders, they are apt to suffer in ways that are significantly worse than nonclaustrophobes. If it is agreed that such added suffering is morally problematic, does this not show that we must be prepared to take the subjective experience of offenders into account in calculating penal severity? Further, if it is admitted that claustrophobes' subjective experiences of the objective losses and deprivations imposed on them matters, then how can we avoid admitting the relevance of other differences among offenders in their subjective experiences of punishment? For instance, many offenders suffer from chronic forms of mental illness that do not suffice, under the law, to excuse them from criminal liability. If they are sentenced to jails or prisons, they will likely suffer in ways and to a degree that other offenders do not. Should we ignore this suffering, or should we, as Kolber might suggest, respond by assigning them noncustodial sentences or, at least, shorter custodial ones?

I would concede that the likely subjective experience of some offenders ought to be taken into account when we punish them, but I am not convinced that it matters in ways that cast doubt on either rights-based accounts of penal severity or retributive proportionality. Due to the special susceptibilities of some offenders, even generally humane and nondegrading imprisonment will cause them so much distress that they will, in relatively short order, deteriorate psychologically. Given this more or less unalterable fact about them, such offenders must be given special accommodations, in such forms as mental-health treatment, larger cells, or more time out of their cells. Yet these accommodations can be, in most cases, accounted for by the nondegradation constraint that retributivists and other penal theorists should embrace. In other words, it is not the simple fact of some offenders having atypically negative subjective experiences of punishment that matters but the fact that such experiences will imperil their moral-reasons responsiveness. In addition, retributivists could urge shorter or noncustodial sentences for certain susceptible offenders on grounds of their reduced culpability for their crimes.

The mentally ill but not insane might have to be treated, by the law, as liable for their criminal acts. However, retributivists could concede that the mentally ill are less culpable for their crimes and so ought to be given reduced sentences on account of it. Notice that this line of argument is unlikely to help claustrophobes, at least on the assumption that their condition does not affect their responsibility for their criminal acts.

Indeed, retributivists might be prepared to take a somewhat tougher line with offending claustrophobes than with mentally ill offenders. Assuming that the former's capacities for responsible conduct are not compromised by their condition, it might be suggested that individuals who realize that they will not do well in smallish, confined spaces ought to take special care to avoid serious forms of criminal conduct. This line is not unlike the one that retributivists might take with rich or sensitive offenders who find nondegrading and humane prisons to be nearly unendurable. The difference, of course, is that it might be thought that claustrophobes have considerably less control over their reactions to confinement than rich or otherwise sensitive offenders. The latter, it might be argued, should be able to adjust gradually to prison conditions that pass moral muster in ways that the former cannot. I can concede this point and fall back on the need to make special accommodations for claustrophobes to forestall their degradation under normal prison conditions. Still, suppose that a claustrophobe persists in serious offending, despite having experienced what life is like in a custodial setting. Should recidivist claustrophobes continue to be accommodated? I am less certain what to say about this.

Another example that Kolber and other penal scholars discuss is the use of fines as criminal sanctions (2009*b*, p. 226). As long as we imagine offenders to be what most of them are—poor or, at least, certainly not rich—it will seem that abridging their property rights in modest ways will convey censure to them that they can presumably grasp. The problem some have raised is with the use of fines as sanctions for rich or super-rich offenders. The impact of the kinds of fines typically used to sanction minor offenses will be negligible with such offenders, or so it seems. As a result, some countries instead use day fines that adjust the amount of the sanction to the income or wealth of offenders. By doing so, it is thought that better-off offenders can be made to feel the "penal bite" of such property-right infringements. But how can we make sense of this without admitting that it is the subjective experience of fines that matters for penal purposes? Is it not the differential suffering caused by fines that leads us to think that larger fines must be imposed on rich offenders?

It might be, but it also might be that we fear that rich offenders will not experience the censure of legal punishment at all or sufficiently if we do not adjust fines to reflect their levels of prosperity. Fines are typically reserved for criminal offenses that are relatively minor; nonetheless, the conduct in question is a public wrong that the state prohibits (Duff and Marshall 2010). When poor or middle-class offenders are fined $500, this will, for most, be a noticeable setback to their interests. When the rich or super-rich are fined $500 for some minor offense, state censure will be barely, if at all, perceptible to them. Or at least, that is the concern that might motivate the use of day fines. Of course, there might be exceptions to these surmises on both sides of the poor–rich divide. There might be poor offenders who view fines as little more than the cost of doing business (where their business consists of illegal activities of various kinds). And there might be rich misers who notice and are aggrieved horribly by every fine they have to pay, regardless of its impact on their wealth. I doubt that we should adjust fines for these outliers, although that is what a focus on subjective experience as the measure of penal severity might seem to suggest that we should do. Instead, we might prefer to have the state keep its distance from offenders and their internal lives by operating with assumptions about standard cases of offenders and what is needed to effectively convey state censure of their misconduct to them (von Hirsch and Jareborg 1991, p. 4).

IV. Conclusion

Other issues would have to be addressed in order to produce a fully elaborated account of penal severity. For instance, should the public infamy of criminal conviction be counted as increasing penal severity, even if it is not usually conceived of as something inflicted by the state as part of offenders' formal penal sanctions (Jacobs 2016)? Also, should the various collateral consequences of criminal conviction, ones typically encountered by offenders after they have served their formal sentences, be counted as increasing the severity of the state's penal response to crimes (Chin 2012; Lippke 2014)? Instead of pursuing these matters further, however, let me close with a point that I have so far ignored.

The account of penal severity that I have defended might seem all well and good as long as the state does indeed secure the basic moral rights of all its citizens, however these are conceived. But what if it does not? Many criminal offenders come from socially and economically disadvantaged backgrounds. Their families were poor, they grew up in economically devastated and crime-ridden neighborhoods, or they were the victims of racial, ethnic, or gender discrimination in some or all of its forms. It is natural to think that as a result, some of them resorted to criminal misconduct out of desperation, in order to eke out livings, or because doing so was almost normative in their communities of origin. The question I want to raise, in closing, is whether the account of penal severity that I have defended can in any way help us to understand qualms we might have about whether and how much to punish poor offenders.

The answer depends, to some extent, on the wider theory of basic moral rights to which one subscribes. Some of these theories, as we have seen, defend a limited array of rights, mostly consisting of liberty rights defined in negative terms (that is, as rights against interferences of certain kinds). Others of these theories defend some combination of liberty and welfare rights, with considerable variation in the robustness of the latter. Partisans of the latter kinds of theories will find social deprivation more worrisome, perhaps believing that the state has failed some of its citizens. One solution might be to urge some mitigation in the punishment inflicted on poor offenders, though not because they have "already suffered enough" or should not be made to suffer more. Instead, the grounds for mitigating their punishment should be understood as stemming from doubts about the extent to which they have freely chosen criminal conduct or have the same moral and prudential reasons the rest of us have against doing so (Morse 1998; Lippke 2011). In these respects, socially deprived offenders are different from most well-off citizens who commit crimes and have little excuse for doing so. The fact, if it is one, that well-off offenders will suffer more from the sanctions they are made to endure, assuming that their sanctions are proportional and nondegrading, arguably is one toward which we should not be inclined to pay much heed.

References

Ackerman, Bruce. 1980. *Social Justice in the Liberal State*. New Haven: Yale University Press.

Alexander, Larry, and Kimberly Kessler Ferzan, with Stephen Morse. 2009. *Crime and Culpability: A Theory of Criminal Law*. Cambridge: Cambridge University Press.

Alexander, Michelle. 2012. *The New Jim Crow*. New York: New Press.

Barnett, Randy E. 1998. *The Structure of Liberty: Justice and the Rule of Law*. Oxford: Oxford University Press.

Beitz, Charles R. 2013. "Human Dignity in the Theory of Human Rights: Nothing but a Phrase?" *Philosophy and Public Affairs* 41:259–90.

Berman, Mitchell N. 2008. "Punishment and Justification." *Ethics* 118:258–90.

Braithwaite, John, and Philip Pettit. 1990. *Not Just Deserts: A Republican Theory of Criminal Justice*. Oxford: Clarendon.

Chin, Gabriel. 2012. "The New Civil Death: Rethinking Punishment in the Era of Mass Conviction." *University of Pennsylvania Law Review* 160:1789–833.

Cohen, G. A. 2008. *Rescuing Justice and Equality*. Cambridge, MA: Harvard University Press.

Cruft, Rowan, S. Matthew Liao, and Massimo Renzo. 2015. *Philosophical Foundations of Human Rights*. Oxford: Oxford University Press.

Davis, Angela J. 2007. *Arbitrary Justice: The Power of the American Prosecutor*. New York: Oxford University Press.

Duff, R. A. 1986. *Trials and Punishments*. Cambridge: Cambridge University Press.

Duff, R. A., and S. E. Marshall. 2010. "Public and Private Wrongs." In *Essays in Criminal Law in Honour of Sir Gerald Gordon*, edited by James Chalmers, Fiona Leverick, and Lindsay Farmer. Edinburgh: Edinburgh University Press.

Dworkin, Ronald. 2000. *Sovereign Virtue: Equality in Theory and Practice*. Cambridge, MA: Harvard University Press.

Feinberg, Joel. 1984. *Harm to Others*. Oxford: Oxford University Press.

Feinberg, Joel. 1986. *Harm to Self*. Oxford: Oxford University Press.

Feinberg, Joel. 1990. *Harmless Wrongdoing*. Oxford: Oxford University Press.

Fischer, John Martin, and Mark Ravizza. 2000. *Responsibility and Control: A Theory of Moral Responsibility*. Cambridge: Cambridge University Press.

Frase, Richard S. 2013. *Just Sentencing: Principles and Procedures for a Workable System*. New York: Oxford University Press.

Gray, David. 2010. "Punishment as Suffering." *Vanderbilt Law Review* 63:1619–2010.

Gross, Hyman. 1979. *A Theory of Criminal Justice*. New York: Oxford University Press.

Hampton, Jean. 1984. "The Moral Education Theory of Punishment." *Philosophy and Public Affairs* 13:208–38.

Hampton, Jean. 1991. "A New Theory of Retribution." In *Liability and Responsibility: Essays in Law and Morals*, edited by R. G. Frey and C. W. Morris. Cambridge: Cambridge University Press.

Haney, Craig. 2003. "Mental Health Issues in Long-Term Solitary and 'Supermax' Confinement." *Crime & Delinquency* 49:124–56.

Haney, Craig. 2006. *Reforming Punishment: Psychological Limits to the Pains of Imprisonment*. Washington, DC: American Psychological Association.

Hayes, David J. 2016. "Penal Impact: Towards a More Intersubjective Measure of Penal Severity." *Oxford Journal of Legal Studies* 36:724–50.

Husak, Douglas. 2019. "The Metric of Punishment Severity: A Puzzle about the Principle of Proportionality." In *Of One-Eyed and Toothless Miscreants: Making the Punishment Fit the Crime?* edited by Michael Tonry. New York: Oxford University Press.

Jacobs, James B. 2016. *The Eternal Criminal Record*. Cambridge, MA: Harvard University Press.

Kant, Immanuel. 1991. *The Metaphysics of Morals*. Translated by Mary J. Gregor. Cambridge: Cambridge University Press.

Kateb, George. 2011. *Human Dignity*. Cambridge, MA: Harvard University Press.

Kolber, Adam J. 2009*a*. "The Comparative Nature of Punishment." *Boston University Law Review* 89:1565–608.

Kolber, Adam J. 2009*b*. "The Subjective Experience of Punishment." *Columbia Law Review* 109:182–236.

Lazarus, Liona. 2004. *Contrasting Prisoners' Rights: A Comparative Examination of England and Germany*. Oxford: Oxford University Press.

Lee, J. Roger, and Laurin A. Wollin Jr. 1985. "The Libertarian Prison: Principles of Laissez Faire Incarceration." *Prison Journal* 65:108–21.

Lippke, Richard L. 2007. *Rethinking Imprisonment*. Oxford: Oxford University Press.

Lippke, Richard L. 2011. "Social Deprivation as Tempting Fate." *Criminal Law & Philosophy* 5:277–91.

Lippke, Richard L. 2012. "Anchoring the Sentencing Scale: A Modest Proposal." *Theoretical Criminology* 16:463–80.

Lippke, Richard L. 2014. "Some Surprising Implications of Negative Retributivism." *Journal of Applied Philosophy* 31:49–62.

Lomasky, Loren E. 1987. *Persons, Rights, and the Moral Community*. New York: Oxford University Press.

Markel, Dan, and Chad Flanders. 2010. "Bentham on Stilts: The Bare Relevance of Subjectivity to Retributive Justice." *California Law Review* 98:907–88.

Masur, Jonathan, John Bronsteen, and Christopher Buccafusco. 2009. "Happiness and Punishment." *University of Chicago Law Review* 76:1037–81.

McDermott, Daniel. 2001. "The Permissibility of Punishment." *Law and Philosophy* 20:403–32.

Moore, Michael S. 1997. *Placing Blame: A Theory of the Criminal Law*. Oxford: Oxford University Press.

Morris, Christopher W. 1991. "Punishment and Loss of Moral Standing." *Canadian Journal of Philosophy* 21:53–79.

Morris, Norval. 1982. *Madness and the Criminal Law*. Chicago: University of Chicago Press.

Morse, Stephen. 1998. "Excusing and the New Excuse Defenses: A Legal and Conceptual Review." In *Crime and Justice: A Review of Research*, vol. 23, edited by Michael Tonry. Chicago: University of Chicago Press.

Murphy, Jeffrie G. 1973. "Marxism and Retribution." *Philosophy and Public Affairs* 2:217–43.

Narveson, Jan. 1988. *The Libertarian Idea*. Philadelphia: Temple University Press.

Nielsen, Kai. 1985. *Equality and Liberty: A Defense of Radical Egalitarianism*. Totowa, NJ: Rowman and Allanheld.

Nozick, Robert. 1974. *Anarchy, State, and Utopia*. New York: Basic.

Pratt, John. 2008. "Scandinavian Exceptionalism in an Era of Penal Excess, Part 1: The Nature and Roots of Scandinavian Exceptionalism." *British Journal of Criminology* 48:119–37.

Quinn, Warren. 1985. "The Right to Threaten and the Right to Punish." *Philosophy and Public Affairs* 14:327–73.

Rawls, John. 1971. *A Theory of Justice*. Cambridge, MA: Harvard University Press.

Roemer, John E. 2000. *Equality of Opportunity*. Cambridge, MA: Harvard University Press.

Rosen, Michael. 2012. *Dignity: Its History and Meaning*. Cambridge, MA: Harvard University Press.

Sadurski, Wojciech. 1985. *Giving Desert Its Due: Social Justice and Legal Theory*. Dordrecht: D. Reidel.

Sen, Amartya. 1995. *Inequality Reexamined*. Cambridge, MA: Harvard University Press.

Sher, George. 1987. *Desert*. Princeton, NJ: Princeton University Press.

Tonry, Michael. 1992. "Proportionality, Parsimony, and the Interchangeability of Punishments." In *Penal Theory and Penal Practice*, edited by R. A. Duff, S. Marshall, R. E. Dobash, and R. P. Dobash. Manchester: Manchester University Press.

Tonry, Michael. 2004. "Has the Prison a Future?" In *The Future of Imprisonment*, edited by Michael Tonry. New York: Oxford University Press.

Tonry, Michael, and Mary Lynch. 1996. "Intermediate Sanctions." In *Crime and Justice: A Review of Research*, vol. 20, edited by Michael Tonry. Chicago: University of Chicago Press.

Von Hirsch, Andreas [Andrew]. 1993. *Censure and Sanctions*. Oxford: Clarendon.

Von Hirsch, Andreas [Andrew], and Nils Jareborg. 1991. "Gauging Criminal Harm: A Living-Standard Analysis." *Oxford Journal of Legal Studies* 11:1–38.

Von Parijs, Philippe. 1995. *Real Freedom for All: What (If Anything) Can Justify Capitalism?* Oxford: Oxford University Press.

Waldron, Jeremy. 1993. "Rights." In *A Companion to Contemporary Political Philosophy*, edited by Robert E. Goodin and Philip Pettit. Oxford: Blackwell.

Waldron, Jeremy. 2012. *Dignity, Rank, and Rights*. Oxford: Oxford University Press.

Wallace, R. Jay. 1996. *Responsibility and the Moral Sentiments*. Cambridge: Harvard University Press.

Wellman, Christopher. 2017. *Rights Forfeiture and Punishment*. Oxford: Oxford University Press.

7

The Time of Punishment

PROPORTIONALITY AND THE SENTENCING
OF HISTORICAL CRIMES

Julian V. Roberts

DI COMMITS A crime in 2008. Police detect and charge him years later, in 2018. Over the decade, sentences imposed for this offense rose substantially as a result of an increase in the crime rate for this and related crimes. Had he been sentenced in 2008, he would have received a 6-year prison term, but as a result of the shift in sentencing practices, he is sentenced to 10 years. Is this fair?

D2, a member of an urban terrorist cell, robs a bank in 1978. She then leads a law-abiding life for the next 30 years, building a successful career and raising a family. D2 now both regrets and rejects her former life. When a routine database review alerts the police to her whereabouts, she is arrested and convicted. Should she be sentenced today as though the crime occurred last year rather than 30 years ago, or should her reformed life be considered in mitigation?

D3 has spent the last 30 years in prison serving a 40-to-life term for drug trafficking. During that time, social attitudes toward the crime have evolved, and awareness of the full (adverse) consequences of long-term imprisonment has grown. Should his sentence be reevaluated in light of these changes?

Julian V. Roberts is Professor of Criminology, Faculty of Law, at the University of Oxford. This essay has benefited from feedback from the participants at the Oxford seminar and from Lyndon Harris, Rory Kelly, Netanel Dagan, Allan Manson, and Lucia Zedner.

In all these cases, the passage of time is raised as a relevant consideration. Crime and punishment are usually separated by a brief period—normally months, seldom up to a year. Yet in a growing number of cases, courts around the world are now sentencing offenders for crimes committed decades earlier. Is the delay legally and normatively significant? One view is that sentencing should be time-insensitive: the court should disregard the interval between the crime and the sentencing, because the passage of time has no effect on the seriousness of the crime, the impact on the victim, or the offender's culpability for the offense. I'm not so sure.

Sentencing is a culturally and historically variant enterprise; attitudes toward crimes and punishments evolve continually, as do conceptions of blameworthiness and moral fault. Scholars have explored the variability across jurisdictions (e.g., Freiberg 2002), but less has been written on variation over time. How does the passage of time affect a court's evaluation of offenses, offenders, and the appropriate level of state sanctions? In this essay, I explore the effects of time within a proportional sentencing framework,[1] in relation both to sentences imposed long ago and to current sentences imposed for crimes committed years earlier.

I assume that proportionality should be the primary, but not the only, principle governing sentences imposed. There are two forms of proportionality: ordinal and cardinal (von Hirsch 1993). The former refers to the relative ordering of crimes on a scale of seriousness: how far above offense X is offense Y on the ordinal ranking? Cardinal proportionality refers to the outer limits of severity: what is the most severe sentence reserved for the most serious crime? The passage of time may affect both components. The ranking of offenses may change over time, as a crime ranked relatively low is "reassigned" to a higher tier of seriousness or rank in a sentencing guidelines grid. The question then becomes: if the offender commits the crime when the offense was ranked low but is sentenced after it has "risen" to a higher level, is he or she liable for the lower or higher punishment? Similarly, the outer limits of the sentencing regime—the most severe punishments that may be imposed— also shift over time. What impact should these changes have on sentencing practices?

---

1. Meyer (2017) provides an interesting discussion of the relationship between time and punishment. She rejects a retributive approach on the grounds that it "requires a time-consciousness" that "freeze-frames and isolates the memory of the crime" (p. 6). In contrast, here I explore the role of time within a sentencing regime based on the retributive proportionality principle.

Several other questions arise. How might the passage of time, including intervening events, affect the primary components of a proportional sentence, namely, harm and culpability? Complex problems of practice and principle engage retributive as well as preventive considerations. On a preventive rationale, a period of 30 years' compliance with the law may justify a highly mitigated sentence; otherwise, the state would be punishing the offender in order to achieve the compliance that he or she has already demonstrated. Offenders may now present a very low risk to reoffend, in which case a milder punishment than would have been imposed at the time of the offense or even a discharge may be appropriate. Incapacitation, specific deterrence, or rehabilitation is also less necessary if the offender has spent the period in the community since the crime occurred without further offending (Flatman and Bagaric 1997). But how does a proportionality-based analysis change when the crime and the sentencing are separated by a significant interval of time? The claims arise in relation to the offense, the offender, and the crime victim.

Prevailing conceptions of the components of a proportional sanction—harm and culpability—continually evolve. Rankings of offense seriousness change as a result of a number of time-related factors, including our evolving awareness of the nature of harms associated with specific criminal acts and societal perceptions of their inherent wrongfulness. Conceptions of culpability also evolve, as can be seen in the relative importance of the two components of a proportional sanction over the centuries. The origins of proportionality in English law can be traced to the Magna Carta and earlier, when key provisions related crimes to punishments—with no reference to offender culpability.[2] The concepts of blameworthiness and distinctions in terms of culpability emerged only much later (Robinson 1980).

In recent years, sentencing has become increasingly responsive to claims for mitigation based on diminished culpability. Courts now recognize an expanding range of mitigating factors that reduce an offender's culpability. These circumstances include diminished capacity, extreme emotional disturbance, fetal alcohol syndrome, social deprivation, incomplete cognitive development (of young adults), aboriginality, and other cultural and historical factors, to name but a few. The relative and absolute severity of punishments

---

2. The laws of Anglo-Saxon England (circa 595) prescribed specific punishments for a list of offenses (e.g., "if a freeman steal from the King, let him pay nine-fold bot"). Offense-based proportionality emerges more explicitly in clause 20 of the Magna Carta but without any reference to the offender's mental state or forms of culpability: "For a trivial offence, a free man shall be fined only in proportion to the degree of his offence, and for a serious offence correspondingly."

also changes over time as we become more aware of the full impact of the sentence on the offender. A term of imprisonment that was proportionate to the crime 50 years ago may now be seen as disproportionate in light of the longer-term effects of imprisonment. The traditional view of a sentence of custody was that severity was almost entirely captured in the duration of the sentence (von Hirsch 2017), yet recent research has revealed much more severe long-term, postsentence effects on the ex-prisoner.

These issues affect the overall architecture of the sentencing regime in terms of the ordinal proportionality of offenses. Sentencing commissions and legislatures periodically respond to evolving standards by reviewing the nature of sentencing guidelines or the nature of statutory sentencing provisions.[3] Such reviews should in principle and as a matter of sound practice reflect research on sentencing factors related to harm and culpability (crime seriousness) and the relative onerousness of different sanctions (sentence severity). Traditionally, such modifications tend to be ad hoc in nature, as are statutory amendments to maximum or minimum penalties. Amendments to offense rankings or statutory sentences are more likely to reflect haphazard political initiatives rather than any systematic examination of whether existing penalties have become outdated (Kelly 2018).

When there is a substantial interval between commission of the crime and determination of sentence, the passage of time may also influence proportionality considerations at the level of individual sentencing decisions. Many examples of delayed conviction and sentencing have arisen, including people who committed sexual assaults long before, members of radical groups in the 1960s and 1970s[4] who committed politically motivated crimes, and war criminals convicted of crimes committed long before their ultimate arrest, trial, and sentencing. Of all forms of historical sentencing, sexual offenses

---

3. Hate-motivated crime is a good example. During the 1980s and 1990s, many countries codified hate motivation as an aggravating factor at sentencing or created aggravated forms of specific offenses. This reflected growing awareness of the increasing prevalence of hate crime and a view that society regarded this form of offending as being more serious.

4. The Weather Underground in the United States was the largest group to launch a nationwide campaign of political violence in the country, beginning in the 1970s (Berger 2006). Urban terrorist cells in Europe also committed crimes of violence and property-related crimes during the 1960s and 1970s. A number of former members were convicted of criminal acts decades later. Some remain in prison more than 40 years later (Burrough 2015, p. 541).

currently account for the greatest volume; the number of "stale" sexual prosecutions has grown significantly in England and Wales in recent years.[5]

Historical cases vary widely in their nature and seriousness. Prosecution and punishment may have been delayed by any number of factors relating to the victim, the offender, official inaction, or the unavailability of modern technologies such as DNA and genealogical analyses. In some cases of historical sexual abuse, the victim may only recently have reported to the police.[6] Alternatively, the prosecution may have been triggered by improvements in criminal-justice databases or cold-case reviews. Finally, the offender may simply have avoided prosecution without taking any extraordinary steps, or he or she may have actively evaded detection by acquiring a new identity and moving to another jurisdiction. Whatever the reason, sentencing cases in which there is a significant gap between crime and sentencing creates challenges for courts.[7]

There is an additional time-related problem involving people who have served lengthy prison terms during the course of which state and societal perceptions of their offenses have changed. Should these prisoners be required to discharge the full penalty imposed all those years ago, or should the recalibration of their crimes not justify some "second look"? If time plays a role for uncharged offenders at liberty, it should also be a consideration for the individual who has been in custody during the same lengthy period. As with the at-large offender, the long-term prisoner can also argue that he or she is no longer the same person. Indeed, if the prison has achieved its purpose, that prisoner should not be the same person who committed the crime decades earlier. A growing literature demonstrates that imprisonment has far

---

5. The high-profile case in England of a disgraced public figure (Jimmy Saville) triggered a wave of reports of historical abuse involving him and other celebrities from the 1970s. Independent statutory inquiries were established in England and Wales, Scotland, and Northern Ireland to investigate child sexual abuse, including historical crimes. Most of the inquiry reports involve offenses committed years or decades earlier (Independent Inquiry into Child Sexual Abuse 2018, p. 5).

6. Statistics on the time between commission of the offense and sentencing are rare. However, one indication comes from a recent report from New South Wales, which found that almost half of sexual abuse cases were sentenced more than 25 years after the offense was committed (Freiberg, Donnelly, and Gelb 2015, p. 89).

7. As Flatman and Bagaric (1997) noted in an early discussion of sentencing historical sexual offenses, a significant delay between the commission of the offense and sentencing "can put a completely different complexion on the sentencing inquiry, given that most of the variables relevant to sentencing are primarily contingent upon the accused's character and predictions of future conduct" (p. 17).

more debilitating and longer-term consequences than was recognized a generation ago. The sentence of imprisonment that appeared proportionately severe 20 years ago may now be disproportionate in light of this additional insight into the effects of penal sequestration. In much of this essay, I deal with offenders being sentenced for crimes committed long before, but I return to the long-term prisoner in the concluding section.

Section I explores the significance of the offense and considers factors affecting calibrations of crime seriousness and the appropriate punishment. Because sentencing levels for many crimes have increased in recent years, section II asks whether current or historical sentencing levels should apply. Section III considers time-based mitigation and aggravation in relation to the culpability of the offender and the consequences of delayed sentencing for the crime victim. Section IV proposes a methodology for sentencing in cases in which the crime and the sentencing are separated by a significant passage of time. This section also briefly addresses the question of whether the passage of time should affect the treatment of long-term prisoners. Their sentences also need some reconsideration in light of developments in society and the prisoner's life. Section V is a brief conclusion.

My key points include the following:

- The penal value of both crimes and punishments evolve over time. Crimes are seen as more or less serious at different times. The perceived severity of legal punishments evolves to reflect research into their consequences for offenders as well as their preventive efficacy. These changes need to be considered at sentencing.
- The context in which the crime occurred, including the defendant's mental state, is a relevant consideration when sentencing takes place years later.
- The period of time between crime and punishment should be carefully examined for relevant sources of aggravation and mitigation. Aggravating factors include attempts to frustrate detection and prosecution and the ongoing suffering of the victim. Yet there are also many sources of mitigation, including moral reformation, changes in perceptions of the seriousness of the crime, and the severity of punishments.
- The sentence normally imposed at the time is an important guide to the seriousness of the offense committed, and courts should not routinely override the historical tariff with the sentence currently imposed.
- Passage-of-time mitigation should also justify second-look sentencing for prisoners who have served lengthy terms in prison.

- While a proportionality framework justifies a close examination of historical developments regarding the offense, the offender, and the victim, preventive rationales also provide a reason to conduct the sentencing exercise in a different way.

I. *The Evolution of Crimes and Punishments*

Time affects many issues in criminal law. For example, the passage of time attenuates the aggravating effect of prior convictions at sentencing. Older convictions are less reliable indicators of the individual's current risk of reoffending or level of culpability (Frase and Roberts 2019). The passage of time also weakens inferences about the propensity to offend that may be drawn from evidence of bad character. The underpinning justification is that the offender (or in the case of bad character evidence, the defendant) may no longer be the same person[8] years after the events in question occurred. Indeed, when many years have passed, the individual may be a very different person (Goldberg-Hiller and Johnson 2013). Most significantly, many jurisdictions place statutory time limits on the state's ability to prosecute.[9] Statutes of limitation may be justified on both practical and normative grounds. On the former, these limits acknowledge the diminishing reliability of witness testimony and the physical degradation of evidence over time. Yet these restrictions also reflect recognition that time affects the legitimacy of prosecuting and punishing offenders many years after the crime. A lengthy delay between the crime and the point of state interest will affect whether the prosecutor decides that the public interest is served by a prosecution (Crown Prosecution Service of England and Wales 2018). If the passage of time can justify restricting the state's ability to prosecute, a temporal delay must also affect the nature and quantum of punishment imposed.

The relationship between time and punishment is therefore a neglected area of sentencing scholarship and law. (For the most recent discussion of the issue, published as this volume goes to press, see du Bois-Pedain [2019]).[10] Few

---

8. I explore the passage of time as it affects the sentencing of individuals. Many of the arguments have relevance for corporate sentencing, where the corporation and its employees may be very different if the crime was committed years earlier (Diamantis 2018).

9. Many, but by no means all; there are no statutory limitations in the United Kingdom (exception for summary offenses) or Australia. In Canada, except for summary offenses and treason, there is no legal bar to prosecution no matter how much time has passed.

10. I discuss only the time between the crime and the sentencing hearing. A substantial literature explores delays between the laying of a criminal charge and the determination of sentence.

sentencing regimes explicitly acknowledge the passage of time as a relevant sentencing factor.[11] The passage of time and the offender's conduct during the protracted delay between crime and punishment do not generally appear on any list of statutory or guideline factors at sentencing. A rare example can be found in the English sentencing guideline for sexual offenses, which notes that "the Court must consider the relevance of the passage of time carefully as it has the potential to aggravate or mitigate the seriousness of the offence" (Sentencing Council of England and Wales 2016, p. 155). The guideline offers little guidance beyond observing that "It will be an aggravating factor where the offender has continued to commit sexual offences against the victim or others or has continued to prevent the victim reporting the offence" (p. 155).

When reference is made to this circumstance in sentencing law, the rationale and consequences for sentencing remain obscure. For example, chapter 29, s. 5(7) of the Swedish sentencing statute (which establishes proportionality as the guiding principle) directs a court to consider "whether considering the nature of the crime, an unusually long time has elapsed since the commission of the crime," without specifying why this should be so.[12] This suggests that the passage of time has some significance at sentencing. Ashworth and von Hirsch (2005) cite the Swedish provision and accept the passage of time as a "basis for compassion . . . with the lapse of time, the possibility increases that the actor may have changed significantly—so that his long-past act does not reflect badly on the person he now is" (p. 278). The sentencing law in Israel also lists "the time that has elapsed since the commission of the offense" as a circumstance to be considered at sentencing, but without clarifying why (Penal Law [Amendment No 113] 2012, s. 40k[10]). If statutory regimes say little about the significance of the passage of time, this consideration does commonly appear in sentencing judgments as a source of mitigation. For example, in one high-profile historical sex case in England, the

---

When excessive, and if due to state failures, these delays may lead to charges being stayed or dropped.

11. English sentencing law explicitly creates a temporal interval in the expectation that the offender may change prior to the determination of sentence. According to section 1ZA of the Powers of the Criminal Courts (Sentencing) Act, a court may defer sentencing so the offender can participate in a restorative activity. Similarly, the Model Penal Code Sentencing contains a "deferred adjudication" mechanism. This encourages courts to defer adjudication in order to facilitate offenders' rehabilitation and reintegration and to restore victims and communities (S.6.02B).

12. A number of authors cite the passage of time as a reason for mitigating or withholding punishment without explaining why (e.g., New 1992, p. 39).

court included the following in its list of mitigating factors: "The offending took place 35 years ago" (*Hall*, [2013] EWCA Crim 1450, para 19). Yet legal judgments that cite the passage of time do not articulate why it is a (potential) source of mitigation. I attempt to supply some justifications.

A. The Evolving Seriousness of Crimes

Changes in the objective or perceived seriousness of the offense carry consequences for the offender. Crimes that are regarded as less serious today are less problematic. Only a Kantian purist would insist on a severe punishment today for a crime currently regarded as trivial, on the basis that the offender committed the crime believing it was more serious. However, offenses that are now regarded as more serious—and punished accordingly—create challenges for courts; most of the historical sexual assault cases appearing for sentencing in England and Wales are subject to levels of punishment significantly higher now than 30 or 40 years ago.

If a given sentence was proportionate to the offense (and the offender) in 1970, what factors determine whether it remains proportionate decades later? Can the mere passage of time alone justify differential sentencing? A crime committed a generation earlier may have become a distant memory for the community (and even the victim), but it has not been effaced. Something needs to have changed with respect to the offense or the offender before a proportionality analysis justifies a different approach to sentencing. The most obvious change is an evolution in the objective or perceived gravity of the conduct, which then generates a different response to the question "What is the proportionate punishment in this case?" Many crimes have "become" more serious in recent decades (domestic violence, drunk driving, environmental offenses), as our evaluation of their harm and relative seriousness has evolved. Others, such as assisting suicide or possession of soft drugs, are considered less serious or have been decriminalized (e.g., homosexual acts).

Ordinal proportionality rankings evolve over time, whether they are derived from analysis of case materials (victim impact statements, medical reports, etc.) or ratings of seriousness derived from samples of the public. Comparisons of public seriousness rankings over time reveal changes. In one early analysis, Coombs (1967) compared public offense rankings from 1966 and 1925 and found significant changes even for the most serious offenses such as murder and rape. Similarly, Cullen, Link, and Polanzi (1982) demonstrated the evolution of public rankings of the seriousness of white-collar crime (Roberts and Stalans 1997, pp. 65–66).

B. Changes in the Perceived and Experienced Severity of Punishments

The relative severity of sanctions also evolves over time. Punishments deemed unproblematic in the past—corporal punishment in the postwar period is an obvious example[13]—have been abolished, a change triggered by the evolving standards of human dignity. But the penal value of punishments has also changed on a shorter time scale. A few decades ago, imprisonment was regarded as little more than the deprivation of liberty through penal sequestration. The effects of the punishment expired with the end of the sentence. Or so we thought; now we're not so sure. This (in retrospect) naive perception may explain how very lengthy terms of imprisonment were imposed, particularly in the United States.

Today there is a large and growing body of research demonstrating the long-term, sometimes irremediable effects of imprisonment on a range of indicators, including life opportunities, employment prospects and lifetime income, physical and mental health, and family relationships (Pridemore 2014). A number of studies have demonstrated that spending time in prison reduces life expectancy long after release. In one of the most careful analyses, Patterson (2013) reports that after controlling for a range of other explanatory factors, each additional year in prison increases the odds of death by approximately 16 percent and that this translates "to an increased odds of death of 78 percent for somebody who spent 5 years in prison" (p. 526). Many people in the United States have served 5 or more years in prison. Schnittker, Massoglia, and Uggen (2012) and Schnittker and John (2007) document the effect of incarceration on mental health and psychiatric disorders. Apel and Sweeten (2010) document the adverse effects of incarceration on employment (see also Massoglia and Pridemore 2015).[14]

We are also much more aware of the impact of imprisonment on family and dependents of prisoners. Arditti (2012) provides a concise summary of this literature: "The available research has indicated the largely negative effects of

---

13. When I was a schoolboy, pupils were subject to official corporal punishment (the strap), as well as spontaneous beatings by choleric teachers. Neither form of punishment aroused any controversy or even commentary at the time. Today such actions would give rise to immediate dismissal of the teacher and criminal charges.

14. All these studies benefit from the increased sophistication of statistical analyses in recent decades, allowing researchers to isolate the effects of incarceration, having controlled for other factors that might also predict adverse life conditions such as unemployment, low earnings, ill health, suicide, and early death.

incarceration on offender parents, children, and spouses or intimate partners such that family health declines, child adjustment is compromised . . . and family relationships deteriorate or cease altogether" (p. 101). The "pains of imprisonment" are more intense and far-reaching than we ever knew. Once paid, a fine's consequences are over; imprisonment does not end so easily. In terms of punishment, it is the sanction that keeps on giving. The consequence of this evolution is that a 20-year prison sentence is, or should be regarded as, a much more severe sentence than hitherto, and this should trigger a greater reluctance to impose such sentences and a second-look review of existing long-term sentences.

A second research-based reason for reevaluating long-term sentences of imprisonment relates to their intended effects on persons other than the offender. Again, until a few decades ago, the general deterrent effect of lengthy prison sentences was unquestioned. Lengthy prison sentences were seen as an effective and appropriate response to rising crime rates, sporadic outbursts of offending, or the occasional exceptional crime.[15] Although courts in many jurisdictions continue to endorse lengthy prison sentences for deterrent purposes, the research evidence suggests they are far from effective. To the extent that this research is accepted, it creates an obligation to revisit the sentences imposed for deterrence decades ago. It is the equivalent of revisiting a lengthy term of quarantine in light of revised medical advice regarding the necessary period of isolation. The US drug laws offer a good example. As a result of the American wars on drugs, launched in the 1970s and 1980s, penalties for drug offenders increased dramatically. The goal was to target and incapacitate or deter major drug dealers. In the event, these laws affected all kinds of drug offenders, even those playing minor roles. The Sentencing Project (2017) noted that "in 1986, people released after serving time for a federal drug offense had spent an average of 22 months in prison. By 2004, people convicted on federal drug offenses were expected to serve almost three

---

15. The so-called Great Train Robbery in England in 1963 is a good illustration. A group of men stopped a night mail train, assaulting the driver in the process. Most of the stolen 2 million pounds was recovered. The courts imposed 30-year prison sentences—far in excess of those handed down for manslaughter and the most serious crimes short of murder. The sentences were justified by reference to general deterrence. One of the defendants became an example of historical sentencing. Ronnie Biggs escaped from prison after 15 months and lived outside the United Kingdom for the next 37 years. Returning voluntarily in 2001, he was committed to custody and remained in prison until 2009, when the parole board recommended his release, in light of his repentance and his ill health. His request for parole was denied by the politician with oversight of parole decisions, and he remained in prison until released on compassionate grounds shortly before his death.

times that length: 62 months in prison" (p. 2). Once it became clear that the increased penalties had failed, there was a need to revisit the sentences.

The perceived seriousness of crimes changes constantly, as does the perceived severity of different punishments. This reality has consequences for the sentencing of historical offenses.

II. Should Current or Historical Sentencing Levels Apply?

Since sentencing standards are constantly evolving, the most fundamental question is whether the offender should be sentenced under the regime applicable at the time of the offense, or under current sentencing standards if the two are disparate? Jurisdictions have taken different approaches.

The position in England and Wales, Canada, and several other jurisdictions is clear. The English Court of Appeal and the Sentencing Council that issues guidelines for courts to follow concur that the offender should be sentenced according to current, not historical, standards. In *R. v. L.*, the court notes: "The only constraint . . . on the powers of the sentencing court is the statutory maximum for the offense."[16] *Forbes*[17] reiterates a previous judgment and notes: "The offender must be sentenced in accordance with the regime applicable at the date of sentence. The court must have regard to the statutory purposes of sentencing *and to current sentencing practice*."[18] The judgment cites the definitive guideline issued by the Sentencing Council, which provides additional guidance, including the following: "The seriousness of the offence, assessed by the culpability of the offender and the harm caused or intended, is the main consideration for the court. The court should not seek to establish the likely sentence had the offender been convicted shortly after the date of the offence. . . . The offender must be sentenced in accordance

---

16. *R. v. L.*, (2017) EWCA Crim 43, at 14.

17. The appellant in *R. v. Forbes*, (2016) EWCA Crim 1388, para. 4, was a 56-year-old man convicted in 2015 of sexual offenses committed 40 years earlier when he was between ages 16 and 21. There were four counts of indecent assault on a male and one count of attempted buggery. He was sentenced to 17 years' imprisonment. The court noted an aggravating factor, namely, that the offender had "intimidated his victims into keeping quiet for years" (para. 48). It went on to state that the passage of time carried "very little weight," since Forbes had "lived a far from exemplary life" (para. 48). The court stressed the need for "positive good character," rather than simply the absence of further offending, thus setting a higher bar for access to mitigation (Doig 2017).

18. *R. v. Forbes*, para. 4; emphasis added.

with the sentencing regime applicable at the date of sentence" (Sentencing Council of England and Wales 2016, p. 155).

Article 7 of the European Convention on Human Rights prohibits the imposition of a more severe punishment than was available when the crime was committed. English courts[19] have interpreted this provision to mean that any sentence within the maximum penalty[20] available at the time of the crime may be imposed and be compliant with Article 7.[21] The application of current sentencing standards would seem particularly problematic when it results in a significant change in the nature of the sentence imposed. It is one thing to add additional months to a sentence on the grounds that the crime is now punished more severely, quite another to imprison the offender when 30 years ago he or she would seldom or never have received a custodial sentence. It seems harsh to imprison an offender in this example and justify the imprisonment simply by noting that custody was a legal option 30 years earlier, even if never actually imposed. Samuels (2017) notes that "the fact that 20 years ago the sentence would have been less, and sentences now are heavier, is not relevant. Trying to ascertain what the sentence would have been in the last century is an unnecessary and pointless exercise" (p. 1). I'm not so sure it is either pointless or unnecessary. There are reasons to question the current-standards position. If contemporary rather than historical standards apply, I advocate a more sustained consideration of issues arising from the passage of time.

---

19. And courts in some other jurisdictions: When sentencing historical cases, Canadian courts apply the criminal code provisions that existed at the time of the offense. These provide the legal framework, but the sentencing approach is the current one and not the one that would have applied at the time of the offense. The time interval between the offense and sentencing may provide either mitigating or aggravating factors, but these will mitigate or aggravate from a sentence based on current levels of severity.

20. Using the maximum penalty as the ceiling would be more defensible if the statutory maximums reflected ordinal proportionality considerations. Because in most common-law jurisdictions they derive from the nineteenth century, they bear little relation to the relative seriousness of the crimes for which they may be imposed.

21. In short, any sentence is compliant with Article 7 as long as it was a legal sentence 30 years ago. It is the difference between "could" have imposed and "would" have imposed. In *R. v. H.*, (2011) EWCA Crim 2753, the court noted that "the common law rule which prohibits retrospective increases in the penalty which may be imposed for an offence, a rule which is reflected in article 7 of the European Convention on Human Rights, applies to changes in the statutory law which defines the powers of a sentencing court, but does not apply to changes in judicial sentencing practice within the scope of the statutory provisions." For further discussion, see Harris and Walker (2017).

In contrast to the English position, courts in other jurisdictions such as Minnesota[22] have taken the opposite view. The presumptively binding Minnesota guidelines provide specific sentence ranges calibrated to the seriousness of the offense. If an offender is being sentenced for a crime that was, say, offense seriousness level six at the time of commission, guideline sentence ranges for this level of seriousness will apply, even if the offense has subsequently been regraded upward to a higher level by the commission. Similarly, Australian courts also apply historical rather than contemporary sentencing levels.[23] A recent government policy paper endorsed this position by noting that "when sentencing for historic offences, the Court has regard to the scope of the offence and maximum penalty for the offence at the time the offence was committed." (Government of New South Wales 2014, p. 16; see also discussion in Freiberg, Donnelly, and Gelb 2015, pp. 91–94).

Judicial practice reveals no consensus regarding the appropriate approach to sentencing historical crimes. Since the respective judgments affirm their positions rather than engage in a more systematic exploration of the merits of different approaches, current practice is unhelpful in resolving the normative issues. What arguments might be advanced to sentence the offender according to the sentencing norms applicable at the time, rather than standards many years later? I see three reasons to give consideration to the historical period in which the crime was committed: fair notice requires citizens to have a clear idea of their liability for breaking the law, imposing contemporary standards is potentially unfair as it represents a retroactive recalibration of the crime and the offender's culpability, and applying current levels of sentencing may violate the principle of parity in sentencing involving defendants convicted of the same crime but punished years apart.

A. Fair Notice and Legitimate Expectations

An offender sentenced for a historical sexual offense in England in 2017 complained that he "was sentenced for historic sex offences and the judge insisted on being told what the law is now. Surely this isn't relevant? My sentence would have been less back when the offences were committed."[24] His

---

22. And also, it would appear, at the federal level; *Peugh v. United States*, 133 S. Ct. 2072 (2013).

23. In *R. v. MJR*, (2002) NSWCCA 129, the court held that it is proper for a court to take into account the sentencing practice at the date of the commission of the offense when sentencing practice has moved adversely to an offender.

24. *Inside Time*, May 3, 2017, p. 1.

surprise at the court's sentence was understandable. Criminal law should be as clear as possible in its definitions of criminal behavior and also the liability for breaking the law. There should be little ambiguity regarding the illegality of specific acts, and citizens should be able to understand the potential consequences of offending. If the maximum penalty in effect at the time of the offense constitutes the appropriate frame of reference for sentencing, two consequences ensue. First, for all serious offenses, the state has a very wide range of sanctions it may impose. Offenses of variable seriousness will share a common maximum penalty, thereby obscuring the utility of the maximums as a guide to relative seriousness of different crimes.

Second, the vast range of severity for even a middle-ranked offense such as burglary means the average citizen can have no accurate idea of his or her likely sentence; for most serious offenses, the sky's the limit. The maximum penalties in most countries convey an inaccurate idea of the seriousness of the crime for which they may be imposed. This creates an interesting paradox to the detriment of the defendant. The state revisits the sentence that should be imposed by applying current, not historical, standards. It holds the defendant to account for current perceptions of the relative seriousness of the offending. At the same time, it adheres to much older and even more antiquated maximum penalties. The offender's sentence is recalibrated, while the state's powers as limited by the maximum sentence are left untouched.

For most crimes, the maximum penalties provide no guide to the average or the relative severity of punishments for different crimes. Domestic burglary is an example. This offense is punishable by any sentence up to and including life imprisonment in England and Wales and most common-law jurisdictions, yet convictions often result in a community penalty[25] and if in custody, for only a short period. If the state may impose anything up to and including life imprisonment, is this sufficient notice for the citizenry of the consequences of offending? Ordinal proportionality requires an orderly correspondence between the seriousness of crimes and the severity of punishments. Yet if the ordinal constraints are either obscure or rapidly changing, how is the censuring action of a proportionate sanction likely to function?

Advocates of imposing current (rather than past) sentencing levels sometimes argue that no offender convicted of a historical offense would have refrained from offending had he or she had a more realistic idea of the

---

25. Approximately half the sentences for domestic burglary are served in the community; the remainder involve a brief period of imprisonment (Sentencing Council of England and Wales 2011).

potential punishment. Yet the offender is still entitled to ask,[26] "When I committed this offense, my perception was that it was of seriousness X and would attract a penalty of severity Y. So why am I being sentenced now to 10Y?" Consider a theft of an ounce of gold in 1970. At the time, gold was worth £250 an ounce. The offender is ultimately convicted of the theft in 2000, when the value of gold has risen to £1,000 an ounce.[27] Should the offender be sentenced for stealing gold worth £250 or £1,000? Or suppose that 40 years ago, D steals a painting by an unknown artist from a local gallery. Since then, the artist has become famous and is now regarded as a modern master. If D is sentenced for the theft today, should he be sentenced for having stolen a masterpiece that is worth millions?

More important, if the historical evaluation of the seriousness of the crime was erroneous, the state was compliant in the error. The historical offender can argue that his or her perception of the seriousness of the crime was guided by the state response to this offense at the time as reflected in sentencing levels. The state clearly shared the offender's view of the relative seriousness of the offense; otherwise, courts at the time would have imposed a harsher sentence. If the state punishes conduct X with a sanction of severity Y at one time and then grants itself the freedom to impose a sentence of severity level 10Y, the state is, in the words of Alexander and Ferzan (2009), "deceptive with respect to the consequences of disobeying the law" (p. 300).

Some authors see no difficulties in this position. Lippke (2018), for example, argues that fair-notice requirements are fulfilled simply by the person knowing (or being expected to know) that the conduct was illegal. I'm not so sure. An individual acts with the knowledge that his or her conduct is illegal and also that it is normally punished by a fine. Twenty years later, the state decides that the crime, in fact, merits imprisonment. Was this degree of notice sufficient? Is it reasonable to now imprison the individual? In discussing the application of retrospective punishment, Lippke suggests that "it might be better to keep 'bad men' a bit in the dark about the exact price they will have to pay for their contemplated criminal offences" (p. 10). It's like keeping restaurant diners guessing about the price of their meal until the bill arrives

---

26. Ashworth (2015) notes the importance of "a person's entitlement to rely on the law as it was at the time of the conduct" (p. 170). He cites the long-accepted dictum of Lord Diplock that there is a rule-of-law requirement that "the citizen should be able to know in advance the legal consequences" of particular acts. O'Malley (2016) concurs: "an offender may claim that at the time of the offence he or she had a legitimate expectation that the punishment for the offence, in the event of conviction, would be within a certain range" (p. 54).

27. Assume that the £1,000 is corrected for inflation.

at the table. If we can keep them in the dark about the severity of the penalty, why not also obscure the nature of the offense itself? We could create an offense of "unlawful sexual activity" and then determine upon a complaint from a victim exactly what constitutes an illicit sexual act. No one would regard such an offense as acceptable.

"Bad men" aside, the criminal law should be as clear as possible about the legality of acts and omissions, as well as the relative severity of attached punishments. That is why most legal systems honor ex post facto principles prohibiting prosecutions for acts that were legal when they were committed. It is not obvious why a similar principle should not be applied to punishments for acts that were criminal but conventionally regarded at the time to be less serious (and warranting less punishment) than at the present. Notwithstanding the importance in everyday life of informal sources of guidance regarding the moral wrongfulness of different acts, the law remains the ultimate authority. Hiding the true severity of the sentencing process undermines both the censuring and the deterrent functions of criminal sanctions. This, of course, is the principal objection to indeterminate sentences of imprisonment.

B. Retrospective Recalibration of Seriousness and Culpability

If the change in severity reflects a systematic and evidence-based reevaluation of the seriousness of the offense, rather than simply a cultural shift in perceptions of seriousness, applying the new regime may be more defensible. The argument runs this way: "We had it wrong all those years ago, and if we'd known then what we know now, we would have sentenced differently. So we should not persevere in that mistaken calibration of harm." Yet if the increase simply reflects a shift in public attitudes,[28] due perhaps to a single high-profile incident or a politically motivated piece of legislation, applying the new sentencing levels is less defensible. History is replete with examples of moral panics that triggered a sudden and dramatic increase in sentence severity in the absence of a systematic and compelling recalibration of the seriousness of the crimes affected. The widespread media coverage of the killing of James Bulger by two 10-year-old boys in England is a good example. Although truly

---

28. A number of judgments cite changes in community views as a justification. For example, in an Australian judgment, the court observed that sexual assault has generally "come to be regarded as requiring increased sentences . . . by reason of a change of community attitudes" (*R. v. MJR*, [2002] 54 NSWLR 368 at 11). In *R. v. Clifford*, (2014) EWCA Crim 22 45, para 30, the English Court of Appeal affirmed that "sentencing [for historical crimes] should reflect modern attitudes."

exceptional, the case changed public perceptions of the seriousness of crime by young persons and has been cited as a cause of tougher sentencing (Hough, Jacobson, and Millie 2003).

Sentencing severity changes over time, often for reasons unrelated to the seriousness of the offense in question. If the prevalence of a category of crime changes over time, sentencing levels often rise. Recent examples of such a shift in England and Wales include terrorism offenses, offenses involving knives, and sexual offenses. In recent years, these crimes have all increased in terms of volume, with a consequent impact on sentencing levels. Sometimes the legislature has intervened to raise statutory penalties, and sometimes the courts have increased the level of severity within existing statutory limits. Where these changes in severity have remained within the maximum penalties in effect at the time of an offense, the offender will be liable for the increase. In such cases, he or she is being held accountable (and punished more severely) for the conduct of other offenders committing crimes years later.[29] The consequence is that an increase in the volume of offending long after the offender's crime was committed is used to justify a harsher sentence if he or she is ultimately sentenced at a later period.

Courts and sentencing commissions that raise the tariff for crimes on the basis that the offense is now appropriately seen as being more serious appear confident that the recalibration is sound. Again, I'm not so sure. Revisionist, upward drifts in the perceived seriousness of some offenses are often unprincipled and reflect something other than a sound theoretical justification. At the very least, the revised seriousness rankings of offenses need to be scrutinized within some conceptual scheme, such as the "living standards" analysis (von Hirsch and Jareborg 1991).[30] Unless the upward recalibration of harm is evidence-based, the historical offender is being overpunished, at least within a proportionality framework. Finally, even if we accept the position that the calibration of harm at T_1 was inaccurate and that the recalibration upward better captures the true harm of the offense, it is hard to see how this should also trigger a reevaluation of the offender's level of culpability.

---

29. There are clear parallels with arguments against general deterrence. The severe penalties imposed on offenders involved in the 2011 English riots were justified by the need to deter future offenders in subsequent incidents of urban unrest ("pour encourager les autres . . . *dans l'avenir*") (*Blackshaw*, [2011] EWCA Crim 2312).

30. Ordinal rankings of crime seriousness reflect many influences, some of which are questionable, including sudden shifts in public opinion, punitive political populism, special-interest or advocacy group pressures, and mass-media campaigns.

C. Violating Parity at Sentencing

Parity is one of the key subcomponents of a proportional sentence (von Hirsch 1993). The principle is codified throughout the common-law world. For example, s. 718.2(b) of the Canadian Criminal Code states that "a sentence should be similar to sentences imposed on similar offenders for similar offenses committed in similar circumstances." Applying contemporary sentencing levels to offenders convicted of older crimes violates the subprinciple of treating offenders convicted of comparable crimes equitably. Consider two offenders, A and B, both convicted of participating in the same crime. The only difference between the offenders accused is that A was sentenced to six months' custody, while B received 18 months' custody a decade later, by which time sentence levels for this crime had risen. The difference in severity arises from the application of current sentencing practices at T_2 for the crime committed prior to T_1. The principle of parity is violated[31] in this case, since in relation to the principal elements of a proportional sentence (harm and particularly culpability), the two cases were equivalent at the critical time when the offending occurred. Comparable cases are now punished differently for reasons unrelated to harm or culpability.

It is not obvious that the normatively appropriate approach to historical sentencing is to apply current sentencing levels. Some consideration of the context of the offense is necessary, particularly when levels of severity have risen markedly during the period between crime and punishment.

III. *The Offender and the Crime Victim: Temporal Mitigation and Aggravation*

A pure Kantian retributivist might argue that the offender's liability remains unchanged over time. A character-based retributivist might argue the opposite, that decades of compliance with the law means that the stale offense was

---

31. Several English commentators and judgments take the view that had the offender wished to avail himself of the less severe sentence, he could have reported himself for sentencing earlier. Samuels (2017) again: "The reason for the long passage of time is presumably that . . . the offender did not confess his offence" (p. 1). Similarly, in *R. v. Forbes*, (2016) EWCA Crim 1388, para. 4, the Court of Appeal noted that "it was [the defendant's] choice not to take the initiative and admit the offences when the earlier more lenient sentencing policy was in operation." This position asks a lot of citizens and raises concerns about self-incrimination. On the other hand, there is some force to the converse argument that by evading prosecution and punishment, an offender assumes the risk of societal and sentencing standards evolving to his or her disadvantage.

sufficiently out of character to be ignored for the purposes of punishment. If the crime occurred 40 years earlier, the state is sentencing a different individual from the one who committed the offense. The 60-year-old offender now sentenced for a crime committed when he was 20 is at once the same and also a different person. He is a living embodiment of the philosophical problem of Theseus's trireme, slowly being repaired, plank by plank; once every plank has been replaced, is it still the same ship? Is he still the same individual?[32] And if he has changed, is the difference between the offender then and now retributively significant? As the offender moves in time away from the crime, why exactly might his liability diminish? His conduct during the period may supply an answer.

The diversity of delayed-sentencing cases may preclude any general rules of application, but the offender's conduct during the period between crime and punishment is a key consideration. Much will depend on the offender's moral trajectory since the crime was committed. Some offenders will have transformed their lives and may reasonably be regarded as different from the individuals who offended. The US case of Sarah Jane Olson is an example. Born Kathy Soliah, she was a member of the Symbionese Liberation Army, a group of would-be urban terrorists responsible for kidnapping heiress Patty Hearst (and several other serious crimes). Having participated in a bank robbery in the 1970s, she assumed a new identity and spent the next 25 years as a law-abiding citizen in Minnesota—until the FBI came calling. This postoffense transformation merits consideration at sentencing for the old crime.[33] Yet recognizing a protracted period of compliance with the law is also problematic. Most German war criminals appear to have led such lives in Latin America for decades after World War II. In their cases, compliance with the law may simply have reflected a desire to evade prosecution and punishment, rather than any moral transformation.

Assuming that the offender has led a law-abiding life since the crime and has not actively avoided detection, the claim for mitigation has been strengthened. This source of mitigation is recognized in English judgments. In the sentencing of Max Clifford for historical sexual offenses, the Court of

---

32. Derek Parfit (1984) has written the most compelling account of the relationship between two periods of the same individual's life, but the account seems too metaphysical to be relevant to contemporary sentencing, and for this reason I do not discuss his work here.

33. Had she been sentenced shortly after the crime, Soliah would have been unable to claim 25 years of legal compliance in mitigation. Yet to what degree is this mitigation offset by the fact that she was also a fugitive from justice, actively evading detection during this period?

Appeal noted that "there is some mitigation available based on the fact that [the appellant] had not offended since the 1980s."[34] The first-time offender claims mitigation based on a protracted period of compliance prior to the offense; the historical offender can place postoffending compliance alongside this claim.[35] First-time offenders claim mitigation on the basis that the offense was preceded by a sustained period of law-abiding living and compliance with the law. Historical offenders can use the same argument to claim mitigation for the sustained compliance occurring after the crime occurred. The first-offense claim in mitigation becomes a "first and only" offense.

A. "Back in the Day" Claims in Mitigation

Husak (2010) makes a compelling case to consider what he describes as the "but everyone does that!" (BEDT) defense. This is the claim by the defendant that the widespread prevalence of the crime with which he is charged exculpates him. If everyone at the time was engaged in this form of wrongdoing, is it fair to single out one individual for punishment? The argument in the present context is related to this defense. Here the claim is more modest, namely, that the existence of certain conditions at the time of the crime (but absent now) mitigate the offender's level of culpability. We might call this BITD mitigation, reflecting the assertion that "back in the day," the offense was regarded as less serious (and, crucially, was punished less severely) than at present. Consider, for example, marijuana trafficking by college students in the 1960s. The argument is not that everyone, or even most people, committed the offense back in the day but simply that the conduct was considered less serious by society and the state.

The strength of the BITD claim for mitigation rests on three related limbs. First, if the crime was widespread during this earlier period, the offender may reasonably claim to be less culpable. Second, if social attitudes at the time were less condemnatory of the conduct, the offender is deserving of less condemnation. Third, if the state tolerated widespread impunity and prosecutions were rare, an offender may reasonably claim to have lacked

---

34. (2014) EWCA Crim 22 45, para. 27.

35. The Canadian case of *R. v. L.F.W.,* [2000] 1 S.C.R is a good illustration. The offender had committed sexual offenses against a child when he was approximately 22 years of age, during 1967–1973. Alcohol was a factor, and since the offending he had abstained from alcohol. He was convicted a quarter century after the offending and had a family, a good work record, and had led an exemplary life. The offenses were undoubtedly serious, but the offender's law-abiding life before and since the offending should carry some substantial weight.

complete awareness of the wrongfulness of the acts or omissions. In practice, the three justifications are likely to be related: an offense that is committed with widespread impunity is unlikely to be regarded as a serious offense and is less likely to be prosecuted.

1. *Prevalence of the Crime at the Time of Commission.* More than a century ago, a Victorian scholar wrote, "Conceive a locality in which a particular class of crime is for the time being rife. If regard were had primarily and directly to the moral nature of the offence, the prevalence of the crime must be looked on as an extenuating circumstance, for an immoral act is less blameworthy when the general moral tone is low than when it is high" (Crackenthorpe 1900, p. 109). That the abuse was far more prevalent than now does not diminish its harm, but there may be some traction with respect to diminished culpability. Two noncriminal examples are illustrative. Today the use of a racist epithet in public is likely to trigger immediate (and strongly expressed) condemnation in almost all contemporary social contexts. Fifty years ago, such language was far more common and often passed without critique. The corollary of this observation is that we would regard someone using a racist, homophobic, or sexist term today as being more blameworthy than someone who used the same language 50 years ago. A similar argument may be made with respect to criminal conduct. Fifty years ago, driving while over the legal limit of alcohol consumption was far more common and far less socially condemned than at present.

A frequent claim in mitigation for young people carrying knives is that such conduct is common and deemed acceptable among their peers.[36] This acceptability of the conduct in the social network legitimizes and diffuses the culpability of the juveniles. Blameworthiness is not restricted to the individual offender; some shared responsibility arises. Yet if I walk into a college meeting with a knife hilt protruding from my belt, ascriptions of blame would be rather different; I have no diffused culpability on which to draw. There is no social context which partially justifies my actions and mitigates my blameworthiness. The current scandals concerning sports doping are also illustrative. Professional athletes in a variety of sports appear to have been

---

36. That conduct is common has not been recognized by the courts as potentially mitigating. On the contrary, the prevalence of the conduct is taken as a justification for aggravating the sentence for reasons relating to general deterrence. For example, in *Povey*, (2008) EWCA Crim 1261, a case involving the possession of knives, the Court of Appeal noted that "for the time being, whatever other considerations may arise in the individual case, sentencing courts must have in the forefront of their thinking that the sentences for this type of offence should focus on the reduction of crime, including its reduction by deterrence."

taking performance-enhancing drugs for years, contrary to sports rules. If all, or most, competitors are taking these drugs, there is a collective diffusion of culpability. Or from the opposite perspective, an athlete who resorts to a proscribed medication knowing this to be truly exceptional in light of the behavior of other athletes is more blameworthy. He has no possible diffused or shared culpability on which to draw in partial mitigation.

There appear, then, to be grounds for some leniency when culpability is diffused across a community, and this may diminish an individual's level of blameworthiness. The context in which the conduct occurs should be considered when evaluating the offender's culpability. Consider two offenders convicted of the same offense, one in 1969, the other in 2019. Assume further that the offense resulted in a short prison sentence in the earlier period and a much longer term in 2019, the difference arising from an evolution in social awareness of the crime's seriousness. Applying the 2019 sentencing standards to both offenders will result in overpunishment of the historical offender. The offender who commits the crime in 2019 is more culpable because the offense is committed in the full, contemporary awareness of its harmfulness. The historical offender committed the same act but in a very different context. This distinction in culpability is lost if contemporary sentencing standards are applied to both offenders.

2. *Societal Attitudes to the Offense at the Time.* Social attitudes are also relevant; people derive cues from the environment with respect to the relative seriousness of proscribed acts, or possibly even the legality of specific actions.[37] Ignorance of the law may be no defense, but an offender convicted of a crime regarded by the community as relatively trivial at least has a claim in mitigation. One factor affecting culpability is the degree to which he or she should have understood the inherent (and relative) wrongfulness of his conduct. Multiple sources of guidance are available, some formal, others informal. The formal sources involve statutory penalties and legal judgments. These are how a citizen becomes aware of a behavior's illegal nature, its inherent wrongfulness, and the legal consequences of violating the law. Duty is reciprocal: on the state to ensure that citizens are aware of the illegal nature of proscribed acts and omissions and on the citizen to inform himself or herself of the legal status of his or her conduct. The state should also ensure that the criminal statutes do not contain offenses that are never prosecuted.

---

37. If defendants believe that reasonable and honest people would regard their conduct as honest, they may not even be guilty of dishonesty; this should surely be relevant to their level of blameworthiness.

More formal, nonstate sources also play a role in affecting culpability. D is convicted of insider trading. In his defense, he demonstrates that this form of trading was endorsed by his superiors, was commonplace among other traders (and at all trading firms), and was subject to minimal institutional prohibitions. For example, rogue trader Kweku Adoboli was responsible for the largest trading loss in British banking history ($2.25 billion) through fraudulent trading. He argued that his trading practices were common among other traders and condoned—if not encouraged—by his superiors. His bank was ultimately fined £30 million for its role, thereby lending some credibility to the offender's claim (*R. v. Kweku Adoboli*, Southwark Crown Court, November 20, 2012). These circumstances are not exculpatory, but they might mitigate—an example of Husak's BEDT defense argument applied in mitigation rather than exculpation. Social norms may not exculpate but do create legitimate sources of mitigation. Informal sources are also relevant. Some acts proscribed by the law are commonplace, others rare. When the crime is a feature of everyday life, the citizen's full awareness of the legal consequences is compromised.

The early prosecutions for offenses occurring during sporting events are also illustrative. In the 1970s, fights were common in professional ice hockey games in the United States and Canada. Spectators approved, and clubs recognized this by hiring players for the speed of their fists rather than their skates. The sports authority's laws punished on-ice fights with indulgence; the penalty for fighting was a short (5-minute) period off the ice, during which time the offending players could be replaced without cost to the teams (Roberts and Benjamin 2000). Players charged with assaults during games argued that professional athletes effectively consented to the assault, a position rejected by the courts. But there was also an appeal in mitigation that these considerations (frequency, public support, and professional endorsement) meant that the defendants were less blameworthy than if the assault had taken place outside the hockey arena. In other words, social and professional norms were invoked as sources of diminished blameworthiness.

3. *State Inaction against Perpetrators.* Is the offender reasonably deemed less culpable because the state fails to prosecute and punish other offenders guilty of the same crime? The nature of the state response represents an additional source of guidance for the offender about the wrongfulness of specific actions. An absence of any prosecutions may lead people to reasonably conclude that the crime is insufficiently serious to justify the state's action.[38]

---

38. In several countries, during the years preceding the legalization of abortion, state prosecutions declined or ceased entirely. This failure to prosecute conveys a message to the public about the moral wrongfulness of the conduct, even if it remained illegal.

The possession of marijuana for personal consumption is a commonly cited example. Homosexual acts are another. These were criminalized until 1988 in Israel, although the last prosecutions occurred in the 1960s. Citizens are entitled to draw some conclusions from this prosecutorial inactivity. Domestic violence also provides a good illustration. Fifty years ago, all but the most serious instances of this form of offending were considered a private matter concerning only the offender and the victim. Few cases were prosecuted, fewer still punished. Finally, if the state declines to prosecute criminal acts committed by significant numbers of people, this conveys a message of indulgence that the offender may raise in mitigation.

Sentencing is complicated when the court is effectively dealing with two offenders: as he or she was at the time of the crime and at the time of sentencing. The offender's liability should reflect the seriousness of the offense as calibrated at the time of the crime. Historical sentencing levels should apply, as they reflect the wrongfulness and harm as recognized by courts at the time. Applying contemporary levels is nothing less than a retroactive recalibration of harm and culpability.[39]

A case may be mounted in favor of recalibrating the gravity of the offense but not the offender's level of culpability. The offender's level of blameworthiness reflects his or her mental state at the time and his or her appreciation of the wrongfulness of the conduct. The state should not retrospectively impute a heightened level of blameworthiness to the offender. The offender may reasonably claim that his or her liability rests on the harm reflected in historical standards applicable at the time. Finally, it is important to recognize that harm and culpability are not independent components of a proportional sanction with discrete liability arising from both elements. The degree of culpability is linked to the level of harm inflicted or threatened; blameworthiness relates to the degree of harm the offender intended to cause. This being the case, if the state revisits (and reinterprets) the seriousness of the crime, it is also, by inference, revising the offender's culpability—retroactively.

The issue of culpability highlights the complexities arising from historical sentencing. One view is that culpability is derived from and therefore directly tied to the seriousness of the offense. Rapists are more blameworthy

---

39. The English courts have taken the view that it was the offender's "choice not to take the initiative and admit the offences when the earlier more lenient sentencing policy was in operation" (*Forbes*, [2016] EWCA Crim 1388, at 4). The defendant should not have to surrender his or her right to a trial in order to be sentenced according to the levels of severity in operation at the time of the crime (for further discussion of the English courts' approach to sentencing historical cases, see Doig 2017; Harris 2017; and Harris and Walker 2017).

than robbers because they are responsible for more harm. On this reasoning, if the state recalibrates the harm of the offense, it should automatically increase the offender's blameworthiness. Yet even the position that culpability is fixed in time is open to debate. The passage of time may not change the offender's moral blameworthiness, but it can change the court's evaluation of that blameworthiness. For example, months after the crime, the offender manifests symptoms of a mental disorder that diminishes his or her culpability in some way. If the disorder was of a long-standing nature, it would have played a role in the commission of the crime, making the offender less blameworthy. Resetting the clock and asking about the offender's blameworthiness without regard to circumstances in the period between the crime and the delayed sentencing hearing would mean that this information would be lost.

The context in which offending took place should be considered at sentencing, particularly if courts are applying current sentencing standards that are manifestly harsher than those operating at the time of the crime.

B. Considering the Crime Victim

The analysis so far consists of a unidirectional claim for mitigation. It is susceptible to the response that the offender may mitigate his or her punishment simply by lying low and refraining from further offending. The offender's liability then slowly decays as time passes. Yet historical offenders must also accept the consequences of delayed punishment relating to the victim. If the offender's moral trajectory since the crime is taken into account (to his or her benefit), it is reasonable to consider any harm arising from the crime over the same period to his or her detriment. The offender cannot claim positive conduct in the period between crime and punishment as mitigation while requiring the victim's situation to be frozen in time. Awareness of the state's inability to identify and prosecute the offender may exacerbate the victim's suffering and prolong any process of healing. The continuing awareness that an offender is "wandering free and unpunished," to use Tomlin's phrase (2014, p. 66), may well be a source of potential distress to the crime victim.

Censure-based sentencing conveys a message to the victim as well as the offender, namely, that he or she has been the victim not of adventitious harm but of a criminal wrong (von Hirsch 1993). If punishment is mitigated on the grounds that 30 years after the crime, the offender is a different person, this message is diluted. The impact of the crime on the victim may be documented in the victim impact statement, where available.

To the extent that a victim impact statement contains legally relevant information to help a court determine the seriousness of the offense, this should include the (possibly lengthy) period between crime and punishment. For this reason, prior to sentencing, crime victims are permitted to update their impact statements completed at the time of first contact with the police. The victim, in short, may be a different person, too, and directly as a consequence of the crime.

IV. A Model Approach to Sentencing Historical Cases

Considering the elements making up a proportionate sentence leads to the following preliminary conclusions regarding the sentencing of historical offenses. The passage of time alone does not change the sentencing exercise, but it does open up fresh avenues of mitigation and aggravation. Applying current sentencing standards decouples the sentence from an individualized determination of the offender's level of culpability. Mitigating and aggravating factors may carry more (or less) weight when the crime occurred decades prior to the determination of sentence. The offender should not be sentenced as if the crime had just occurred, nor should he or she be sentenced as if the court could move backward in time, weighing circumstances exactly as they existed at that time. The period between crime and punishment must be considered. Treating the offense and the parties as though the crime were committed yesterday is artificial and unreal; the crime has not just occurred, the offender is not the same individual who committed the offense, and the victim is not the same person harmed years earlier.

A. Qualifying Passage-of-Time Mitigation

The impact of most forms of mitigation often diminishes when the offense is extremely serious.[40] If the offense entails the intentional taking of human life—murder, for example—claims of good character, remorse, or other mitigations pale in significance to the harm inflicted and the culpability of

---

40. For example, the Sexual Offences Guideline in England and Wales notes the following with respect to good character mitigation: "The more serious the offence, the less the weight which should normally be attributed to this factor" (Sentencing Council of England and Wales 2016, p. 155; Ashworth 2015, p. 200).

the offender.[41] Exactly why mitigation counts for less in these cases is unclear. One possible explanation is that when the crime is most egregious (intentional homicide), pleas in mitigation become less credible. For example, first-offender mitigation is more plausible when there is some ambiguity about the harm inflicted or about the full impact of the crime on the victim.[42] No such ambiguity can reasonably be claimed in the context of murder. Citizens do not need to be arrested, charged, prosecuted, and punished before they fully appreciate the wrongfulness of this crime.

The same diminished-mitigation argument should apply to historical offenses,[43] and this may suggest that offenders convicted of offenses such as homicide may be exempt from passage-of time-mitigation. This may be why war-crimes prosecutions should generally be exempt from passage-of-time mitigation. I would also exclude such offenders on the view that the exceptional seriousness of mass human-rights violations removes these cases from a proportionality sentencing framework devised for more conventional crimes. Let's face it, can a court really calibrate a proportional sentence in response to the murder of thousands of people? Murder is also excluded from statutes of limitations in most jurisdictions. The character change that may justify mitigation will always be heavily outweighed by the severity of the crime in these cases.[44]

The significance of passage-of-time mitigation is related to the seriousness of the offense. Statutes of limitation are sensitive to the seriousness of

---

41. Cases in which the offender takes the life of a dying or comatose spouse or family member are an obvious exception to this general position. See, for example, *R. v. Inglis*, where the defendant had taken the life of her severely disabled son and was convicted of murder, carrying a mandatory life sentence. On appeal, the Court of Appeal imposed a relatively lenient minimum term of 5 years' imprisonment ([2010] EWCA Crim 2637).

42. D is convicted of claiming false business-related expenses to reduce his tax liability. Two factors combine to reduce his culpability. First, he has never been charged with tax avoidance before (and is entitled to first-offender mitigation), and second, there is ambiguity surrounding the legitimacy of certain deductions. However, if he fails to include payments from a large overseas contract in his world income, his "but I've never done it before" plea in mitigation is less plausible, as the wrongfulness of the omission was much clearer (Roberts 2010).

43. In sentencing Max Clifford for eight counts of indecent assault committed decades earlier, the Court of Appeal noted that "his claim to credit based on his not having offended since the mid-1980s and his charitable work were much reduced by this being offending of a serious nature" (*R. v. Clifford* [2014] EWCA Crim 2245; [2015] 1 Cr. App. R. [S.] 32 [CA (Crim Div)]).

44. The same logic applies to compensatory responses to the most serious crimes. You may be able to compensate the victim for 6 months' loss of income or some similar harm, but you cannot compensate a community for a mass atrocity. Some things just can't be squared away by the offender.

the offense, with more generous limits available to the state when the alleged offense is more serious.[45] An analogy may be made with prior convictions. Although retributivists disagree about the exact role of prior crimes at sentencing, there is consensus that more serious crimes "decay" more slowly than less serious crimes. This is reflected in criminal history counting rules in the US sentencing guidelines, as well as judicial practice. For example, a 12-year-old felony is counted in criminal-history calculation, whereas a misdemeanor of the same age will have "washed out" (Frase et al. 2015). In a similar fashion, the most serious historical offenses should attract less consideration in terms of mitigation.

B. The Process

A stepped sentencing process is therefore necessary in passage-of-time cases. Crime seriousness is calibrated according to historical standards as indicated by the severity of punishments imposed at that time. The court determines a provisional sentence proportionate to the harm ascribed to the offense as reflected in historical sentencing patterns. This sentence is then adjusted to reflect any relevant passage-of-time mitigation and aggravation. In aggravation, the victim's continued suffering over the period between commission of the crime and sentencing should be set against any claim in mitigation relating to law-abiding life or exemplary conduct during the same period. If the offender had benefited from the crime over the period in question, this gain should be offset by a harsher punishment. Another postcrime source of aggravation would arise from active efforts by the offender to avoid detection and prosecution—for example, by changing his or her identity, appearance, or country of residence. Attempts to prevent or inhibit crime victims from reporting to the police should also aggravate the ultimate sentence.[46]

Courts should consider passage-of-time mitigation claims, including the possibility that at the time, the offense was regarded as less serious (and punished accordingly). The passage-of-time mitigation should include disproportionate impact in light of the passage of time since the offense and the

---

45. Most statutes apply the seriousness-of-the-crime criterion. For example, the US federal code places a 3-year limitation on most crimes but longer limits for more serious offending. There is no limit on capital offenses.

46. Even this position may be too simplistic. An offender's efforts to efface his or her past identity may be interpreted as an attempt to repudiate an earlier criminal identity, in the way that efforts at desistance often invoke similar steps.

offender's current circumstances,[47] an extended period of compliance with the law, voluntary compensation to the victim, and evidence of significant moral transformation.[48] Many long-term offenders in the United States convicted of drug-related offenses are serving sentences that today seem draconian but were deemed proportionate decades ago. These prisoners have a justiciable claim for a second-look sentence review.

C. Second-Look Sentencing Reviews

What of the second category of cases in which the passage of time may play a role, the individual who has served many years in prison? Space limitations here prevent a thorough analysis, but some comments may be offered. Long-term prisoners in the United States, in particular, serve decades in prison. If the passage of time creates opportunities for mitigation in the case of the unprosecuted offender at liberty, it would be unfair to deny similar consideration to the long-term prisoner. In addition, knowledge of the debilitating effects of confinement, particularly long-term imprisonment, has grown considerably. Consideration should therefore be given to whether the sentence imposed all those years ago remains proportionate. The American Law Institute's Model Penal Code Sentencing provision permits such a second-look approach to long sentences of imprisonment. Its S.305.6 authorizes a judicial panel or other judicial decision maker to hear and rule on applications for modification of sentence from prisoners who have served 15 years of any sentence of imprisonment. The code notes that "the inquiry shall be whether the purposes of sentencing in S.1.02 would better be served by a modified sentence than the prisoner's completion of the original sentence."

There may also be reason to question whether the degree of penal censure deemed appropriate many years earlier has diminished as a result of developments in the intervening period. In determining the level of censure (and the stringency of the sanction), a court should recognize any offense-related conduct by the prisoner. Once sentence is imposed, there should be an opportunity for the offender to demonstrate postsentence behavior that

---

47. For a less serious offense that might attract a short period of imprisonment, the sentence may become disproportionate due to a change in the offender's circumstances since the crime.

48. What if the offender has acquired additional criminal convictions since the original offense that is only now being sentenced? He or she should be sentenced on the first offense as a true first offender; the subsequent string of offenses should only serve to disentitle the offender from good-character mitigation in the period separating the first offense and his or her current sentencing for that offense.

may justify recalibration of the amount of appropriate censure. The longer the sentence—whether served in prison or in the community—the stronger the censure-based reasons for allowing the offender an opportunity for some reconsideration of his or her sentence. Life prisoners have the strongest claim to a court revisiting their censure level and their time in detention. After, say, 30 years in prison, such prisoners may reasonably ask whether the degree of censure expressed all those years before is still necessary (Roberts and Dagan 2019).

I have explored the role of time within the context of a proportional sentencing framework, but no regime is purely retributive. All jurisdictions consider multiple objectives at sentencing, including rehabilitation, deterrence, and incapacitation. These other purposes should also be sensitive to the passage of time. Assuming that there has been no further offending, a lengthy delay between crime and punishment reduces the need for a deterrent or incapacitative sentence. From the perspective of rehabilitation, the law-abiding-for-20-years offender can plausibly argue that this has been achieved without state intervention.[49] As noted many years ago: "The criminal who has avoided prosecution for several years and who seeks to rehabilitate himself would be encouraged in this objective by the assurance that whatever progress he makes will not be shattered by enforcement of some long-dormant claim of the state to his freedom" (University of Pennsylvania Law Review 1954, p. 634).

V. *Conclusion*

A purely retributivist account ascribes no relevance to even a lengthy passage of time between commission of the crime and punishment of the offender. The crime and the offender remain fixed in the same retributive state. I have suggested reasons to see retributive and preventive significance in developments in the passage of time between crime and punishment. Sentencing the offender as if the crime occurred recently and imposing current sentencing levels without regard to the penal context at the time of the crime are insufficiently sensitive to the seriousness of the offense at the time or the offender's true level of culpability.

---

49. A lengthy delay between the crime and the point of state interest will affect whether the prosecutor decides that the public interest is served by a prosecution (Crown Prosecution Service of England and Wales 2018).

References

Alexander, Larry, and Kimberly Ferzan. 2009. *Crime and Culpability: A Theory of Criminal Law*. Cambridge: Cambridge University Press.

Apel, Robert, and Gary Sweeten. 2010. "The Impact of Incarceration on Employment during the Transition to Adulthood." *Social Problems* 57(3):448–79.

Arditti, J. 2012. *Parental Incarceration and the Family*. New York: New York University Press.

Ashworth, Andrew. 2015. "Case Comment on *R. v. Clifford*." *Criminal Law Review* 2:167–70.

Ashworth, Andrew, and Andreas [Andrew] von Hirsch. 2005. *Proportionate Sentencing*. Oxford: Clarendon.

Berger, Dan. 2006. *Outlaws of America: The Weather Underground and the Politics of Solidarity*. Oakland, CA: Oakland Press.

Burrough, Bryan. 2015. *Days of Rage: America's Radical Underground, the FBI, and the Forgotten Age of Revolutionary Violence*. New York: Penguin.

Coombs, C. H. 1967. "Thurstone's Measurement of Social Values Revisited Forty Years Later." *Journal of Personality and Social Psychology* 6:85–91.

Crackenthorpe, M. 1900. "Can Sentences Be Standardised?" *The Nineteenth Century* (January):103–15.

Crown Prosecution Service of England and Wales. 2018. *Code for Prosecutors*. London: Crown Prosecution Service of England and Wales.

Cullen, Frank, Bruce Link, and Craig Polanzi. 1982. "The Seriousness of Crime Revisited." *Criminology* 2:83–102.

Diamantis, Mihailis. 2018. "Corporate Essence and Identity in Criminal Law." *Journal of Business Ethics* 154(4):955–66. https://doi.org/10.1007/s10551-018-3892-4.

Doig, Gavin. 2017. "The Sentencing of Historic Sexual Offences: *R. v. Forbes and Others* [2016] EWCA Crim 1388." *Journal of Criminal Law* 81:9–19.

du Bois-Pedain, Antje. 2019. "Penal Desert and The Passage of Time." In *Penal Censure: Engagements within and beyond Desert Theory*, edited by Antje du Bois-Pedain and Anthony Bottoms. Oxford: Hart.

Flatman, Geoff, and Mirko Bagaric. 1997. "Problems in Prosecuting Cases Involving Historical Child Sexual Abuse: The Victorian Experience." *Deakin Law Review* 4(1):1–20.

Frase, Richard, and Julian V. Roberts. 2019. *Paying for the Past: Prior Record Enhancements in the US Sentencing Guidelines*. New York: Oxford University Press.

Frase, Richard, Julian V. Roberts, Kelly Mitchell, and Rhys Hester. 2015. *Sourcebook of Criminal History Enhancements*. Minneapolis: Robina Institute, University of Minnesota.

Freiberg, Arie. 2002. "What's It Worth? A Cross-Jurisdictional Comparison of Sentence Severity." In *Sentencing and Society: International Perspectives*, edited by Neil Hutton and Cyrus Tata. Aldershot: Ashgate.

Freiberg, Arie, Hugh Donnelly, and Karen Gelb. 2015. *Sentencing for Child Sexual Abuse in Institutional Contexts*. Report for the Royal Commission into Institutional Responses to Child Sexual Abuse. Sydney: Royal Commission into Institutional Responses to Child Sexual Abuse.

Goldberg-Hiller, Jonathan, and David Johnson. 2013. "Time and Punishment." *Quinnipiac Law Review* 31:621–76.

Government of New South Wales. 2014. *Sentencing of Sexual Assault Offenders*. Victoria: Joint Select Committee.

Harris, Lyndon. 2017. "Sentencing: *R. v. L.*" *Criminal Law Review* 7:567–69.

Harris, Lyndon, and Sebastian Walker. 2017. "Old Law and Young Offenders: Sentencing and the Limits of Article 7." *Criminal Law Review* 2:78–92.

Hough, Mike, Jessica Jacobson, and Andrew Millie. 2003. *The Decision to Imprison: Sentencing and the Prison Population*. London: Prison Reform Trust.

Husak, Doug. 2010. "The 'But Everyone Does That!' Defense." In *The Philosophy of Criminal Law: Selected Essays*. New York: Oxford University Press.

Independent Inquiry into Child Sexual Abuse. 2018. *Interim Report*. London: House of Commons.

Kelly, Rory. 2018. "Reforming Maximum Sentences and Respecting Ordinal Proportionality." *Criminal Law Review* 6:450–61.

Lippke, Richard. 2018. "Retroactive Sentencing Changes: Exploring the Complications." *Oxford Journal of Legal Studies* 38:147–67.

Massoglia, Michael, and W. Pridemore. 2015. "Incarceration and Health." *Annual Review of Sociology* 4:291–310.

Meyer, Linda. 2017. *Sentencing in Time*. Amherst: Amherst College Press.

New, Christopher. 1992. "Time and Punishment." *Analysis* 52(1):35–40.

O'Malley, Tom. 2016. *Sentencing Law and Practice*, 3rd ed. Dublin: Round Hall.

Parfit, Derek. 1984. *Reasons and Persons*. Oxford: Clarendon.

Patterson, Evelyn. 2013. "The Dose-Response of Time Served in Prison on Mortality: New York State, 1989–2003." *American Journal of Public Health* 103(3):523–28.

Pridemore, W. 2014. "The Mortality Penalty of Incarceration: Evidence from a Population-Based Case-Control Study of Working-Age Males." *Journal of Health and Social Behavior* 55(2):215–33.

Roberts, Julian V. 2010. "Re-Examining First Offender Discounts at Sentencing." In *Previous Convictions at Sentencing: Theoretical and Applied Perspectives*, edited by Julian V. Roberts and Andreas [Andrew] von Hirsch. Oxford: Hart.

Roberts, Julian V., and Cynthia Benjamin. 2000. "Sports Violence in North America: Scope of the Problem and Nature of the Response." *European Journal on Criminal Policy and Research* 8:163–81.

Roberts, Julian V., and Netanel Dagan. 2019. "Just Deserts, Penal Censure, and Parole." In *Penal Censure: Engagements within and beyond Desert Theory*, edited by Antje du Bois-Pedain and Anthony Bottoms. Oxford: Hart.

Roberts, Julian V., and Loretta Stalans. 1997. *Public Opinion, Crime, and Criminal Justice*. Boulder: Westview.

Robinson, Paul. 1980. "A Brief History of Distinctions in Criminal Culpability." *Hastings Law Journal* 31:815–53.

Samuels, Alec. 2017. "Sentencing the Historic Sex Offender." *Criminal Law and Justice Weekly* 181(June 3):21.

Schnittker, Jason, and Andrea John. 2007. "Enduring Stigma: The Long-Term Effects of Incarceration on Health." *Journal of Health and Social Behavior* 48:115–30.

Schnittker, Jason, Michael Massoglia, and Christopher Uggen. 2012. "Out and Down: Incarceration and Psychiatric Disorders." *Journal of Health and Social Behavior* 53:448–64.

Sentencing Council of England and Wales. 2011. *Overview of Burglary Offences*. https://www.sentencingcouncil.org.uk/wp-content/uploads/Analysis_and_research_bulletin_-_burglary_offences.pdf.

Sentencing Council of England and Wales. 2016. *Sexual Offences: Definitive Guideline*. https://www.sentencingcouncil.org.uk/wp-content/uploads/Sexual-Offences-Definitive-Guideline-web5.pdf.

Sentencing Project. 2017. *Trends in U.S. Corrections*. https://www.sentencingproject.org/wp-content/uploads/2016/01/Trends-in-US-Corrections.pdf.

Tomlin, Patrick. 2014. "Time and Punishment." *Law and Philosophy* 33:655–82.

University of Pennsylvania Law Review. 1954. "The Statute of Limitations in Criminal Law: A Penetrable Barrier to Prosecution." *University of Pennsylvania Law Review* 102:630–53.

Von Hirsch, Andreas [Andrew]. 1993. *Censure and Sanction*. Oxford: Clarendon.

Von Hirsch, Andreas. 2017. *Deserved Criminal Sentences*. Oxford: Hart.

Von Hirsch, Andreas [Andrew], and Nils Jareborg. 1991. "Gauging Criminal Harm: A Living Standard Analysis." *Oxford Journal of Legal Studies* 11:1–38.

8

The Time-Frame Challenge
to Retributivism

Adam J. Kolber

MOST PEOPLE HAVE the intuition that good people deserve good things and bad people deserve bad things. Retributivists take this intuition quite seriously. They argue that criminal offenders should suffer or be punished in proportion to their moral desert. It is offenders' moral desert, they believe, that justifies the harsh treatment offenders receive.

It turns out to be quite difficult, however, to decide exactly what counts in assessments of moral desert for criminal justice purposes. Even if we assume that desert depends on actions (as opposed to, say, character or virtue), retributivists must decide whether to examine offenders' desert for crimes and other misdeeds across their entire lives (the whole-life approach) or only for what are typically recent crimes under consideration at a current sentencing proceeding (the current-crime approach).

Neither view is acceptable. The whole-life view examines all of offenders' good and bad deeds and all of the good and bad things that have happened to them in order to impose penal treatment proportionate to moral desert. Unfortunately, we have limited evidence of offenders' prior conduct and of the good and bad things that have happened to them since birth. Moreover,

Adam J. Kolber is Professor of Law at Brooklyn Law School. For helpful comments on earlier drafts, he thanks Mitch Berman, Mihailis Diamantis, Doug Husak, Rocío Lorca, and Michael Tonry, as well as conference participants at Cardozo Law School, Oxford University, and Syracuse University. This project was generously supported by a summer research stipend from Brooklyn Law School and a visiting fellowship at the Center for Research in Crime and Justice of the New York University School of Law.

punishing those who have suffered great misfortune risks augmenting the mismatch between their well-being and what they deserve. In some cases, the whole-life approach could lead to unworkable "moral madness" (Ezorsky 1972, p. xxv) in which a person has suffered so much that he or she could knowingly break the law and still be immune to punishment.

Some retributivists might cling to the whole-life approach but view it as an idealization. They might say recent crimes are proxies for whole-life desert given available evidence. But retributivists widely endorse a firm prohibition on purposely, knowingly, or recklessly overpunishing (Alexander and Ferzan 2009, p. 102, n. 33). In any world we can plausibly imagine, using recent crimes as a proxy for overall moral desert would make the risk of overpunishment enormous and could be deemed knowing overpunishment whenever a judge deliberately ignores evidence from an offender's past that would mitigate.

Our actual sentencing practices, to the extent that they contain retributivist features, largely reflect a different approach. Most judges purport to sentence offenders only for crimes for which they have been recently convicted (the current-crime approach). To the extent that judges consider offenders' broader history at all, they typically believe that it informs the seriousness of the crimes currently being sentenced. Outside of prior criminal history, an offender's broader history has limited effect on sentencing. Sentencing practices vary substantially, however, often in nontransparent ways, and likely reflect both the whole-life and current-crime approaches to varying degrees.

Even if the current-crime view predominates among judges in the United States, retributivists cannot simply rely on what a legal system actually does. They must show that whatever practices they advocate are morally justified. And if desert matters so much to retributivists that it can justify punishment, it's not obvious why we generally fail to examine desert holistically. Looking narrowly at recent crimes risks ignoring offenders' positive desert and prior suffering and might cause offenders to get even less of what they deserve than if the state hadn't intervened at all.

Retributivists must choose a time frame in which to analyze desert, but the choice puts them in an unenviable position. The whole-life view is impractical to the point of absurdity, while the current-crime view is theoretically unsound. Hence the choice of a pertinent time frame in which to evaluate desert presents a serious challenge to retributivist justifications of punishment (and, implicitly, a challenge to many hybrid theories of punishment that have substantial retributivist components), particularly when such justifications are meant to apply to real-world punishments such as incarceration. Retributivists have often ignored the choice, perhaps because it is so difficult to make. But to uphold the retributivist justification, they must select a time frame and explain why the choice is neither theoretically unsound nor hopelessly impractical.

1. *The Whole-Life View*

In 1930, W. D. Ross described what has come to be known as the whole-life view of desert (Ross 1930, pp. 55–64).[1] On this view, we assess an offender's overall moral desert by examining the offender's life so far, looking both at whether he or she has qualities warranting good or bad things and at the extent to which he or she has already received or endured good or bad things.

Regarding whether the offender deserves good or bad things, most retributivists make the determination by focusing on the offender's actions. In other words, they take the "desert basis" (Feinberg 1970, p. 58)—the substrate that determines whether a life should go better or worse—to be actions. Did a person do (or refrain from doing) good or bad? I follow the majority in speaking of the desert basis in terms of actions, even though some retributivists prefer to focus on character or intentions or other plausible criteria. (I suspect that the brunt of the time-frame challenge would apply to these other forms of retributivism as well.)

The second part of the analysis of what an offender deserves looks not at their good and bad deeds but at how their lives have gone so far. The criminal justice system can step in to help ensure that offenders have been, all things considered, subjected to the bad things they deserve. On this view, we seek proportionality between all of an offender's conduct and his or her overall well-being (or pleasure or quality of life or the like).

The whole-life view appears, at least at first, to be an elegant option. If moral desert matters, it seems as though all moral desert matters. And if we believe that people should get what they deserve, then it seems we should examine what offenders have already received (in terms of life circumstances and experiences) when evaluating whether their well-being is in proportion to what they deserve.

The whole-life view also resolves a puzzle about pretrial detention (Kolber 2013, pp. 1147–58). Detainees awaiting trial are usually given credit, if subsequently convicted and sentenced, for time they already spent detained. Crediting time served in detention is puzzling, because such confinement

---

1. On the whole-life view generally, see also Ezorsky (1972, pp. xxii–xxvii); Parent (1976); Ryberg (2004, pp. 18–19); and Tadros (2011, pp. 68–73).

isn't normally thought to be punishment. Yet we reduce the duration of incarcerative punishment by time spent detained. The whole-life view yields an explanation: suffering in pretrial detention, even if it's not punishment, is still suffering. And a day of pretrial detention is similar enough to a day of prison that it counts against prison time on a day-for-day basis.

A. Special Challenges for Whole-Life Retributivism

Despite its elegant initial appearance, the whole-life view has three major drawbacks that do not afflict all versions of retributivism, at least not to the same degree.

1. *Impractical and Invasive.* The first and most devastating drawback is that whole-life retributivism is extraordinarily impractical. We are unlikely to have sufficient evidence to assess the good and bad actions people have taken throughout their lives, nor sufficient evidence to identify the good and bad things that have happened to them. Offenders themselves may know little about the life circumstances they experienced as small children.[2] Moreover, merely attempting to assess the quality of offenders' lives and the morality of all of their actions may unacceptably burden their privacy (von Hirsch 1981, pp. 607–13) and the privacy of those with whom they have ever interacted.

2. *Get-Out-of-Jail-Free Cards.* Second, the whole-life approach puts some beyond the reach of the criminal law. Those who commit bad acts may have already endured so much suffering that punishing them for recent crimes would only make the relationship between their well-being and desert more divergent. Similarly, some offenders may have committed many good deeds that have gone unrewarded; their lives might be best proportioned to their desert if we simply refused to punish their recent crimes.

As Gertrude Ezorsky has noted, a person may have engaged in so many good deeds or have suffered so much that he or she could bank up the opportunity to commit a crime yet still deserve no punishment (1972, p. xxv). Suppose, for example, that Smith is erroneously convicted of a pickpocketing committed by someone else. After six months' incarceration, he is released and then actually does pickpocket someone under circumstances identical in seriousness to the crime for which he erroneously served the six-month sentence.

---

2. Given how dramatically personal identity can change, whole-lifers should arguably exclude information about a person who has changed so much that he or she is, in effect, a new person. This "whole life of a person" variation would, however, be only a little more practical and would require us to resolve persistent tricky questions about the nature of personal identity.

Assume he is arrested for doing so, and all the facts of both pickpocketing incidents come to light. Should Smith now be incarcerated for six more months for the crime he actually committed?

If we assume that Smith's well-being and moral desert were well aligned prior to his erroneous incarceration, it would seem that we ought not punish him for the pickpocketing he actually committed. After all, just prior to pickpocketing, his suffering exceeded what he deserved by six months' incarceration. We can now easily realign his desert and well-being by not punishing him for the pickpocketing he committed. The problem is that if the criminal justice system refused to punish people like Smith when they have already accrued unjust punishment, they will effectively have been given get-out-of-jail-free cards (Alexander 2012, pp. 315–18). A person erroneously punished for murder would be entitled to a future punishment-free murder. Such a possibility is unthinkable from a deterrence perspective but seems inevitable from a whole-life perspective.[3]

3. *Moral Desert We Usually Ignore.* Third, the whole-life approach seems to create obligations to adjust desert in domains extending well beyond the criminal law. Some repeatedly engage in morally odious acts that are not crimes. Nevertheless, the state doesn't see fit, as a general matter, to make sure that noncriminal bad actors' lives become somewhat worse because of their legal but morally inappropriate behavior. Yet why should the state worsen the life of a petty thief but not that of a law-abiding scoundrel who creates far more moral disvalue in the aggregate?

Similarly, if bad deeds yield negative desert, good deeds would seem to yield positive desert. Yet we rarely use the machinery of the state to give people the good things they deserve. While good deeds may have inherent benefits and are often rewarded by market mechanisms, many good deeds go unrewarded or underrewarded and would seem to warrant state intervention as well if the state is going to be in the desert-adjustment business in the first place (Tadros 2011, p. 69).

---

3. One might argue that the person erroneously punished for murder should be compensated for his or her erroneous punishment but still serve the sentence for the murder he or she actually committed. While there are obviously consequentialist reasons to favor that approach, as I discuss below, it is hard to believe that as a matter of desert, there is any better way to remedy the undeserved infliction of X than by refusing to inflict X when it is deserved. Moreover, in this example, we might suppose that serving a second sentence for murder will take away so much of the offender's remaining life span that it would effectively eliminate his or her ability to enjoy the compensation for the earlier erroneous sentence. The inferiority of compensation is also clear when the person erroneously convicted has such enormous wealth that there is no meaningful way to remedy the unjust incarceration with money.

While some have argued that the state needn't reward good deeds or punish noncriminal bad deeds (Berman 2013, p. 107), failure to do so raises questions about whether we really have strong reasons to bring lives into line with what they deserve. Maybe incentives are simply too weak in ordinary cases to create broad-scale state-level efforts to give people what they deserve. Only when consequentialist reasons for punishment are sufficiently strong do retributivists seem to take up the task of bringing desert into alignment. But if that's true, it makes us wonder whether desert is really playing an important role at all—one strong enough, for example, to deprive people of liberty and close association with their loved ones for decades. Those who think desert should play an important role in criminal justice owe us an explanation for why we don't have state institutions that regularly adjust people's lives for their good deeds and noncriminal bad deeds (or a concession that we ought to).

B. Ideal Theory and Absurd Impracticality

The whole-life view is reminiscent of divine reward and punishment in which an all-knowing being wants us to get what we deserve in this life or the next and has the omniscience and omnipotence to make it happen.[4] The criminal justice system, however, is neither omniscient nor omnipotent. Many decry the limited resources available for criminal defense in the real world, but a whole-life approach would make sentencing unfathomably more expensive and complicated. (And while it may not bear on deep theoretical questions, a whole-life approach might exacerbate the disparity of treatment between those who can hire expensive lawyers and expert witnesses and those who cannot.) Even though theorists can abstract away from many real-world complexities, some idealizations are simply too unrealistic to serve as justifications of punishment in anything like our own world. Even if we could avoid get-out-of-jail-free cards and explain away our limited interest in rewarding positive desert, the impracticality challenge seems insurmountable.

Few consider whole-life retributivism to be a serious real-world contender. Kim Ferzan is "somewhat sympathetic to a whole life view" (2018, pp. 286), but Joel Feinberg called it "an obvious impossibility" (1970, pp. 116–17). Thomas Hurka simply declared that "legal retributivism is not a whole-life theory" (2003, p. 52), as though no one really considers it to be one.

---

4. For comparisons of sentencing and divine justice, consider Nigel Walker on the Recording Angel (1991, pp. 101, 138) and Norval Morris on Saint Peter at the Pearly Gates (Morris, Bonnie, and Finer 1986, pp. 121, 139–40).

Whole-life retributivism may be most relevant, as Victor Tadros has used it (2011, pp. 68–73) and as I do here, to point out theoretical deficiencies in more practical forms of retributivism.

II. *The Current-Crime View*

Under what I call the current-crime view, we consider only the crimes an offender is currently being sentenced for and try to make his or her sentence proportionate to the seriousness of those crimes. Those who adopt the current-crime view needn't think an offender's history entirely irrelevant. For example, they may think reoffenders are more culpable than first-timers because they didn't learn from their mistakes when they chose to reoffend. But if current-crime advocates do consider an offender's history, they give no weight to it beyond the light it sheds on culpability for current crimes. Hence, the view principally focuses on a comparatively brief period of an offender's life instead of his or her whole life.

Note that the current-crime view deviates in three important ways from the whole-life view. First, it shifts focus away from any bad deeds a person has engaged in and toward those that are crimes. Second, by focusing only on crimes, it largely ignores positive desert. While whole-lifers offset bad deeds with good ones, there's no obvious positive analogue to crime (although cooperation with law enforcement may have this quality to some extent). Third, consistent perhaps with their narrow focus on crimes, advocates of the current-crime approach focus not on all the ways offenders suffer but only on the ways they suffer or are deprived as a result of state punishment.[5]

These changes make the current-crime view far more practical than the whole-life view. By focusing only on crimes, current-crime retributivists needn't investigate all of a person's conduct since birth. They can develop a rough sense of the seriousness of a recent offense and a rough sense of the amount of punishment proportionate to it. While there are reasons to doubt that we have coherent proportionality intuitions (Kolber 2013), if we do, there is a chance that our criminal justice system can accommodate the current-crime view.

As noted earlier, the criminal justice system in the United States, to the extent that it is characterized by retributivism, is better approximated by a current-crime than a whole-life approach. Criminal history does factor into

---

5. While we can certainly imagine variations of a current-crime view with different assumptions, I believe I've described a rather common version.

sentencing, although it is often understood to simply inform the serious-ness of the crime for which the offender is being sentenced. While judges sometimes mitigate the sentence of an offender who had a deprived or abu-sive upbringing or a history of exceptional public service, doing so is rel-atively uncommon, and the explanation will typically focus on how such considerations bear on the seriousness of recently committed crimes. While real-world sentencing contains features of both whole-life and current-crime approaches, the current-crime approach likely plays a larger role.

A. The Inaccurate-Desert-Basis Challenge

What current-crime retributivism gains in feasibility, however, it loses as a theory. First and foremost, the current-crime view can be faulted for ignoring offenders' more general history of good and bad deeds and life experiences. The whole-life view has been likened to divine justice for a reason. When we picture divine justice, we tend to imagine an omniscient deity that dispenses good or bad treatment based on full knowledge of a person's desert. We might think the current-crime approach deficient to the extent that it ignores aspects of moral desert. What started as the relatively attractive intuition that good people deserve good things and bad people deserve bad things turns out to ignore much of (and probably most of) a person's moral desert. It's as if entry to the Pearly Gates were calculated based only on weekend behavior while entirely ignoring weekday behavior.

Relative to the whole-life view, the current-crime approach will inevi-tably punish inaccurately, overpunishing those with moral credit (for ex-ample, those with distinguished service to the poor or the sick), while underpunishing those with nonlegal moral discredit (for example, those who have taken advantage of the poor and the sick without committing a crime). The overpunishing criticism is particularly serious because retributivists usu-ally have a firm deontological commitment to never purposely, knowingly, or recklessly overpunish. We can safely assume that offenders who fare worse under the current-crime approach would readily offer evidence of their good deeds for which they deserve moral credit. If judges deliberately ignore such evidence when offenders offer it, they have violated a core retributivist commitment. If retributivism required us only to get "close enough" to ac-curate desert, current crimes might serve as rough proxies for the more ele-gant whole-life theory. But given their firm prohibition on overpunishment, current-crime retributivists must explain why they can deliberately ignore evidence of positive moral desert that, at least at first appearance, seems to mitigate negative desert. More generally, they owe us an explanation for why they restrict the kind of moral desert that figures into sentencing.

1. *Moral versus Legal Desert Reply.* Current-crime retributivists cannot respond by purporting to focus only on legal desert rather than moral desert. They cannot say that someone deserves a particular punishment simply because the law provides for that punishment. The whole endeavor of punishment theory is supposed to provide a moral justification of punishment (if, indeed, there is one). Since our current sentencing practices may be wrong from a moral perspective, retributivists must rely on moral arguments to show that punishment can be just.

Institutional practices, such as those of a legal system, only reveal what people deserve relative to some particular institution. If I play a poker hand foolishly but get lucky and win, I am entitled to the pot because the rules of poker say so. Relative to the institution of poker, I deserve the pot. But that alone doesn't mean I morally deserve it. Similarly, rules of a college fraternity may dictate the excommunication of those who share secrets. Within the institution, secret sharers could be said to deserve to be ousted. But that doesn't speak to what they morally deserve. Hence, an offender may deserve two years' incarceration relative to the institution of criminal justice without morally deserving it.

2. *Public-Private Distinction Reply.* The restricted scope of current-crime retributivism might be explained by radically different kinds of moral desert. Betraying a friend might warrant social ostracism, while viciously assaulting strangers might warrant incarceration. Such a strategy might help explain ignoring vast amounts of desert information that would be required by a whole-life approach. The current-crime approach might only consider, say, public moral wrongs rather than private moral wrongs. Public moral wrongs are addressed by the state (often in the form of punishment), while private moral wrongs, if they receive attention at all, are addressed by private individuals and groups.

I am skeptical that the public-private distinction is meaningful for this purpose. For example, enabling and immorally pressuring a family member to cease life support is likely to be a private wrong (not a crime), but enabling and immorally pressuring someone to commit suicide may be a crime and hence a public wrong. Sex between spouses is public if it involves sexual assault but private if it concerns the freedom to use contraceptives (*Griswold v. Connecticut*, 381 U.S. 479 [1965]).

There are important distinctions to draw in these cases, but it's not clear that the demarcation is between what is private and what is public. Naturally, serious crimes such as murder more dramatically alter a person's moral desert than legally permissible transgressions against a friend. But that some desert claims are weightier than others is not enough to show that there are different kinds of desert. Moreover, minor transgressions can be substantial in the aggregate: acts of duplicity and betrayal over a period of years—even if they do not constitute crimes—can create more pressing moral desert concerns than minor criminal offenses such as petty theft.

It would be exceedingly difficult, if not impossible, to make the line between crimes and noncriminal bad behavior match up perfectly with the line between negative desert that should and should not be punished. Decisions to criminalize require society-wide estimations of, for example, the harmfulness of certain conduct and the costs and invasiveness of police efforts to stop it. There's no obvious reason why such variables, heavily dependent on empirical considerations and falling along various spectra (Kolber 2014, 2016a, 2016b), would also draw an appropriate line regarding the kind of treatment people deserve. A new law-enforcement technology could make it cheap enough to criminalize conduct that couldn't practically be criminalized before. Presumably, that wouldn't change the treatment that offenders now morally deserve. Unless desert were somehow the only consideration in determinations of what to criminalize, the criminalization line is not likely to demarcate an appropriate boundary regarding the kinds of desert warranting punishment.

B. The Inaccurate-Desert-Object Challenge

Another challenge to the current-crime view focuses on the desert object, meaning that which offenders are deemed to deserve (Berman 2011, p. 437). By moving from deserved suffering under the whole-life view to deserved punishment under the current-crime view, current-crime retributivists once again risk punishing inaccurately. That is, they may overpunish offenders who suffered tremendously outside of the criminal justice system (for example, those who have been abused or have suffered from severe physical or mental illness) and underpunish those gifted with every life advantage in terms of undeserved talents, money, and parental love.

Once again, the overpunishment concern is the more serious one given retributivists' firm refusal to purposely, knowingly, or recklessly overpunish. And again, offenders who are harmed by the current-crime approach would surely offer evidence of their undeserved suffering for which they deserve credit. The challenge to current-crime retributivists is to explain why they can ignore such evidence and still punish individual offenders.

   1. *The Intuition Reply.* One reply simply describes intuitions more consistent with the current-crime approach: "I don't think a bank robber should be punished less *simply* because he was accidentally paralyzed during a robbery." Or "I don't think the celebrity vilified in the press should receive lighter treatment because of his especially acute shame and embarrassment."[6] The problem with these intuitions is that others report opposite ones, believing that both the bank robber and the celebrity should have their punishments mitigated.

   Moreover, I have already suggested one intuition that challenges the view that deserved punishment is the appropriate desert object. We give offenders credit for time served in pretrial detention, even though detainees have not been proven guilty of anything. They are waiting while we determine whether they will be punished. Nevertheless, we regularly reduce amounts of punishment offenders receive by amounts of unpunished time spent in detention. If unpunished time in detention is comparable to time punished in prison, then there are likely other sources of suffering that are equivalent to punishment as well.

   Compare the practice of giving credit for time served with the earlier pickpocketing scenario. Due to a series of strange coincidences, Smith is erroneously convicted of pickpocketing. After serving six months in jail for it, he is released and then commits a pickpocketing of equal seriousness. Must he now spend six months in jail for the crime he really did commit? I suspect most will say that he must; otherwise, he essentially gained a six-month get-out-of-jail-free card while erroneously confined.

   But why are we inclined to credit time in pretrial detention that is, at best, punishment-like, while disinclined to credit time actually punished that precedes a crime?[7] Deterrence concerns are what really seems to drive differential treatment of these scenarios. We want to avoid giving the erroneously

---

6. For discussion, see Husak (1990).

7. Is pretrial detention precondemnatory in some way that conviction can somehow retroactively turn into punishment? I doubt it. That would imply an unnatural definition of punishment. We'd have to shift the typical requirement that punishment be "intended to be burdensome or painful" (Duff 2001, pp. xiv–xv) to something like punishment either "is or subsequently was intended to be burdensome or painful" (Kolber 2013, p. 1150). Moreover, I doubt we would readily recharacterize in the opposite direction. If an erroneously convicted person spent 10 years in prison, we would be loath to deny that he was punished. Indeed, we would think he should be compensated precisely because he was erroneously punished.

convicted pickpocket a get-out-of-jail-free card that can be used upon release. We don't have the same worry about the pretrial detainee whose alleged crime is already in the past.[8] Hence, current-crime retributivists may be smuggling in consequentialist considerations to punish people who would not otherwise be deemed to deserve it.[9]

Current-crime retributivists could disavow the practice of crediting time served by making pretrial detainees serve their full punishments upon conviction. Someone detained for one year who is later convicted and sentenced to a year in prison would spend a total of two years in confinement. Ferzan is "willing to bite the bullet" and accept such results (2018, p. 286), but they deviate radically from consensus practices in the United States and from what I take to be most people's desert intuitions.

Refusing to credit time served might be more palatable if we financially compensated pretrial detainees for their detention. But such compensation seems second best. If only two mint-condition copies of the first *Superman* comic book existed and the holder of one negligently destroyed the other copy, the tort victim would more appropriately be compensated with the remaining copy rather than a monetary payment. There may be policy reasons for courts to order monetary compensation, but requiring transfer of the remaining comic book would more accurately compensate. Similarly, financial compensation for pretrial detainees is better than nothing but not as accurate from a desert perspective as simply allowing them to forgo a day of confinement for each day previously confined. Well-to-do detainees might consider no amount of money sufficient to compensate them, and terminally ill offenders would be better compensated by credit for time served than with money they will never have the liberty to spend.

The view that compensation is always adequate for pretrial detainees may be premised not on desert interests but on other sensible policy considerations. To my mind, these policy considerations are infected with consequentialist concerns about deterrence and public safety that are off limits to more pure forms of retributivism. To be sure, desert and compensation are not the same,

---

8. An interesting borderline case arises when a pretrial detainee assaults a cellmate but is acquitted of the offense that put him in detention in the first place. Should judges credit time served in pretrial detention prior to the assault against the punishment for the assault? Deterrence considerations might counsel against credit, as an offender who believes he'll be acquitted of the initial offense has less incentive to refrain from crime while detained: he is accruing credit against future punishment for crimes committed in detention.

9. Of course, some retributivists explicitly allow consequentialist considerations at sentencing, but few, if any, would rely on consequentialist reasons to punish in excess of desert.

but those who would not remedy undeserved jail time with forgone deserved jail time should probably bear the burden of explaining why monetary payments are the better choice.

In short, if we had good reason to use the current-crime approach, doing so would not be entirely impractical. Indeed, it seems we currently use a current-crime approach (or a hybrid approach with a strong current-crime focus). Unfortunately, it is not at all clear that there are good theoretical reasons for adopting a current-crime approach. Mere practicality cannot turn a bad theory into a good one.

2. *The Incommensurability Reply.* Putting aside the specifics of pretrial detention, current-crime retributivists might argue that there is a broader incommensurability problem that bolsters their approach. To the claim that positive desert offsets negative desert, current-crime retributivists could argue that when you do something good and something bad, what you deserve is both something good and something bad.[10] If so, we needn't worry about punishing someone already below his or her desert baseline. He or she may simply deserve something good, say, to make up for an abusive childhood and something bad, say, to address the thefts he or she committed.

This again strikes me as too convenient a way to smuggle consequentialist considerations into the nature of desert. Certainly, some positive desert offsets some negative desert. If you deserve both to receive a new car and to forfeit one, we needn't go through the formality of giving you the car in the first place. Similarly, we regularly offset positive and negative desert. When Robin Hood steals from the rich to give to the poor, we don't punish him to the fullest extent of the law and then give him the Presidential Medal of Freedom and a celebratory roast at the Rotary Club. Rather, we take all of the pertinent circumstances into account when punishing him, because what he deserves is a function of both his positive and his negative desert.

Current-crime retributivists already seem to accept the additivity of negative desert in many contexts. The more crimes you commit, generally speaking, the more punishment you deserve, even when those crimes are quite varied in nature. Most would think it unremarkable to add together the sentences for someone who commits both assault and insider trading, even though these bad acts are rather different in kind. Why be so ecumenical when summing up negative desert but so picky when combining positive and negative desert?

---

10. I thank Doug Husak for raising this objection.

We often support rewarding positive moral desert with generalized good fortune. Many would be pleased, for example, if an engineer who sacrifices precious time each weekend to volunteer at a soup kitchen happens to receive a salary increase at work, even when the increase is unrelated to morally praiseworthy behavior. But if positive moral desert can be rewarded generically and negative moral desert can be punished generically (as may be the case at least for incarceration), it is hard to see why positive and negative desert are incommensurable.

Even substantive criminal law arguably nets out good and bad desert on some occasions. Under the Model Penal Code, when a defendant attempts a crime but then fully and voluntarily renounces it prior to completion, he or she has a full defense (American Law Institute 1985, § 5.01[4]). Similarly, if a person aids and abets a crime but then gives timely warning to law enforcement or otherwise makes appropriate efforts to undo the help he or she provided, that person, too, has a complete defense (American Law Institute 1985, § 2.06[6]).

In some of these cases, defendants may have walked down the road toward crimes they would never really complete and arguably have no negative desert. In others, though, defendants engaged in genuinely reprehensible conduct for which punishment was warranted but then made praiseworthy decisions to cease or foil crimes. For members of this group, retributivists who accept the Model Penal Code approach may be inclined to say that these defendants deserved punishment but then engaged in at least partially offsetting praiseworthy behavior such that we are willing to negate their desert. In any event, I doubt current-crime retributivists believe such defendants deserve both punishment and reward. And if we allow positive and negative desert to offset on short time scales, what in the moral universe would keep us from doing so on longer time scales as well?

Consider now a scholar, Jones, who writes an excellent but overlooked article that deserves praise. Might we not think she deserves both praise for the article and punishment for some minor crime she commits rather than think the praise she deserves must be netted out against her punishment? First, it is not at all clear that excellent articles should be praised as a matter of moral desert. Our interests in promoting good scholarship could be consequentialist or a matter of nonmoral desert. Second, suppose we gave the scholar the choice of being rewarded with praiseworthy citations or with a loving and devoted new puppy certain to bring joy for years to come. If the scholar chose the latter, I wouldn't feel that her moral desert (assuming there was some) went unrewarded. The scholar simply received something of more value to her than praise. The scholarly community might be at a loss for failing to recognize the paper properly, but that has little to do with moral desert.

Admittedly, there are many ways to argue that rewards and sanctions fail to combine, but retributivists arguably bear the burden of explaining why positive and negative desert have rather asymmetric properties. For example, while one might say that doing good can sometimes be its own reward, doing bad can also sometimes be its own punishment. And if the reward we deserve for good deeds is typically something minimal, such as gratitude, why isn't the punishment for bad deeds something minimal as well, such as condemnation? We are indeed inclined to respond quite differently to good and bad deeds, but that may be a function of instrumental reasons that have little to do with desert.

In short, current-crime retributivists owe us an explanation for why we cannot commensurate positive and negative moral desert. Retributivists who endorse something like our current criminal justice system would have to implausibly believe that negative moral desert is sufficiently important that it can justify locking people up and separating them from their children, but positive moral desert is so inconsequential that we can ignore it when we deliberately make offenders suffer. Even if positive and negative desert are not perfectly commensurable, they often seem close enough. Nobody thinks that money accurately compensates someone for the wrongful death of a loved one, but in the absence of a better mechanism, we do compensate with money. When positive desert goes otherwise unrewarded, it is not obvious why we wouldn't use it to offset negative desert.

3. *The "Retributivism Is Localized" Reply.* Another strategy that current-crime retributivists might use is simply to restrict the domain of punishment to negative moral desert. According to Mitch Berman, what people deserve is not measured against some external "absolute norm of individual welfare" but is measured by an "*intra*-personal standard" (2013, pp. 103–4). What offenders deserve, according to Berman, is that their lives go less well than they would have gone had they not offended.[11] To the charge that current-crime retributivism punishes those already worse off than they deserve to be, he could simply deny the relevance of offenders' current sorry states to retributivism.

---

11. Note how smoothly Berman's view comports with deterrence: "What is thought good," on Berman's view, "is precisely that people's wrongful choices don't avail them and, to the contrary, make them worse off" (2013, p. 103).

But even if the state has a special role in the infliction of negative desert on criminals (Berman 2013, p. 107), the state presumably still has other legitimate desert obligations. State actors are also people, and presumably, it should count against whatever punishments they inflict that they are thereby aggravating net desert imbalances. Correctional institutions may be designed to inflict punishment rather than clean up the environment, but that doesn't mean they can ignore moral issues related to the environment, even if those issues run counter to punitive goals. If negative moral desert is powerful enough to justify punishment, other moral desert considerations outside of the criminal justice system presumably can be quite weighty and should influence our actions as well. This is all the more true given that reducing punishment for a history of good deeds might well save the state money overall.

Berman anticipates these concerns, arguing that retributivism needn't respond to all concerns of justice. To Berman, "retributivism is a localized theory of justice, not a comprehensive theory" and "does not claim or aspire to be a theory about what we should do taking all justice-relevant considerations into account" (2013, p. 104). Rather than arguing that positive desert is incommensurable with negative desert, retributivists could simply delegate the task of examining positive desert to some other aspect of moral theory. Berman deliberately and avowedly sets out a modest role for retributivism (2016).

Berman's view is so modest, however, that it cannot respond to the concerns raised by the time-frame challenge. It simply delegates questions about prior suffering and prior deeds to other unspecified moral theories. So delegated, of course, the time-frame challenge would not apply to Berman's retributivism. But many theorists, I believe, have grander expectations for what retributivism is supposed to accomplish. David Gray writes that the "core challenge to any theory of criminal law" is "to justify punishment generally and to rationalize the punishments inflicted in particular cases more specifically" (2010, p. 1640). Similarly, Göran Duus-Otterström writes: "In order to reliably establish retributive justice, we must not only be able to say with reasonable confidence that a supposed offender deserves punishment. We must also be able to say how much punishment a deserving offender deserves" (2013, p. 459).

More generally, retributivists adopting a version of H. L. A. Hart's separate-questions approach (1968, pp. 8–13) may treat the general justifying aim of punishment to be consequentialist but still consider the distribution of punishment to particular offenders to be retributivist. For them, there may be broad criminal justice questions requiring resort to theories outside retributivism, but the narrower question of whether some punishment is proportionate to some particular offender's crime falls squarely in the domain of retributivism. If retributivism cannot tell us even in principle what punishment we ought to impose on particular offenders, at least in a wide range of cases, it is rather incomplete, striking me more as a component of a justification of punishment than as a justification itself. To the extent that we believe a justification of punishment should speak to the amount we punish offenders (and this essay appears in a collection arguably devoted to the topic), we may feel unsatisfied by Berman's approach.

Berman never denies that positive desert and prior suffering matter from a moral perspective; he simply treats retributivism as the first stop on the path to assessing whether we ought to impose some particular sentence. When all justice-relevant considerations are taken into consideration, perhaps Berman would even be led back to the results given by whole-life retributivism. Hence, Berman's approach postpones the time-frame challenge but does not resolve it.

III. Challenges to Both Views

So far, I have made some arguments challenging the whole-life view and some challenging the current-crime view. Here are three arguments challenging both but in somewhat different ways.

A. Punishment as a Worsening

Though removed somewhat from the time-frame debate, there is a further problem with the suggestion by Berman and others that crimes warrant reductions in how well an offender's life goes. They envision punishment as exacting a reduction proportionate "to the blameworthiness of [the offender's] wrongdoing" (Berman 2013, p. 88). In other words, retributivist proportionate punishment is generally understood as imposing proportionate worsenings.

Proportionate worsenings work well enough in the limited domain of criminal fines. If you commit a minor offense with a $100 fine, we reduce your net worth by $100, and your life goes a little worse than it would have otherwise. Similarly, a more serious offense with a $1,000 fine reduces your net worth by this substantially higher figure, and your life goes even worse than it would have had you committed the less serious offense. While it's puzzling that we focus on fines in objective terms rather than their experienced disutility (von Hirsch, Wasik, and Greene 1989, pp. 607–8; Ashworth and Player 1998, pp. 251–61; Kolber 2009*b*), if we could somehow get past that problem, these fines might preserve proportionality between the seriousness of these offenses and the amounts by which offenders' lives are worsened.

But even if proportionate worsenings are consistent with criminal fines, they are not consistent with our treatment of incarceration (Kolber 2009*a*, pp. 1566–73). We do not measure the severity of incarceration as a worsening of anything at all; rather, we have a duration fetish that ignores almost everything relevant to the severity of incarceration except for the passage of time. We measure the severity of incarceration as a duration of time spent in bad conditions. True, incarceration is usually a worsening, but even when it is, we do not measure its severity as such, and so offenders are not punished in ways that can possibly be proportionate except by chance.

To see how we ignore any true measure of incarcerative harm, imagine what we would have to do to measure incarceration as a worsening (which is precisely what seems to be required by theorists who speak of incarceration as a deprivation of liberty). When understood as a deprivation of liberty, incarceration deprives someone of liberty relative to his or her baseline. An offender with lots of liberty prior to incarceration (a wealthy fraudster with substantial holdings of land and personal property) is deprived to a large extent by 100 days of incarceration. However, a person with less liberty in his or her baseline state (a computer hacker who—due to no fault of his own— is quarantined with a contagious illness) is deprived much less by 100 days of incarceration. Both are worsened by incarceration, but unless we measure offenders' prepunishment baseline levels of liberty (and we seldom do), the extent of their worsenings cannot be proportionate to their wrongdoing except by chance.

True, the typical offender does not have a dramatically limited baseline liberty. But there surely are people with reduced baseline liberties, including, for example, asylum seekers in detention, civilly confined sexual predators, and teenagers required to attend school or observe state-imposed curfews. More generally, everyone varies somewhat in his or her baseline liberties, even if only in terms of property rights. A wealthy rancher has more liberty of movement than a homeless person. Nevertheless, we seem disinclined to care about these baselines when sentencing to prison, no matter how much individual offenders deviate from the norm.

The disproportionality of incarcerative sentences is easiest to see when we consider two equally blameworthy offenders with different baseline liberties. Equally blameworthy wealthy fraudsters and quarantined hackers receive punishments of quite different severity when incarcerated for the same period of time because they are differentially deprived of liberty. They can't both be equally worsened when we know that imprisonment will reduce the wealthy fraudster's liberty dramatically but the quarantined hacker's just a little.

Most people probably don't want the wealthy fraudster and the quarantined hacker to have equal deprivations of liberty. Depriving them equally might mean subjecting the quarantined hacker to an extremely liberty-deprived state relative to that of the fraudster. Proportional worsening that we accept when fining seems unacceptable when incarcerating. Our proportionality intuitions seem to vary, perhaps inexplicably, based on the mode of punishment. The results are so hard to reconcile that one might question whether we can make sense of retributive proportionality at all.

Another way to see what's wrong with the way we measure the severity of incarcerative sentences is to imagine using the same technique to measure the severity of fines. Suppose that monetary fines were not measured as worsenings but as imposed life conditions in the same way incarceration is measured. We could use "forced poverty" punishments to limit the net worth of offenders for certain periods of time. For one offense, we might set an offender's maximum net worth at $20,000 for, say, two years. For a more serious offense, we might set maximum net worth at only $500 for two years. Such punishments are clearly not proportionate worsenings, since they pay no attention to offender's baseline property rights. We could be sentencing wealthy Jeff Bezos, who would be severely worsened, or poor Charlie Chaplin's Little Tramp, who, having essentially no property rights before or after punishment, would not be punished at all. (I have posed my examples in terms of deprivations of liberty, but similar examples can be framed in terms of suffering. A happy person and a mildly depressed person brought to the same level of misery in prison are worsened to quite different degrees.)

Notice that, like incarceration, forced-poverty punishments consist of placing people in bad conditions for periods of time. If forced-poverty punishments seem clearly disproportionate, then we ought to feel the same way about incarceration. Prison is a forced-poverty punishment (we require inmates to give up most of their rights to personal property for a sustained period) combined with deprivations of liberties of motion. If forced poverty is disproportionate, so is incarceration.

Given that our actual punishment practices treat fines as worsenings but prison sentences as periods of time spent under particular conditions, our practices are inconsistent and seemingly incoherent. It is impossible for our approach to both fines and incarceration to be proportionate in the same sense, because they measure punishment severity in very different ways. Moreover, since punishment theorists need to justify the harms that punishment inflicts, retributivists who endorse the conventional approach to proportionality cannot hope to justify prison sentences, because they incorrectly measure the magnitude of the harm inflicted. Thus, the conventional approach to proportionality conflicts with the theorist's need to measure punishment as a worsening. These concerns are quite serious for those whole-life and current-crime retributivists who endorse our conventional approach to incarceration and raise questions about the extent to which our practices reflect Berman's suggestion that punishment should be understood as a worsening.

B. Bulk Offense Discounting

Many of the well-known difficulties with proportionality infect both whole-life and current-crime views (for example, how do we anchor units of culpability or harm to units of desert?) (Ryberg 2004, pp. 123–49). One sentencing practice is particularly relevant to the time-frame challenge because it concerns the aggregation of culpability over extended periods of time.

Many jurisdictions give far lighter sentences to offenders who engage in several crimes close in time than they give to offenders who commit the same crimes spaced out over many years and distinct sentencing proceedings (Ryberg, Roberts, and de Keijser 2018). Known as the "bulk discount" for multiple crimes, the practice is widespread. For example, a 1994 German study found that the average sentence for one burglary was 7.9 months of incarceration but only 24.6 months for seven burglaries when all seven were sentenced at the same time.[12] The average for the seven was 3.5 months each, less than half the sentence for a single burglary sentenced by itself. A study of Finnish sentencing around the turn of the last century found bulk discounts "at least proportionally more substantial than the discount provided in Germany," at least for the first several offenses (Hinkkanen and Lappi-Seppälä 2011, pp. 363–66).

Retributivists believe that deserved punishment should be proportionate to wrongdoing. But how can punishment for a burglary be proportionate if the same acts constituting one's first burglary lead to more than double the punishment of one's seventh in bulk-discount contexts? While there may be good consequentialist reasons for bulk discounts (for example, offenders are deterred more by the prospect of getting caught than by long sentences), the extent of the discounts seems harder to square with retributive

---

12. I rely on the analysis in Jareborg (2004, p. 135) of Albrecht (1994, pp. 387–98), published in German.

proportionality.[13] The topic deserves more attention than I can give it here, but among the many mysteries of proportionality, bulk discounting is particularly mysterious, at least for those retributivists who endorse the surprisingly common practice (Tonry 2018, p. 246).

While bulk discounts challenge all retributivists who support them, they may be particularly challenging for whole-life retributivists. From a whole-life perspective, punishment should be proportionate to an offender's overall moral desert. Yet people are constantly engaging in multiple good and bad deeds. Which time scales warrant bulk discounts, and which do not? How do whole-lifers make sense of our inclination to aggregate deeds across some time frames but not others? Whole-lifers might be tempted simply to disavow bulk discounts, but given that proportionality is often defended on the ground that strong moral intuitions support it, such whole-lifers would have to explain away the apparently strong intuitions supporting bulk discounts.

C. The Epistemic Challenge

The whole-life and current-crime approaches are incompatible. Results under one approach will often be inconsistent with the other. Ignoring the praiseworthy history of an offender under a current-crime view will overpunish relative to the whole-life view, while considering the history of noncriminal wrongdoing under a whole-life view will overpunish relative to a current-crime view.[14] So while it might be tempting to select the approach that seems less objectionable, uncertainty about the correct approach, as I have discussed elsewhere in more detail,[15] reduces our confidence in retributivism more generally.

Consider just some of the propositions retributivists likely believe if they think some particular person can be sentenced without relying on consequentialist motivations. They likely believe:

---

13. For discussion of some attempts to square bulk discounts with retributive proportionality, see Tonry 2018.

14. A hybrid theory that sentenced offenders under whichever scheme is more lenient would reduce the risk of overpunishment. It would, however, increase the risk of underpunishment and, more important, would be about as impractical as the whole-life theory because it would often require the same infeasible data gathering. It may also provide unacceptable get-out-of-jail-free cards.

15. See Kolber (2018), as well as Vilhauer (2009); Gross (2012); Tomlin (2013); and Hanna (2014). For criticism, see Atiq (2018); Flanders (2018); Galoob (2018); Rosenthal (2018); and Sigler (2018).

1. The person satisfies all the criteria for moral responsibility, including having metaphysical free will.
2. Suffering (or punishment) is an appropriate response to wrongdoing.
3. The state itself is justified in punishing, and punishment can justifiably be imposed.
4. This defendant engaged in the conduct alleged.
5. The alleged conduct was morally wrongful.
6. Police conduct and judicial proceedings were not so unlawful as to preclude just punishment.
7. The costs of giving this offender what he or she deserves do not so grossly exceed the benefits as to make punishment morally inappropriate.
8. Punishment should be proportionate, and this offender's punishment is proportionate (or at least not disproportionate).

It's difficult to be highly confident about many of these propositions, let alone the conjunction of all of them. Can we even be 90 percent confident that anyone has metaphysical free will in light of the centuries-long dispute on the topic?

Consider your confidence in each of the numbered propositions, but when you examine numbers 2–8, take the truth of prior propositions as given. Doing so allows us to multiply confidence in these (suitably revised) propositions to assess confidence in their overall conjunction.[16] If you were 90 percent confident in the revised version of each of these propositions, your confidence in the conjunction would be only 43 percent.[17] You would be more confident that punishment of this offender is not justified by retributivism than that it is.

Now add a ninth proposition:

9. We can adequately analyze a defendant's background history to assess what he or she deserves (taking prior propositions as given).

If you're ambivalent about whether retributivists should follow a current-crime or a whole-life approach, you will likely have limited confidence in proposition 9. Such limited confidence would dramatically diminish your

---

16. The formula for conditional probability holds that the probability of both A and B equals the probability of A given B times the probability of B (Papineau 2012, p. 106).

17. We raise 90 percent to the eighth power and get 43 percent.

already low 43 percent confidence even further. If you believed each proposition to be true, including the ninth one, with a perhaps unreasonably high 95 percent confidence level, your total confidence that punishment of some particular offender is justified on pure retributivist grounds would still be a paltry maximum of 63 percent.[18]

William Blackstone famously claimed, "the law holds that it is better that ten guilty persons escape than that one innocent suffer" (1860, p. 358). His claim is usually understood to speak of factual guilt, but the values animating it suggest that we should be hesitant to punish someone when our confidence that punishment is justified is not much better than that for a coin flip. While my discussion here is quite abbreviated, the general point remains that whole-life and current-crime retributivism are inconsistent and that punishment under one theory might constitute violation of a deeply held principle against overpunishment under the other. Moral uncertainty over the correct approach should arguably make us insufficiently confident to use either.

IV. Conclusion

I suspect many readers would happily give up the whole-life view. It is impractical and would not only fail to adequately deter crime but might encourage it with get-out-of-jail-free cards. While a justification of punishment can idealize away from some real-world complications, the whole-life view does so too much to be of practical use.

The whole-life view nonetheless highlights how much is missing from the current-crime view. Imagine if every drugstore sold omniscient desert-o-meters that revealed exactly what a person deserved. Would current-crime retributivists still insist on only considering desert for current crimes? If we had desert-o-meters, I suspect current-crime retributivists would find a limited desert menu less appetizing. But they cannot easily admit that their view is just a rough-and-ready proxy for whole-life retributivism. Doing so would likely conflict with their strict commitment to never purposely, knowingly, or recklessly overpunish.

I have, of course, only discussed certain whole-life and current-crime views. Changing some assumptions may fix some problems. Some hybrid views may do better than either kind of view on its own. Real-world sentencing systems seem to take intermediate positions. Perhaps some intermediate position

---

18. We raise 95 percent to the ninth power and get 63 percent.

better gets at the truth. Or we may simply have intuitions about retributivist proportionality that are irreconcilable.

References

Albrecht, Hans-Jörg. 1994. *Strafzumessung bei schwerer Kriminalität: Eine vergleichende theoretische und empirische Studie zur Herstellung und Darstellung des Strafmasses.* Berlin: Dunker and Humblot.

Alexander, Larry. 2012. "You Got What You Deserved." *Criminal Law and Philosophy* 7:309–19.

Alexander, Larry, and Kimberly Kessler Ferzan. 2009. *Crime and Culpability: A Theory of Criminal Law.* New York: Cambridge University Press.

American Law Institute. 1985. *Model Penal Code.* Philadelphia: American Law Institute.

Ashworth, Andrew, and Elaine Player. 1998. "Sentencing, Equal Treatment, and the Impact of Sanctions." In *Fundamentals of Sentencing Theory*, edited by Andrew Ashworth and Martin Wasik. New York: Oxford University Press.

Atiq, Emad H. 2018. "What Unconditional Credence in Individual Desert Claims Does Retributivism Require?" *University of Illinois Law Review Online* 2018:138–48.

Berman, Mitchell N. 2011. "Two Kinds of Retributivism." In *The Philosophical Foundations of Criminal Law*, edited by R. A. Duff and Stuart Green. Oxford: Oxford University Press.

Berman, Mitchell N. 2013. "Rehabilitating Retributivism." *Law and Philosophy* 32:83–108.

Berman, Mitchell N. 2016. "Modest Retributivism." In *Legal, Moral, and Metaphysical Truths: The Philosophy of Michael S. Moore*, edited by Kimberly Kessler Ferzan and Stephen J. Morse. New York: Oxford University Press.

Blackstone, William. 1860 (reprint). *Commentaries on the Laws of England, Vol 4.* Philadelphia: Childs and Peterson.

Duff, R. A. 2001. *Punishment, Communication, and Community.* New York: Oxford University Press.

Duus-Otterström, Göran. 2013. "Why Retributivists Should Endorse Leniency in Punishment." *Law and Philosophy* 32:459–83.

Ezorsky, Gertrude. 1972. "The Ethics of Punishment." In *Philosophical Perspectives on Punishment*, edited by Gertrude Ezorsky. Albany: State University of New York Press.

Feinberg, Joel. 1970. *Doing and Deserving: Essays in the Theory of Responsibility.* Princeton: Princeton University Press.

Ferzan, Kimberly Kessler. 2018. "Defense and Desert: When Reasons Don't Share." *San Diego Law Review* 55:265–89.

Flanders, Chad. 2018. "How Much Certainty Do We Need to Punish? A Reply to Kolber." *University of Illinois Law Review Online* 2018:149–57.

Galoob, Stephen. 2018. "Kolber's Teaser." *University of Illinois Law Review Online* 2018:168–74.

Gray, David. 2010. "Punishment as Suffering." *Vanderbilt Law Review* 63:1619–93.

Gross, Hyman. 2012. *Crime and Punishment: A Concise Moral Critique*. New York: Oxford University Press.

Hanna, Nathan. 2014. "Retributivism Revisited." *Philosophical Studies* 167:473–84.

Hart, H. L. A. 1968. *Punishment and Responsibility*. New York: Oxford University Press.

Hinkkanen, Ville, and Tapio Lappi-Seppälä. 2011. "Sentencing Theory, Policy, and Research in the Nordic Countries." In *Crime and Justice in Scandinavia*, edited by Michael Tonry and Tapio Lappi-Seppälä. Chicago: University of Chicago Press.

Hurka, Thomas. 2003. "Desert: Individualistic and Holistic." In *Desert and Justice,* edited by Serena Olsaretti. Oxford: Oxford University Press.

Husak, Douglas N. 1990. "Already Punished Enough?" *Philosophical Topics* 18:79–99.

Jareborg, Nils. 2004. "Why Bulk Discounts in Multiple Offense Sentencing?" In *Fundamentals of Sentencing Theory: Essays in Honour of Andrew von Hirsch*, edited by Andrew Ashworth and Martin Wasik. Oxford: Oxford University Press.

Kolber, Adam J. 2009*a*. "The Comparative Nature of Punishment." *Boston University Law Review* 89:1565–609.

Kolber, Adam J. 2009*b*. "The Subjective Experience of Punishment." *Columbia Law Review* 109:182–236.

Kolber, Adam J. 2013. "Against Proportional Punishment." *Vanderbilt Law Review* 66:1147–58.

Kolber, Adam J. 2014. "Smooth and Bumpy Laws." *California Law Review* 102: 655–90.

Kolber, Adam J. 2016*a*. "The Bumpiness of Criminal Law." *Alabama Law Review* 67:855–86.

Kolber, Adam J. 2016*b*. "Smoothing Vague Laws." In *Vagueness and Law: Philosophical and Legal Perspectives*, edited by Geert Keil and Ralf Poscher. Oxford: Oxford University Press.

Kolber, Adam J. 2018. "Punishment and Moral Risk." *Illinois Law Review* 2018:487–532.

Morris, Norval, Richard Bonnie, and Joel J. Finer. 1986. "Should the Insanity Defense Be Abolished—An Introduction to the Debate." *Journal of Law and Health* 1:113–40.

Papineau, David. 2012. *Philosophical Devices: Proofs, Probabilities, Possibilities, and Sets*. Oxford: Oxford University Press.

Parent, W. A. 1976. "The Whole Life View of Criminal Desert." *Ethics* 86:350–54.

Rosenthal, Chelsea. 2018. "Response to Adam Kolber's 'Punishment and Moral Risk.'" *University of Illinois Law Review Online* 2018:175–83.

Ross, W. D. 1930. *The Right and the Good*. Oxford: Oxford University Press.

Ryberg, Jesper. 2004. *The Ethics of Proportionate Punishment*. Dordrecht: Kluwer Academic.

Ryberg, Jesper, Julian V. Roberts, and Jan W. de Keijser, eds. 2018. *Sentencing Multiple Crimes*. New York: Oxford University Press.

Sigler, Mary. 2018. "Humility, Not Doubt: A Reply to Adam Kolber." *University of Illinois Law Review Online* 2018:158–67.

Tadros, Victor. 2011. *The Ends of Harm: The Moral Foundations of Criminal Law.* Oxford: Oxford University Press.

Tomlin, Patrick. 2013. "Extending the Golden Thread? Criminalisation and the Presumption of Innocence." *Journal of Political Philosophy* 21:44–66.

Tonry, Michael. 2018. "Solving the Multiple-Offense Paradox." In *Sentencing Multiple Crimes,* edited by Jesper Ryberg, Julian V. Roberts, and Jan W. de Keijser. New York: Oxford University Press.

Vilhauer, Benjamin. 2009. "Free Will and Reasonable Doubt." *American Philosophical Quarterly* 46:131–40.

Von Hirsch, Andreas [Andrew]. 1981. "Desert and Previous Convictions in Sentencing." *Minnesota Law Review* 65:591–634.

Von Hirsch, Andrew, Martin Wasik, and Judith Greene. 1989. "Punishments in the Community and the Principles of Desert." *Rutgers Law Journal* 20:595–618.

Walker, Nigel. 1991. *Why Punish?* Oxford: Oxford University Press.

9

Humane Neoclassicism

PROPORTIONALITY AND OTHER VALUES IN NORDIC SENTENCING

Tapio Lappi-Seppälä

What is not just and fair cannot be law either; for it is on account of the fairness which dwells in the law that the law is accepted. All law is to be wielded with wisdom because the greatest right is the greatest wrong; and there must be mercy in justice as well.
"*The Rules for the Judges*"
Olaus Petri, 1552[1]

TRUST IN THE rehabilitative potential of criminal justice started to erode in the Nordic countries in the 1960s. By the early 1970s, treatment ideology and involuntary institutional treatment were under severe attack. Extensive use of confinement and compulsory treatment in healthcare, child welfare, and prisons was criticized for being inhumane, arbitrary, and ineffective.[2] Critical findings on the modest effects of treatment influenced a shift in criminal justice policy priorities from custodial sanctions to community alternatives and open-care measures. Justifications offered for imprisonment shifted from individual prevention and treatment toward general prevention, with the last term understood in Nordic theory to refer mostly to moral education and reinforcement of basic social norms rather than to general deterrent effects

Tapio Lappi-Seppälä is Professor of Criminal Law and Criminology and Director of the Institute of Criminology and Legal Policy at the University of Helsinki.

1. Propositions collected by 16th-century Swedish theologian Olaus Petri.

2. For influential critics, see Anttila (1967).

of punishment. The new approach stressed legal safeguards against coercive care, more effective protection of offenders' rights, and use of less punitive measures in general. Discretionary powers in public administration and in the courts were to be restricted. Proportionality and predictability became the central values in sentencing.

Principles for Nordic penal reforms were formulated in four important documents published in 1976–1978. The 1976 report of the Finnish Criminal Law Committee provided the basis for total reform of the penal code. Two key reformers offered this summary: "The Committee's reform program favored rationality in terms of Scandinavian general prevention tempered with a new emphasis on classical principles of justice. Judicial discretion was to be limited in an asymmetrical fashion, punishments were to be lowered and the area of criminal behavior redefined" (Anttila and Törnudd 1996, p. 137). A contemporaneous Swedish report, *Nytt straffsystem* (*New Penal System*) (1977), outlined principles for sanctions reform, to be further elaborated in three reports in 1986 (Statens offentliga utredningar1986, pp. 13–15). The Danish reform plan "Alternativ til frihedsstraf—et debatoplaeg" ("Alternatives to Imprisonment") (1977) and the Norwegian Ministry of Justice report *Om kriminalpolitiken* (*On Crime Policy*) (1978) concentrated mainly on new penalties to be used to reduce the prison population.

All the reports, with differing emphases, stressed the need to reduce the severity of sanctions, replace short prison sentences with new community alternatives, restrict the use of indeterminate sentences, and develop a sentencing system that respected principles of proportionality and humanity. The ensuing reform proposals and law reforms followed much the same path.[3] Criminal justice ideologies find their most explicit formulations in rules and principles regulating the use of punishment. Finland undertook the first major sentencing reform in 1976.[4] The new Swedish sentencing law was enacted in 1988.[5] The two reforms shared the same "neoclassical" basic

---

3. These reforms and their effects since the mid-1960s are discussed in detail in Lahti (2000) and Lappi-Seppälä (2007, 2016a).

4. The Finnish provisions are contained in chapters 6 and 7 of the Finnish Criminal Code. On sentencing principles in Finland, see Lappi-Seppälä (1987, 2001). The provisions were amended in a comprehensive reform of the general part of the Finnish Criminal Code in 2003 (GovProp 44 2002).

5. In Sweden, sentencing is regulated in the Swedish Penal Code, chapters 29 and 30. For a general description, see Jareborg (1995) and in greater detail Borgeke and Heidenborg (2016) and two special issues of *Svensk Juristtidning* (February 1999 and February 2003). Sentencing reforms in Denmark and Norway took place later and less visibly. Denmark

orientation. They placed the principle of proportionality at the center and moved forward-looking instrumental considerations including individual and general deterrence to the margin.

The new penal ideology was referred to as neoclassical because of its increased emphasis on principles central to the 18th-century German classical school of criminal law, but the labels created misunderstandings (see, e.g., the discussion between Christie and Törnudd in Hecksher et al. 1980). In order to distinguish the Scandinavian approach from both the emerging "just deserts" movement in the United States and the combination of retribution and deterrence associated with the old German penal theory, it gradually became common in Finland to refer to "humane neoclassicism." That is how the title of this essay should be understood. It refers to a penal orientation that combines the requirements of legal security with the aim of humanization of the criminal justice system. Reduction in the severity of punishment was emphasized more heavily in Finland, which at the time suffered from extraordinarily high use of imprisonment compared with the other Nordic countries (on this background, see Lappi-Seppälä 2007).

Nordic sentencing reforms paralleled similar shifts in other Western countries toward tighter regulation of judicial discretion. While some common-law countries adopted or considered various forms of numerical sentencing guidelines, especially in the United States, the Nordic countries followed the civil-law tradition based on the primacy of written law and the division of powers between legislatures and courts. Legislative guidance, thus, takes the form of penalty scales (ranges with minimums and maximums), graded descriptions of offenses, and statutory sentencing criteria.[6] The merits of this rule-based approach include better protection from short-term politically motivated populist initiatives. Downsides include weaker legal force and a slower pace of change. However, during times when criminal justice policy is becoming ever more politicized and when changes, as a rule, increase the

---

revised its sentencing provisions in 2004 (Danish Penal Code, chapter 10). Norway adopted new sentencing laws in connection with reform of the Norwegian Penal Code in 2005 (Law 2005/05/28 no. 28 [chapter 14]). Scandinavian sentencing principles are discussed in legal commentaries (Andenaes, Matningsdal, and Rieber-Mohn 2004; Greve, Jenson, and Nielsen 2013; Jareborg and Zila 2000); for an English overview, see Hinkkanen and Lappi-Seppälä (2011, pp. 355–76).

6. Complementary legal material is to be found in the preliminary works relating to changes in law (travaux préparatoires), court decisions (from higher and lower instances), and legal doctrine. For discussions of the sources of Nordic sentencing law, see Hinkkanen and Lappi-Seppälä (2011).

scope of penal control, weaker guidance, shielded judicial discretion, and more time-consuming reform processes may be benefits.

Sentencing reforms motivated scholarly work. Swedish discussions were influenced especially by the works of Nils Jareborg (1985, 1995, 2000) and Dag Victor (1999, 2003, 2015) and—from outside the Nordic countries—Andreas von Hirsch (e.g., 1976). The Finnish theory built on discussions at the time of criminal justice policy and legal theory. The issues were much the same in all the Nordic countries, reflecting long and intensive interactions among Nordic scholars.

In this essay, I examine the role of proportionality in Nordic sentencing systems: how the principle is understood and how its relation to other penal aims is conceived in theory and in sentencing norms. I begin in section I with an overview of general aims and values in sentencing and proceed in section II to a more detailed examination of the relations between proportionality and general prevention. In section III, I discuss proportionality and judicial discretion. Section IV discusses relative proportionality. Section V examines absolute proportionality and the social and political conditions that determine it at any time and place.

I. Aims and Values in Sentencing

The aims and values of humane neoclassicism—proportionality, predictability, and equality—are set out in the opening paragraphs of the Finnish and Swedish sentencing laws. The Finnish law provides: "The sentence shall be determined so that it is in just proportion to the harmfulness and dangerousness of the offense, the motives for the act, and the other culpability of the perpetrator manifest in the offense" (FPC 6:4).[7] The new Swedish law obliged the courts to set the sanction according to the "penal value" of the offense (SPC 29:1). The pre-1988 law obliged the courts to take "into account the requirements of upholding the general compliance to the norms" and to choose a sanction that is "best suited to promote the offender's reintegration" (former SPC 1:7). Denmark added a proportionality-oriented general provision to its penal code in 2005 (DPC 80).

---

7. I use the abbreviations FPC (Finland), SPC (Sweden), DPC (Denmark), and NPC (Norway) to refer to the national penal codes.

A. Proportionality

The principle of proportionality receives its most explicit formulation in the Finnish law. The wording of the law requires a "just proportion" between crime and punishment. It also specifies the main criteria to be taken into account ("the harmfulness and dangerousness of the offense, the motives for the act, and the other culpability of the perpetrator manifest in the offense"). Neither Swedish nor Danish law names the principle. The Swedish governmental bill, however, devoted substantial attention to "penal value." Subparagraph SPC 29:1.2 provides: "In assessing the penal value, special consideration shall be given to the damage, wrong, or danger occasioned by the criminal act, to what the accused realized or should have realized about this, and to the intentions or motives he may have had. Especially the court must take into account whether the act involves an infringement of someone's life, health or personal security."[8] In addition, all Nordic criminal codes include specific lists of aggravating and mitigating criteria, most of them specifying the degree of culpability and the factors to be taken into account in assessing the extent of harm and other consequences of the act.[9]

Nordic sentencing theory distinguishes between absolute and relative proportionality. Absolute proportionality provides a link between offenses and specific penalties, between the seriousness of an offense and the severity of a sanction. Relative proportionality concerns comparisons between offenses. A claim about relative proportionality is that offense X deserves a more or less severe sanction than offense Y (e.g., Jareborg and Zila 2000, p. 68). Sentencing criteria provided by the law and developed in legal doctrine deal primarily with relative differences. They provide the courts with tools to grade penalties in a manner that reflects differences in the seriousness of crimes. This applies both within offense categories (how serious an assault it was) and between different offenses (assault compared with theft).

---

8. The Danish law does not explicitly mention proportionality or penal value but requires the court to "take account" of the "seriousness of the crime and the information concerning the offender" (DPC 80:1.2). Two starting points are indicated: "In considering the seriousness of crime, account shall be taken of the harm and danger caused by the crime, which the offender has foreseen or should have foreseen. In considering information about the offender, his personal characteristics and social circumstances before and after the crime, as well as his motives, shall be taken into account."

9. DPC sections 81 and 82; FPC chapter 6; SPC chapter 29; and NPC sections 77 and 78; see also Ågren (2013); Andenaes, Matningsdal, and Rieber-Mohn (2004); Borgeke and Heidenborg (2016); Greve, Jenson, and Nielsen (2013); Hinkkanen and Lappi-Seppälä (2011); Holmqvist (1999); Jareborg (1995, 2000); Jareborg and Zila (2000); Lappi-Seppälä (1987).

This understanding of the proportionality principle is articulated, for example, in a Finnish Supreme Court sentencing decision (Decision 2017:9) on drug offenses. Sentencing practice had been guided by semiofficial court-based guidelines that graded penalties according to the type and amount of drugs. As amounts of trafficked drugs increased over time, sentences increased and reached the legal maximum (10 years). The court decided that this endangered achievement of relative proportionality both internally (within drug offenses) and externally (drug offenses compared with others). The court acknowledged the value of the semiofficial guidelines as a means to promote the "uniformity and predictability of sentencing practice" but noted also:

> Drug offenses consist of ever larger amounts of drugs and an increasing number of new and highly dangerous drugs. This, together with a schematic sentencing practice, has led to the situation that penalties are approaching maximum penalties also in offenses that cannot be deemed to represent the offense's most serious forms. *The most severe penalties are therefore not reserved for the most serious offenses, and penal values of offenses are no longer sufficiently distinguishable from each other.* At the same time, *sentencing practice in aggravated drug offenses has divorced/differentiated from other types of crimes, with the same penalty-scales.* (emphasis added)

The court reduced the penalty for a drug courier from 8.5 to 5.5 years, noting the offender's minor role in the offense. But the main message was that guidelines for drug offenses needed to be recalibrated to maintain just proportion among sentences for drug offenses and in relation to sentences imposed for other offenses.[10]

B. Consistency

All codes stress the need to pay special attention to the "uniformity" or "consistency" of sentencing practice. The Finnish Penal Code provides: "In

---

10. The Swedish Supreme Court revised its sentencing practice in drug offenses in the early 2010s using similar arguments. See Asp (2011, p. 659): "a necessary step towards the normalization and differentiation of the assessment of penal value in drug offenses." This provoked a quick response from the minister of justice and a promise to increase penalties by introducing a new "especially aggravated" form of drug offense (see Minister Beatrice Ask: "Vi skärper straffen för narkotikabrott" ("We will increase penalties for drug offenses"). https://www.expressen.se/debatt/vi-skarper-straffen-for-narkotikabrott).

sentencing, all grounds according to law affecting the amount and type of punishment, as well as the uniformity of sentencing practice, are taken into account" (FPC 6:3.1). In Sweden: "Punishments shall, with due regard to the need for consistency in sentencing, be determined within the scale of punishments according to the penal value of the crime or crimes taken" (SPC 29:1). And in Denmark: "In determining the penalty, the court shall, under due consideration of legal consistency in sentencing, take account of the seriousness of the crime and the information concerning the offender" (DPC 80.1).

The wordings differ in translation but mean essentially the same thing (even if *uniformity* and *consistency* have a somewhat different meaning in the English language). The original Nordic terms (*yhtenäisyys, enhetlig, ensarterthed*) have more or less the same meaning. They signify consistent application of law that satisfies the demands of the principle of equality and avoids unwarranted disparity in sentencing.

Nordic commentaries take account of this phrase in different ways. The standard Danish commentary barely mentions it (Greve, Jenson, and Nielsen 2013). The Swedish commentary discusses it only briefly (Borgeke and Heidenborg 2016). In Finland, it occupies a central position as a symbol of the current sentencing approach and the notion of normal punishment (Lappi-Seppälä 2001, pp. 135–36, with references). Respect for values of consistency and uniformity directs courts to take general sentencing practice into account and to use punishments normally imposed in similar cases, unless there are special reasons to do otherwise. This provides a workable starting point for decision-making and emphasizes the relevance of empirical information to sentencing practices.

C. Humanity

Proportionality and consistency provide stability and legal security in the form of predictability. But general rules that aim to cover as many cases as possible in order to create stability in social relations also need ad hoc adjustments to take into account extraordinary and unexpected circumstances not accounted for in formulation of the rules. This incompleteness of abstract rules was well reflected in the 16th-century Nordic "Rules for the Judges," which stressed that "there must be mercy in justice as well"[11] and concluded, "It is better to

---

11. These propositions from the 16th century have never been officially enacted and are not, strictly speaking, part of the positive law but have been included as a preamble to the official

have a good and wise judge than good law, because he can always settle the matter fairly."

There is an element of "reasonableness" in traditional Nordic legal thinking (Aarnio 1986). Other values besides the requirements of "strict" proportionality need to be included. The application and administration of law need to reflect values such as compassion, tolerance, solidarity, forgiveness, and humanity (Jareborg 2000). To this end, sentencing provisions provide the courts general authority to impose sentences below minimum penalties in exceptional cases. Laws also indicate sets of factors that fall outside the scope of strict proportionality. They are unrelated to the severity of the offense or the culpability of the offenders but nevertheless deserve to be taken into account.[12]

D. Rehabilitation

The reform movement of the 1970s moved away from treatment in the penal system but not from treatment itself. The criminal justice system was not conceived to be the proper place to provide support and care; people in need should be entitled to receive this care from general welfare services (which were rapidly expanding at that time), whether they committed offenses or not (*Nytt straffsystem* 1977, p. 185). Care by coercion was banned, because it overlooked the offenders' fundamental rights and was unable to deliver what it promised. But this did not mean that the aims and values of rehabilitation and reintegration were to be ignored in the administration of criminal justice.

There was no discussion of abolition of the structural arrangements that traditionally served rehabilitative aims, such as conditional and suspended sentences, early release procedures, reoffending rules, and specific regulations for juveniles, even if the application of these instruments rested more strongly on backward-looking considerations.

This differentiation of sanctions structures (in which different sanctions serve different aims in different ways) has continued through the emergence of new community alternatives (Lappi-Seppälä 2016b). The usefulness of

---

law books in Sweden and Finland since 1635. They are firmly embedded as central values in Nordic legal culture.

12. Humanity-related arguments falling outside the (strictly understood) principle of proportionality are discussed in more detail in Ågren (2013); Holmqvist (1999); Jareborg (2000;, and Lappi-Seppälä (1987, pp. 188–95, 487–510). For discussions in English sentencing theory, see von Hirsch and Ashworth (2005, chap. 5).

rehabilitative practices is seen today in a much more positive light than in the 1970s. The use of new community alternatives is often linked to a combination of proportionality-oriented criteria and presumed individual preventive effects. These new alternatives have also reshaped sentencing structures. Simple two-dimensional sentencing schemes have been modified to include additional dimensions and qualitative elements that allow comparisons between sanctions of roughly equal severity but with different (assumed or sought) preventive outcomes on the individual level (Lappi-Seppälä 2001, 2011).

This partial "revival of the rehabilitative ideal" complicates sentencing theory, but it does not take us back to the time when people were institutionalized on the basis of false or unrealistic hopes of treatment effectiveness. Now the issue concerns making choices between alternative community sanctions or is about use of these alternatives instead of custodial sanctions on rehabilitative grounds. The question for the courts is not which of these alternatives is the most efficient but rather if it would be justified to replace a prison sentence (the normal penalty for an offense of this gravity) with a community alternative that would, according to our general knowledge, be less detrimental for the offender's future life in his or her specific circumstances.[13]

D. Risk-Based Sentencing and Predicted Dangerousness

Indeterminate sanctions provide the most notable exception to the proportionality principle. Proportionality can be completely ignored or consciously breached by prolonging the deserved sentence for consequentialist (usually public safety) reasons. The Nordic countries abolished almost all indeterminate sentences in the 1970s and 1980s, but some maintained restrictive arrangements for high-risk violent recidivists. Norway and Denmark allow the release dates of a small number of serious violent recidivists (two or three cases per year) to be based on assessment of the risks they present to public safety. In Finland, the same group of offenders may be denied regular parole release but be placed instead under intensive supervision (lasting 1 year). In Sweden, this group is usually sentenced to psychiatric treatment.

---

13. Ideas about individual prevention to avoid more harmful consequences in sentencing (referred to as "negative individual prevention") were formulated in the 1970s (Bondeson 1994). While expectations of positive treatment effects have recently increased (partly influenced by the "What Works?" movement), new community alternatives have been introduced mainly to avoid harmful effects of imprisonment. The value of rehabilitation was never contested at the enforcement level (see Victor 1999; on rehabilitation in juvenile justice, see Lappi-Seppälä 2011).

All these arrangements are problematic in relation to the proportionality principle. In these few cases, proportionality is trumped by the belief that the offender presents an exceptional and imminent risk, in Sweden and partly in Denmark, in relation to treatment needs. The justification for these deviations depends on the persuasiveness of these considerations.[14] Much could be said to defend these practices. However, there is a risk that they will applied ever more extensively as "risk orientation" gains greater emphasis in the administration of criminal justice.

II. Proportionality and General Prevention

I have not yet discussed the central aim attributed to criminal punishment: to secure general obedience to the law. The shift to a neoclassical approach did not disconnect the justification of criminal justice practices from consequentialist considerations. The general aim of crime policy, as specified in Finnish textbooks and official documents, is to minimize the harms and suffering caused to victims and offenders both by crime and by crime control. They are inevitable and cannot be avoided and should be distributed in a socially just and fair manner (Törnudd 1996). Supporters of the new emphasis on proportionality believed that effective crime prevention mostly takes place outside the criminal justice system. Punishment has a role to play but perhaps a smaller one than in earlier times. Justification of the institution of punishment rests on its ability to protect important individual and collective interests through its general preventive effects.

If, however, punishment as an institution is justified by general prevention and the protection of public interests, why do these same considerations not also apply to sentencing practices? Or do they? To answer that question, we need to examine the theory of general prevention.

A. Forms of General Prevention

General prevention became a primary subject in Nordic criminology in the 1970s.[15] This discussion revitalized the theory of indirect moral education,

---

14. Some supporters of these sanctions argue that they do not violate proportionality principles because they are not "punishments." However, the more closely treatment conditions and placement criteria resemble conventional punishments, the weaker that argument becomes. The role of preventive detention and measures for high-risk violent offenders in the Nordic countries is discussed in detail in Lappi-Seppälä (2016a).

15. For a fuller analysis, see Andersson (2002).

which was developed earlier under the shadow of treatment ideology, first in the writings of Scandinavian realism and the Uppsala School (Ekelöf 1942, with references). It reappeared later in the works of the Norwegian Johannes Andenaes.[16] Punishment is disapproval, and disapproval influences behavior, he wrote: "punishment as a concrete expression of society's disapproval of an act helps to form and strengthen the public's moral code and thereby creates conscious and unconscious inhibitions against committing crimes" (1974, p. 8).

Sociologists identified other submechanisms and functions (Aubert 1972; Mäkelä 1975), but the core distinction between direct/external/instrumental and indirect/internal/normative effects of punishment remained and was adopted in textbooks and accepted in official planning documents. The Finnish Criminal Law Committee observed: "The guiding function of criminal law takes place through both direct and indirect routes, including compliance based on mere habit, norm internalization (personal morality), wish to avoid others' resentment, fear of detection, fear of punishment, and fear of other consequences" (Rikosoikeuskomitean mietintö 1976, p. 41).

Moral disapproval, along with its guiding influence, is a central element in the punishment process. Danish legal philosopher Alf Ross put it this way: "When disapproval is expressed by a person in authority or collectively by the social environment," it shall be "accepted by the recipient, taken up to his own moral consciousness, and in this way come to be determining factor in his own future behavior" (1975, pp. 90–91). People usually refrain from illegal behavior not primarily because it is followed by unpleasant punishment but because the behavior itself is regarded as morally blameworthy (or just by the force of habit, which is in turn shaped by social norms). Promotion of prosocial behavior is, on this reasoning, best served by a system of sanctions that maintains a moral character and confirms and reinforces the blameworthiness of criminal acts. It is imperative for this "norm setting function of public denouncement" (Törnudd 1996, p. 62) that procedures are perceived

---

16. Similar views appeared in late-19th- and early-20th-century German and Anglo-Saxon theory and again in the 1970s and 1980s in the form of "Positive General Prevention" (Germany), "denunciatory" and "expressive functions" of punishment (Feinberg 1965; Walker 1980), and "normative compliance" in writings of the procedural school of justice (Tyler 1990; Crawford and Hucklesby 2013). Distinctively, though, that early Nordic approach more clearly connected moral disapproval and its communication to behavioral effects. Another important difference is that the reformulation of this theory became in the 1970s the guiding ideology that justified liberal and humanizing practices while not disavowing the aim of effective crime prevention.

to be fair, just, and respectful of the rights and intrinsic moral value of all parties involved.[17] This places proportionality in the center.

B. General Prevention in Sentencing

Proportionality-oriented sentencing criteria are consistent with the mechanisms and preconditions of indirect general prevention (punishment as an expression of society's disapproval). But punishment also works, so it is assumed and accepted, as a plain and immediate motive for potential lawbreakers. There remains the question of whether deterrence is a legitimate sentencing purpose that justifies punishments that exceed the requirements of proportionality. Finnish legislation took a negative position; Swedish legislation did also but with reservations. The background documents for the general part of the Finnish criminal code condense this argument:

> The judge's primary role in sentencing is to follow the principle of proportionality, not the pursuit of preventive effects of various forms. This is not in conflict with the general justifying aim of criminal law, emphasizing ultimately pragmatic rational arguments related to crime prevention and the protection of important individual and collective interests. The issue concerns rational and reasoned distribution of labor and tasks between the various levels of criminal law and the institution of punishment. The requirements of general prevention are taken into account when deciding on the penalty scales and individual sentencing criteria. But deterrence is not a court-level argument in the sense the judge should consider the impact of his/her individual decisions on the future behavior of potential law-breakers. . . . The principle of proportionality guides the work of the sentencing. Arguments related to individual prevention become first and foremost relevant during the enforcement stage. (GovProp 44 2002, p. 178)

---

17. "Of crucial importance is the indirect effect of the society's authoritative reproach on citizens' values and views. The precondition that criminal justice system can effectively influence on attitudes and norms is that its aims and means are generally accepted, and that people trust in the fairness of its functioning" (Rikosoikeuskomitean mietintö 1976, p. 41).

Similar arguments appear in the Swedish sentencing report (Statens offentliga utredningar 1986, p. 13).[18] This hardly settles the issue. Legislators can't solve theoretical or moral disputes, and their solutions can be contested. But the position adopted in Finland can be justified by both empirical and theoretical arguments.

To the extent that direct deterrence plays a role in influencing behavior, there is strong empirical evidence that this effect is mainly dependent on the certainty of sanctions and not on their severity (most recently, Chalfin and McCrary 2017). Getting caught has immediate consequences; being sentenced is a distant and uncertain event with weaker motivational effects (Nagin 2018). The weakness of the empirical foundation of deterrent crime-prevention strategies based on the severity of penalties is evident when we consider the effects on offenders' criminal choices of increases in punishments (Hassemer 1979; Beyleveld 1980; Jareborg 1985; von Hirsch and Bottoms 2010). If an "extra dose" of 4 months' punishment for street robbery is to have an effect, the difference must be effectively communicated to potential offenders, they must believe it will be carried out, they must believe there is a significant risk of apprehension, and they must take the punishment increase sufficiently seriously to abandon a planned offense. In relation to ethically tolerable marginal changes, these are unrealistic assumptions. Courts that make them have no valid basis for doing so. Basing sentences on marginal deterrent logic would constitute treating similar cases dissimilarly for indefensible empirical and ethical reasons.

Even if decisions in individual cases have few, if any, general deterrent effects, individual cases added together form practices, and practices may have general preventive effects. To the extent that a sentencing decision based on deterrent considerations represents a practice or a norm to be followed in future cases, deterrent considerations may be as valid for the judge as for the legislature. However, it is unclear to what extent even supreme courts' decisions influence penalty levels; views vary among the Nordic countries.[19] Even so,

---

18. Swedish law, however, allows resort to deterrent considerations when deciding about the use of imprisonment for certain offenses that have gained high priority in political discussions as offenses that need to be prevented (such as drunken driving). This "Artbrott" construction was introduced into the law for political reasons in 1989 and has been a target of scholarly criticism ever since, without, however, much influence (Borgeke 1999; Victor 2003; von Hirsch 2003).

19. Nordic countries may also differ in this respect. The Norwegian Supreme Court has long provided detailed guidance for lower courts on penalty levels, which may partly explain why Andenaes (1974, pp. 137–38), a Norwegian, seems to accept general deterrent considerations in setting the general penalty levels through sentencing. The Finnish Supreme Court has only recently begun to establish precedents on sentence levels (and not only on application of specific

courts in routine cases are not setting norms but dealing with individual cases. Thus, except possibly for supreme court decisions that aim to set sentencing norms for lower courts, deterrent considerations have no place in individual sentencing decisions.

Does this conclusion contradict the overall aim of criminal justice to protect important social interests? Not if we look beyond prevention of single criminal events to the wider goal of cost-effective minimization of harms caused both by crime and by crime control. Proportionality considerations call for setting of penalties according to both culpability and harm. Regarding harm, it is more important (and rational) to prevent serious offenses than lesser ones. Regarding culpability, premeditation and planning signify higher levels of guilt. But offenses committed after premeditation and planning may also be more easily deterred due to the element of conscious deliberation in the motivational process. Thus, focusing preventive actions in that direction is also goal-rational. Culpability concerns call for grading penalties according to the offender's ability to conform to the law. Factors that impair this ability reduce blame and thus should mitigate sanctions. This is both just and rational. One might argue for increases in penalties to compensate for the loss of prevention. However, given that penalty resources are limited, the most rational approach is to invest fewer punishment resources when there is less to gain (minor offenses and offenders with reduced ability to control their actions) and more when the stakes are higher (more severe consequences, easier to prevent) or prospects for more effective prevention are greater (planned and premeditated offenses).[20] The core message remains that proportionality-based sentencing makes pragmatic sense even in a forward-looking criminal justice system.

---

sentencing criteria or use of different sanction options). However, the setting of sentence levels in Finland continues to be based on proportionality-oriented criteria, tempered by equity-based mitigation (*billighet*), and not general deterrence.

20. For detailed discussion, see Lappi-Seppälä (1987). This is one application of the distinction made in analytical philosophy between justifying a rule and justifying a decision under that rule. In real-life sentencing, punishment resources are limited: there is a certain "penalty cake" to be delivered. It makes sense to deliver this cake in a manner that best serves the aims of the system and to direct resources to those crimes that are most important to prevent and to those areas where there is the best hope of achieving something.

C. Theories on Punishment and the Division of Labor

Forward-looking and general preventive considerations are within the legislature's domain. Backward-looking considerations and moral assessment of individual offenses are within that of the judges. They are better equipped and trained for this task. But the practices that grow out of these backward-looking decisions are also germane to rational pursuit of criminal law's goals.

This division of labor, general prevention at the systemic level, proportionality in sentencing, and individual prevention in law enforcement, clarifies the main roles of each theory at different levels. It does not exclude the need for balanced compromises in specific cases. Humanitarian deviations from application of the principle of proportionality in sentencing are often necessary and justifiable. Political pragmatism and pursuit of rehabilitative goals can also justify deviations.

III. *The Role of Proportionality: Asymmetric Limitation of Judicial Discretion*

Sentencing involves more than application of theories of punishment. It also implicates principles that guide and constrain the use of state punishment in legislative, judicial, and law-enforcement settings. The overall aim of criminal law is to promote safety, security, and well-being. Limits on how this is to be done are provided by the rule of law and by principles of legality, proportionality, predictability, equality, and inviolability of human rights. The principle of proportionality has its roots in the concept of the rule of law (*Rechtstaat*), legal safeguards, and citizens' guarantees against abusive treatment, arbitrariness, and excessive use of force. From this point of view, it is more important to prevent overly harsh penalties than to prevent overly lenient ones.

The main function of the proportionality principle is, thus, to specify upper limits that punishments may never exceed. It is much less restrictive concerning punishments less severe than the offender's act might prima facie deserve (Törnudd 1996). This ordering of priorities and the view that the proportionality principle is best understood asymmetrically were influential in the Finnish criminal law reform of the 1970s (Anttila and Törnudd 1996). Applications appear in all the Nordic criminal codes.

The courts have authority to go below a prescribed minimum whenever they believe there are exceptional reasons to do so. Provisions of sentencing law authorize mitigation of punishment on grounds unrelated to the principle of proportionality. The mitigating criteria provide greater authority to judges than do the aggravating criteria.

Grading of offenses reflects the same idea. In Finland, the lists of criteria that make an offense aggravated are always exhaustive, but lists of mitigating criteria are "open-ended"; courts may impose a mitigated punishment for reasons other than those specified.

IV. Relative Proportionality in Crime Definitions and Sanction Structures

The sentencing process consists of several subdecisions. Assuming that the offense type has been determined, there are three main decisions: assessments of the appropriate subcategory of the offense (aggravated, basic, or petty), decisions about the type of punishment, and decisions about its amount. These decisions are interwoven and interconnected normatively and empirically.

A. Sentencing Ranges and the Grading of Offenses

The Nordic criminal codes provide statutory offense definitions and punishment ranges with a minimum and a maximum for each offense. Almost all offenses are graded according to different degrees of seriousness with corresponding minimum and maximum penalties.[21]

Grading of offenses is based on two elements. First is the importance of the protected interests and the extent to which the offense threatens them. The weighting of these interests is ultimately a political decision, guided and influenced by changing societal attitudes and beliefs. These changes can be radical. In the 19th century, criminal courts handled large numbers of offenses against marriage and honor, and in the early 20th century, they handled many alcohol-related offenses; recent decades have witnessed a reevaluation of the seriousness of sexual offenses. The second element in grading is the offender's culpability, reflected in the differentiation between intentional crimes and crimes of negligence and in the internal grading of both.

---

21. For examples, see Hinkkanen and Lappi-Seppälä 2011. The Danish criminal code contains only a few minimum punishments (although their number seems to be increasing).

"Penal value" is expressed in offense-specific punishment ranges. The upper limit is set by life imprisonment in Finland, Denmark, and Sweden.[22] There is no "life without parole," although there is no fixed maximum time to be served under a life sentence. All lifers are released on parole. The average period to be served varies in the Nordic countries from 15 to 18 years. Otherwise, maximums are controlled by general limits. For Finland, the maximum for a single offense is 12 years; for multiple offenses, it is 15 years. The situation is roughly the same in the other Nordic countries (except Norway). Offense-specific maximum penalties are binding and may not be exceeded.[23]

Minimums are different from mandatory minimums in some common-law countries. First, they are not usually severe (for traditional aggravated offenses, a few months) and almost never require judges to impose more severe penalties than they otherwise would. Second, the minimums are not mandatory but only presumptive. Judges may impose sentences below them when they believe circumstances justify it.

B. Sentencing Ranges and Practice: The Tendency toward Leniency

In practice, penalties tend to concentrate close to the minimum, usually in the lower quarter or third of the statutory range. In Finland, for example, the authorized range for aggravated assault is 1 to 10 years, and the average imposed sentence is a little more than 2 years. That pattern repeats for all offenses.

Sentences in the middle or at the top of the range are uncommon, for good reason. One might suppose that the normal sentence, absent aggravating or mitigating circumstances, should be in the middle of the range, but this is based on a false assumption that the average crime is of middling seriousness. In reality, in any category of crimes, the majority of cases are of comparatively low seriousness; the statistical distribution of crime seriousness does not follow the bell curve. There are, for example, fewer brutal murders (10 to 20 per year in Finland) than normal manslaughters (100 per year), fewer aggravated assaults (2000 per year) than simple assaults (20,000 per year),

---

22. Norway abolished life sentences in 1979, in reaction to indeterminate sanctions in general, and replaced them with a 21-year maximum. Life imprisonment in the Nordic countries is discussed in detail in Lappi-Seppälä (2016*a*).

23. Three partial exceptions: (1) extensions of ranges for multiple offenders, (2) specific ranges for repeat offenders in some cases in Norway and Sweden, and (3) a recent Danish law on gang criminality that allows doubling of penalties in connection with organized crime.

and a much larger number of minor breaches of bodily integrity of which a clear majority are not reported to the police (around 600,000 per year). One should not expect that the average punishment for any offense would be in the middle of the range. If that happened, either the range or the sentencing practice should be reviewed.

C. The Choice of Sanction: On Type and Amount

The principle of proportionality requires penalties to be graded in terms of severity. The Nordic countries share a roughly common structure: warnings, usually in the form of nonprosecution or court-ordered warnings; fines, imposed normally as day fines and for minor offenses as fixed summary fines; community sanctions; and imprisonment.

Variation is greatest for community sanctions. Typically, they encompass four to five basic options: conditional imprisonment or suspended sentence, possibly combined with other sanctions; probation or supervision as an independent or a complementary sanction; community service as an independent or a complementary sanction; treatment orders, usually as a complementary sanction; and electronic monitoring, either as a form of court-ordered supervision (Finland) or as a way of serving a prison sentence as decided by prison authorities (Denmark, Sweden, and Norway).

The ordering of penalties follows similar patterns but differs in details. Conditional imprisonment or a suspended sentence is everywhere regarded as more severe than a fine. Conditional imprisonment is followed by community service (or community punishment in Norway). Next in severity are combinations of conditional imprisonment and community service, in those countries that treat these options as separate sanctions. After that is electronic monitoring, either as a court-ordered penalty or as a form of enforcement.

All Nordic countries reserve imprisonment for use only when other alternatives are not appropriate. There is a general presumption in favor of noncustodial alternatives. This presumption must be overcome by other considerations for a prison sentence to be imposed. Swedish law provides that "in choosing a sanction, the court shall pay special attention to any circumstance or circumstances that argue for the imposition of a less severe punishment than imprisonment" (SPC 29:4). Finnish law does not contain a comparable provision but specifies that community sanctions should be the first option and requires courts to explain why they instead choose a custodial sanction.

In Swedish theory, the first step in sentencing is to establish a crime's "penal value," which is expressed first in day fines and, if the penal value exceeds the scope of fines, then in prison days and months. If the penal value is less than 12 months, the courts should choose a community sanction unless previous convictions or the type of offense justifies imprisonment. Finnish law does not use the penal value concept but refers directly to general sentencing criteria (harm and culpability and related aggravating and mitigating factors). The Finnish judge is assumed to proceed one step at a time from less severe toward more severe penalties, each time considering whether that sanction is sufficient or whether something more severe is needed. The Swedish system, by contrast, for more serious cases converts the penal value into abstract prison days and month and only then considers whether they should be converted to community sanctions.

V. Assessing the Level
of Sanctions: Absolute Proportionality

Much that I have written concerns relative proportionality: trying to ensure that offenses of similar seriousness receive similar punishments and that offenses of different seriousness receive correspondingly different ones. Much less can be said about the absolute severity of sanctions. Proportionality theory provides little guidance. Still, for US penal reformers, proportionality was a tool that could help set proper limits on the use of punishment (von Hirsch 1976). In the Nordic countries, the resurgence of retributivism beginning in the 1970s was generally resisted, partly because emphasis on proportionality might favor more punitive sentencing policies and lead to increased severity of punishments (Hecksher et al. 1980).

The reductionist aspirations in the United States were not achieved, but neither did the expansionist fears in the Nordic countries materialize. In Finland, increased emphasis on proportionality coincided with dramatic declines in both punishment severity and imprisonment rates. In Sweden, penalties remained at fairly constant levels, at a time when punishment severity was increasing in many Western countries. Principles alone do not make the difference.

A. Proportionality and Values

The principle of proportionality acquires its content from prevailing social and moral values. Among the key issues are how highly we value the different interests sought to be protected by the criminal law against those interests threatened by criminal punishments and how much importance we attach to the burdens caused by punishments and the beliefs, feelings, and experiences of those subjected to them.

The latter assessment is affected by our perceptions of the nature and causes of crime. If crime is primarily understood to result from social and environmental factors, punishment can play at best a minor role in maintaining public safety. This is a fundamentally different view from that held by people who perceive of criminality as a problem primarily resulting from the actions of evil individuals.

Assumptions of the effectiveness of criminal sanctions are also important. It is easier to justify harsh sentences if there are reasonable bases for believing they can lead to good results. The more clearly the limited or adverse effects of punishments are understood, the more difficult it becomes to justify their use and severity.

The question of how much preventive effect to expect from punishment is inseparable from society's other means of crime prevention. Severe sentences are difficult to justify if other more effective instruments are available. The development of convincing crime-prevention strategies outside the domain of criminal law thus can reduce the political strains on the criminal justice system.

The level of penalties is determined by the prevailing political culture, including the extent to which policymaking is influenced by rational analyses of aims and means and, conversely, by the media, extraneous political considerations, and politicians' quest for popularity. Socioeconomic and political conditions provide more and less favorable contexts. Nordic moderation in penal policy has benefited much from a consensual negotiating political culture (which has tempered extreme positions and enabled consistency in planning), a strong universalistic welfare state (which provides social and economic security, low welfare differences, high levels of social and institutional trust, and low levels of fear and public punitiveness, all relevant for policy formation), (fairly) reasonable media, strong civil servants (who have brought consistency and professional deliberation to decision-making), and a highly professional judiciary (working independently and with high expertise). Some of these background conditions can be influenced; some probably cannot.

B. Proportionality and Policy

Taking into account the complexity of these processes and the diverse factors involved, it is not surprising that the problem of absolute (cardinal) proportionality remains unsolved. Proposed theoretical solutions tend to assume that all options are possible, and nothing has been decided. However, as Duff pointed out, "There is no Archimedean point, independent of all existing penal practice, from which we could embark on such an enterprise" (2001, p. 134). Every society already has a status quo.

A more sensible way to conceptualize consideration of "the decision on the level of sanctions" is to see these decisions as a continuous process in which offenses are assessed in relation to one another and sentences imposed are proportioned to different offenses. Decisions about the absolute level of sanctions (cardinal proportionality) are necessarily connected with decisions about the relative level of sanctions for different offenses (ordinal proportionality).

Nor, at least in the Nordic countries, is it clear what single body or decision maker could make this decision. In countries with a civil-law tradition, the sanction level is determined through different discourses and on different levels. Arguments are presented in legislative proposals, in legislators' statements of purpose, in decisions from higher and lower courts, in theoretical analyses, in policy research, and in public debates. Professional discussions occur in training programs, seminars, and meetings for judges, prosecutors, researchers, and, sometimes, also politicians. Political debates occur in parliaments and in the media.

The level of sanctions is fundamentally a question of policy values. Strong ethical and empirical arguments support a stepwise "decremental strategy" (Duff 2001) and a gradual mitigation of sentences. The Nordic countries provide some successful examples in recent decades. The policy results of the resurgence of penal neoclassicism in the 1960s and 1970s are very different from those a little later in the English-speaking countries. These differences are products of structural differences and cultural characteristics (Lappi-Seppälä 2012, 2017; Pratt and Eriksson 2013) but also of the influence of an active and liberal-minded generation of penal reformers in all the Nordic countries. Put differently, perhaps the Nordic countries also benefited from some good luck—at least so far.

C. Proportionality and Politics

The Nordic countries experienced the late-20th-century "punitive turn," albeit in different forms, scales, and times (Lappi-Seppälä 2016*b*). On some subjects, especially concerning violent and sexual offenses, the stepwise decremental strategy of the past became a stepwise "incremental strategy." Compared with the 1970s and 1980s, crime policy has become more aggressive, more politicized, and more responsive to the views and voices of the media. Crime victims have come to occupy a central position in policy debates, with deep ramifications for political discourse, public perceptions, and penal practices. There is a shift away from pragmatic and rational policymaking toward invoking public opinion as a justification for changing sentencing laws.

The "general sense of justice" has become the standard rationale for penalty increases for sexual and violent offenses, as the program for 2015–2019 of the current conservative Finnish government, for example, states. In Sweden, demands for proportionality and "just deserts" have prevailed as the key argument for penal increments in recent years (Tham 2018). Current political discourse increasingly identifies proportionality with public demands and public opinion. Informed and principled argument about the penal value of different offense types has been replaced by references to the demands of the general sense of justice. Swedish commentators worry that politicians have hijacked the principle of proportionality. Political discourse treats the public as customers of crime policy whose wants and needs must be satisfied by the products offered by the penal state (Andersson and Nilsson 2017). Proportionality in textbooks and in political debate has become two different things.

This populist proportionalism may change the structure of criminal justice policy debate. Until recently, pragmatic approaches calling for careful assessments of evidence and experience provided barriers against unfounded expansions of use of the criminal law. It was, for example, possible to influence policy decisions by providing research-based evidence showing that it would be wiser, from a pragmatic crime-prevention perspective, to invest scarce public resources in social and situational prevention programs rather than in imprisonment. If an argument for the use of criminal law fails on empirical grounds, we should reconsider whether a particular use of penal power is justified. Justifications for policy derived from the general sense of justice may put an end to this approach. What now matters is what people think.

However, we may still find the first type of reasoning in a recent report of the constitutional committee of Finland, a committee consisting of members of parliament tasked to oversee the constitutionality of law reforms. In a report from 2016, the committee summarized its view of the principles to be followed in penal legislation and criminalization:

> The penal system's generally accepted aim is prevention of crime . . . as well as the minimization of the costs and suffering caused by crime and crime control and the fair distribution of these cost among different parties. The

legislator's task is to formulate the elements of the system in a way that best reduces the human and material damages and suffering caused by crime and crime control. The proper level of penalties is determined, along with the considerations of justice, according to how successful criminal punishment is in its efforts to prevent crimes, what kind of social and human cost and suffering its implementation brings, and what other means to society would be at its disposal with the same goal in mind. (PevL 2016, p. 5)

This summarizes the central message of Finnish criminologists in recent decades about the aims of crime policy and the principles of criminalization. To what extent these principles will be honored in parliamentary work in the future remains to be seen.

Perhaps we should not place our hopes too high. Moderation in the use of punishment is not a high political priority in most countries in our time. The Swedish Social Democratic party declared in its 2017 program "Strong Rule of Law" that "The rule of law must always react strongly against crime. Through the sanctions established to punish a crime we demonstrate our values and strengthen what is right and wrong. Those who commit crimes must expect severe punishment." And while the principle of equality before the law is esteemed in the Nordics, the Danish government plans to double penalties for crimes committed in 22 deprived "ghetto" areas.[24] Most recently, the conservative Finnish minister of justice has put forward a list of bills for penal aggravations with references to the requirements of the public sense of justice and the need to "uphold the credibility and legitimacy" of the criminal justice system.[25]

Nothing about crime patterns or trends explains these changes, as most forms of traditional crime have been in decline in all the Nordic countries. However, several of the structural underpinnings of moderate Nordic penal policy have substantially changed since the 1990s. One should be careful about offering causal claims, but it is more than probable that these changes are reflected in political processes, priorities, and penal policies. In some cases, this connection is more than probable.

---

24. See http://www.bbc.com/news/world-europe-43214596.

25. No evidence is provided that the system is experiencing any sorts of legitimation problems or other crises. Given that the comparative Rule of Law Index, published by the World Justice Project in Washington, D.C., has repeatedly ranked the Finnish criminal justice system (i.e., its effectiveness, legitimacy, and impartiality) in the top position among 113 countries, one may seriously question the need and motives for these proposals. For the WJP Rule of Law Index, see https://worldjusticeproject.org/our-work/wjp-rule-law-index/wjp-rule-law-index-2017%E2%80%932018.

Demographic changes, increased immigration, and populist right-wing politics have lifted the general political profile of crime and security issues in all Nordic countries, especially Denmark and Sweden. The economic consequences of the early-1990s recession and scaling down of welfare services have contributed to increased income and welfare differences, threatening the visions of egalitarian, solidary, and secure Nordic societies. Less visible but equally important in the long term are processes that have gradually altered political and economic power relations. Tripartite centralized wage bargaining belongs now to history. Nordic multiparty systems have evolved toward bipolar political blocs, especially in Sweden with right and left alliances of equal size. As elsewhere in Europe, social democratic parties are ever more forcefully challenged by populist right-wing parties. The moderate parties seem to have but two options: keep their voters by endorsing elements of right-wing parties' programs, or collaborate with them as coalition partners.

It is too simplistic to assume that changes in one or two of these conditions will necessarily lead to identifiable and immediate repercussions in national penal policies. There is no mechanical connection between income distribution and sanction severity. But there are connections between political processes that enable negotiations and listen to all voices and political willingness to support redistributive social policies that provide social and economic security for all. Penal moderation is linked to social equality, solidarity, trust, legitimacy, and a sense of security. There is also a link between diminished political legitimacy and heightened feelings of insecurity on the one hand and, on the other, politicians' temptation to respond by offering tougher policies to voters in order to maintain political credibility—and success. That seems to be happening in more than one Nordic country.

References

Aarnio. Aulis. 1986. *Lain ja kohtuuden tähden* [*For Law and Reasonableness*]. Helsinki: WSOY.

Ågren, Jack. 2013. *Billighetsskälen i BrB 29:5—Berättigande och betydelse vid påföljdsbestämning.* Stockholm: Jure Förlag.

"Alternativ til frihedsstraf—et debatoplaeg" ["Alternatives to Imprisonment"]. 1977. Betaenking no. 806. Copenhagen.

Andenaes, Johannes. 1974. *Punishment and Deterrence.* Ann Arbor: University of Michigan Press. (Originally published in Norwegian 1952.)

Andenaes, Johannes, Magnus Matningsdal, and Georg Fredrik Rieber-Mohn. 2004. *Strafferett. Alminnelige del*, 5th ed. Oslo: Universitetsforlaget.

Andersson, Robert. 2002. *Kriminalpolitikens väsen*. Kriminologiska Institutionen. Avhandlingsserie No. 10. Stockholm: Stockholm universitet.

Andersson, Robert, and Roddy Nilsson. 2017. *Svensk kriminalpolitik*, 2nd ed. Stockholm: Liber.

Anttila, Inkeri. 1967. "Konservativ och radikal kriminalpolitik i Norden." *Nordisk Tidsskrift for Kriminalvidenskab*:237–51.

Anttila, Inkeri, and Patrik Törnudd. 1996. "Dynamics of the Finnish Criminal Code Reform." In *Facts, Values and Visions: Essays in Criminology and Crime Policy*, edited by Patrik Törnudd and Inkeri Anttila. Helsinki: National Research Institute of Legal Policy Publication.

Asp, Petter. 2011. "Högsta domstolen revolutionerar narkotikabrotten." *Svensk Juristtidning*:659–69. https://svjt.se/svjt/2011/659.

Aubert, Vilhelm. 1972. *Om straffens sosiale funksjon*, 2nd ed. Oslo, Bergen, and Tromso: Universitetforlaget.

Beyleveld, Deryck. 1980. *Deterrence: Bibliography on General Deterrence Research*. Farnabourgh: Saxon House.

Bondeson, Ulla. 1994. *Alternatives to Imprisonment: Intentions and Reality*. Boulder: Westview.

Borgeke, Martin. 1999. "Brottets art—några tankar kring en svårgripbar förteelse." *Svensk Juristtidning* 2:218–40.

Borgeke, Martin, and Mari Heidenborg. 2016. *Att bestämma påföljd för brott*, 3rd ed. Stockholm: Norstedts Juridik.

Chalfin, Aaron, and Justin McCrary. 2017. "Criminal Deterrence: A Review of the Literature." *Journal of Economic Literature* 55(1):5–48.

Crawford, Adam, and Anthea Hucklesby. 2013. *Legitimacy and Compliance in Criminal Justice*. New York and London: Routledge.

Duff, R. A. 2001. *Punishment, Communication, and Community*. Oxford: Oxford University Press.

Ekelöf, Per-Ole. 1942. *Straffet, skadeståndet och vite*. Uppsala: A. B. Lundquist.

Feinberg, Joel. 1965. "The Expressive Function of Punishment." *Monist* 49(3):397–423. https://doi.org/10.5840/monist196549326.

GovProp 44. 2002. "Hallituksen esitys Eduskunnalle rikosoikeuden yleisiä oppeja koskevan lainsäädännön uudistamiseksi" ["Government's Proposal for the New General Part of Criminal Code.] Copenhagen. https://www.edilex.fi/he/fi20020044.pdf.

Greve, Vagn, Poul Dahl Jenson, and Gorm Toftegaard Nielsen. 2013. *Kommenteret Straffelov: Almindelig del*. Copenhagen: Jurist-og Okonomforbundets Forlag.

Hassemer, Winfried. 1979. "Generalprävention und Strafzumessung." In *Hauptprobleme der Generalprävention*, edited by W. Hassemer, K. Lüderssen, and W. Naucke. Frankfurt am Main: Metzner.

Hecksher, Sten, Annika Snare, Hannu Takala, and Jørn Vestergaard. 1980. *Straff och rättfärdighet—ny nordisk debatt*. Stockholm: Norstedts.

Hinkkanen, Ville, and Tapio Lappi-Seppälä. 2011. "Sentencing Theory and Sentencing Research in the Nordic Countries." In *Crime and Justice in Scandinavia*, edited by Michael Tonry and Tapio Lappi-Seppälä. Vol. 40 of *Crime and Justice: A Review of Research*, edited by Michael Tonry. Chicago: University of Chicago Press.

Holmqvist, L. 1999. "Billighetssyn." *Svensk Juristtidning*:188–99.

Jareborg, Nils. 1985. "Straffets syfte och berättigande." *Tidskrift for Rettvitenskap*:1–17.

Jareborg. Nils. 1995. "The Swedish Sentencing Reform." In *The Politics of Sentencing Reform*, edited by Chris M. V. Clarkson and Rod Morgan. New York: Oxford University Press.

Jareborg, Nils. 2000. "Humanitet och Straffbestämning." *Tidskrift utgiven af Juridiska Föreningen i Finland*:435–50.

Jareborg, Nils, and Josef Zila. 2000. *Straffrättens påföljdslära*. Stockholm: Norstedts Juridik.

Lahti, Raimo. 2000. "Toward a Rational and Humane Criminal Policy: Trends in Scandinavian Penal Thinking." *Journal of Scandinavian Studies and Crime Prevention* 1:141–55.

Lappi-Seppälä, Tapio. 1987. *Rangaistuksen määräämisestä I: Teoria ja yleinen osa [Sentencing I. Theory and General Part]*. Vammala: Finnish Lawyers Association.

Lappi-Seppälä, Tapio. 2001. "Sentencing and Punishment in Finland: The Decline of the Repressive Ideal." In *Punishment and Penal Systems in Western Countries*, edited by Michael Tonry and Richard S. Frase. New York: Oxford University Press.

Lappi-Seppälä, Tapio. 2007. "Penal Policy in Scandinavia." In *Crime, Punishment, and Politics in a Comparative Perspective*, edited by Michael Tonry. Vol. 36 of *Crime and Justice: A Review of Research*, edited by Michael Tonry. Chicago: University of Chicago Press.

Lappi-Seppälä, Tapio. 2011. "Nordic Youth Justice." In *Crime and Justice in Scandinavia*, edited by Michael Tonry and Tapio Lappi-Seppälä. Vol. 40 of *Crime and Justice: A Review of Research*, edited by Michael Tonry. Chicago: University of Chicago Press.

Lappi-Seppälä, Tapio. 2012. "Explaining National Differences in the Use of Imprisonment." In *Resisting Punitiveness: Welfare, Human Rights and Democracy*, edited by Sonja Snacken and Els Dumortier. London and New York: Routledge.

Lappi-Seppälä, Tapio. 2016a. "Life Imprisonment and Related Institutions in the Nordic Countries." In *Life Imprisonment and Human Rights*, edited by Dirk van Zyl Smit and Catherine Appleton. Oxford: Hart.

Lappi-Seppälä, Tapio. 2016b. "Nordic Sentencing." In *Sentencing Policies and Practices in Western Countries: Comparative and Cross-National Perspectives*, edited by Michael Tonry. Vol. 45 of *Crime and Justice: A Review of Research*, edited by Michael Tonry. Chicago: University of Chicago Press.

Lappi-Seppälä, Tapio. 2017. "American Exceptionalism in Cross-Comparative Perspective." In *American Exceptionalism*, edited by Kevin Reitz. New York: Oxford University Press.

Mäkelä, Klaus. 1975. *Om straffens verkningar*. Oikeustiede Jurisprudentia. Vammala: Suomalainen lakimiesyhdistys.

Nagin, Daniel. 2018. "Certainty versus Severity of Deterrence." In *Deterrence, Choice, and Crime: Contemporary Perspectives*, edited by Daniel S. Nagin, Francis T. Cullen, and Cheryl Lero Jonson. New York: Routledge.

Nytt straffsystem [*New Penal System*]. 1977. Brottsfölrebyggande rådet. Rapport 1977:7. Stockholm: Brotts.

Om kriminalpolitiken [*On Crime Policy*]. 1978. St.meld. no.104. Oslo: Justis og Politidepertamentet.

PevL [Constitutional Committee Report] 9/2016. 2016. Perustuslakivaliokunnan lausunto HE 1/2016. https://www.eduskunta.fi/FI/vaski/Lausunto/Sivut/PeVL_9+2016.aspx.

Pratt, John, and Anna Eriksson. 2013. *Contrasts in Punishment: An Explanation of Anglophone Excess and Nordic Exceptionalism*. London: Routledge.

Rikosoikeuskomitean mietintö [Finnish Criminal Law Committee]. 1976. *Komiteanmietintöjä 1976:72* [*Committee Reports 1976:72*]. Helsinki: Rikosoikeuskomitean mietintö.

Ross, Alf. 1975. *On Guilt, Responsibility and Punishment*. London: Stevens.

Statens offentliga utredningar. 1986. *Påföljd för brott* [*Criminal Sanctions*]. Huvudbetänkande av Fängelsestraffkommittén. Stockholm: Justitiedepartement.

Tham, Henrik. 2018 *Kriminalpolitik: Brott och straff I Sverige sedan 1965*. Stockholm: Norstedts Juridik.

Törnudd, Patrik. 1996. *Facts, Values and Visions: Essays in Criminology and Crime Policy*. Helsinki: National Research Institute of Legal Policy.

Tyler, Tom. 1990. *Why People Obey the Law*. New Haven: Yale University Press.

Victor, Dag. 1999. "Påföljdsbestämning i ett differentierat påföljdssystem." *Svensk Juristtidning*:132–44.

Victor, Dag. 2003. "'Artbrotten' och de korta fängelsestraffen—teoretiska frågor." *Svensk Juristtidning*:121–35.

Victor, Dag. 2015. "Straffmätningsvärde och påföljdsval." *Svensk Juristtidning*:173–20.

Von Hirsch, Andreas [Andrew]. 1976. *Doing Justice*. New York: Hill and Wang.

Von Hirsch, Andreas [Andrew]. 2003. "Reducing Use of Short-Term Imprisonment: The Role of Prior Convictions and 'Artbrott.'" *Svensk Juristtidning* 2:111–20.

Von Hirsch, Andreas [Andrew], and Andrew Ashworth. 2005. *Proportionate Sentencing: Exploring the Principles*. New York: Oxford University Press.

Von Hirsch, Andreas [Andrew], and Anthony E. Bottoms. 2010. "The Crime-Preventive Impact of Penal Sanctions." In *The Oxford Handbook of Empirical Legal Research*, edited by Peter Cane and Herbert M. Kritzer. Oxford: Oxford University Press.

Walker, Nigel. 1980. *Punishment, Danger and Stigma: The Morality of Criminal Justice*. Oxford: Basil Blackwell.

Index

For the benefit of digital users, indexed terms that span two pages (e.g., 52–53) may, on occasion, appear on only one of those pages.

Note: Tables are indicated by *t* following the page number

Index